W9-BHF-222

The Best

Baby
Names

for Canadians

The Best
Baby
Names
for Canadians

Collins
An Imprint of HarperCollinsPublishers

The Best Baby Names for Canadians
© 2007 by HarperCollins Publishers Ltd except for material
originally published in *Collins Gem: Babies' Names* by Julia Cresswell
© HarperCollins*Publishers* 2004

All rights reserved.

Published by Collins, an imprint of HarperCollins Publishers Ltd,
by arrangement with HarperCollins Publishers Ltd

No part of this book may be used or reproduced in any manner
whatsoever without the prior written permission of the publisher,
except in the case of brief quotations embodied in reviews.

HarperCollins books may be purchased for educational, business,
or sales promotional use through our Special Markets Department.

HarperCollins Publishers Ltd
2 Bloor Street East, 20th Floor
Toronto, Ontario, Canada
M4W 1A8

www.harpercollins.ca

Library and Archives Canada Cataloguing in Publication

The best baby names for Canadians.

ISBN-13: 978-0-00-639151-7
ISBN-10: 0-00-639151-6

1. Names, Personal—Dictionaries. 2. Names, Personal—Canada—Dictionaries.

CS2377.B465 2007 929.4'403 C2007-901304-X

KRO 9 8 7 6 5 4 3 2 1

Printed and bound in Canada
Text design by Sharon Kish

Contents

1
Naming Your Baby

This is one of the best times for parents to name a baby. One of the most remarkable trends in recent years is the meteoric rise in popularity of rare and exotic names. As you'll see elsewhere in this book, today's babies are more likely to have very rare names than very common ones, which means parents don't have to shy away from an unusual name. This trend also means that even the most common names are less common. So if the name you hoped was different has suddenly appeared on the Top 30 list, you shouldn't necessarily be put off. Even runaway favourites like Emma and Emily are not so common that your child's kindergarten class will be full of them. If you like a name, whether it's popular or rare, go ahead and use it!

Consider abbreviations and nicknames
Think about how the name will be abbreviated—remember, whether you want it to or not, the name may well be abbreviated—and consider how the abbreviated version sounds with the surname.

How does it sound?

It's a good idea to focus on the sound of the name, rather than how it looks on paper. Most names will be spoken aloud far more often than they are seen in writing. As a very general rule, names sound better if the number of syllables in the first name and surname is different. Short first names often go well with long surnames and vice versa. Alliteration (where first and last names begin with the same sound or letter), or even the judicious use of rhyme, can make a name distinctive. Watch out for names that end with the same letter or sound that the surname begins with. Names like Jack Casey or Jasmine North may end up being pronounced "Jackasey" and "Jasminorth." Again, though, consider abbreviated versions too. You may love the euphonious qualities of Samantha Lamb, but she'll likely end up as Sam Lamb.

Avoid arbitrary spellings

While unusual names are trendy—and seem likely to remain so—you may want to think twice about names that are made unusual merely by respelling a more common name. If you like names such as Gabrielle and Alexander, use them as they are. Attempts to make them more exotic by spelling these names as Gabreeyelle and Allakzander merely condemn children to a life of spelling out their names every time they are asked. If you really want to give a "creative spelling" name, try to choose one that is short and can be spelled out quickly. Better yet, if you want a more unusual name, why not choose a variation on the name like Gabriella or Alexis?

Don't exclude "common" names

Many names that you may think are commonplace have become quite rare as baby name choices. (Examples include Ann, Rodney, Lloyd, Dora, Carol, Anita, Guy, Diane, Tracy.) If you want a name that is unusual, but that is easily spelled and won't raise any eyebrows, these may be good choices.

Don't fret the middle names

Many parents work hard to find a first and middle name that sound good with the last name. Don't get so distracted by this that you don't pay enough attention to how the first name and the surname sound on their own. Remember, after they've been so carefully chosen, most middle names will never see the light of day—most don't even turn up on baby name surveys! Don't feel the need to give your child a dull middle name to offset an unusual first name—with more parents making unusual name choices, this precaution is unnecessary. If you have to deal with family politics—relatives and in-laws who expect to see their name reflected in your child—using the relative's name as one of your child's middle names can be an effective compromise. At best, these middle names represent a tie to the child's family history. At worst, middle names may serve as a kind of graveyard for unwanted names.

Check the initials

When considering first and middle names, look at the initials they form with the surname. Most parents are more flexible with middle names than first names, and playing around with middle name choices can give a child a more interesting monogram.

Make it easy to spell

Consider ease of spelling. It's nice to have a name that most people can spell as soon as they hear it. A surprising number of names that were commonplace in previous decades have now become very rare, and these may be good choices for distinctive but easily spelled names.

Choose names from a region

If you have a certain ethnic background, you may want to consider names associated with that country of origin—but why not research the names that are common within a specific area in that country? Many baby name books list "Italian names," but different regions of Italy have names associated with them, which can help narrow down the choices. For example, the name Brizio is associated with the Italian region of Umbria. Those with British or Irish ancestors will find the same variation among regions. For example, a search for specifically Cornish names turns up such unusual examples as Jago, Merryn, and Steren.

Think about geography

Place names can be good choices for names. They're familiar and easy to spell. In fact, several of today's most popular girls' names—Montana, Dakota and Brooklyn—are derived from place names. Among boys, Logan, while not exclusively a place name, suggests Canada's highest mountain, while Hudson suggests Henry Hudson and Hudson Bay. If there is a place name, Canadian or otherwise, that has special meaning for you and your family—or one that you just like the sound of—why not consider it?

Think about history

If you want a name that is exotic but not invented, you may want to use the name of a significant figure from history—particularly if it's the name of an important person from your family's region, or a character from the past whom you like. Such names often aren't listed in baby name books and may require some research. Historic surnames can be a rich source of interesting first names. We know of one university professor who greatly admired a 17th-century English political figure named John Pym, so he used Pym as a name for his daughter—a charming and original girl's name. Other sources of very exotic names include the names of ancient kings or rulers from a region. For example, the ancient kings of England include such unusual boys' names as Hengest, Penda, Alfric, Ferrex, and Runo. They're unusual but have the weight of history behind them.

A name for the Net

Google the name—first name and surname—to see if there are any good or bad associations. (If you put the name in double quotes, the computer will search for the entire name.) This will help avoid inadvertently giving a child the name of, say, a

famous mass murderer. It's also a way of seeing how unusual the name is. And if you want to give a baby an unusual birthday present, why not spend a few dollars and register his or her name as an Internet domain name?

Write in this book

At first, the number of possible baby names can be overwhelming—especially when two parents, with different choices, must agree on a name. One simple, methodical approach is to go through this book and put check marks or ratings against the names you like, and perhaps Xs against names you dislike. Special favourites can be written in the back. If you have a specific reason for being interested in the name, make a note of that too. It is much easier to choose a name from a list of all your favourites than to go back each time to the same huge lists. It will also be fun, in years to come, for your children to look back at the names you considered and see what they were nearly called.

Match it to the rest of the family

If a new baby has brothers or sisters, think about how the name you are considering will sound when compared with those of the siblings. If two of your daughters are given unisex names like Sydney and Taylor, don't give the third an ultra-feminine name like Angelina. You should also consider whether the names of siblings combine in a way you don't want. One mother we know already had a boy named Quinn. When her second child came along, she considered the name Aidan but realized that, taken together, it might look as if her children had been named for actor Aidan Quinn.

Be sensitive in choosing twins' names

If you're naming twins, think about how each child will deal with the name both as an individual and as one of a pair. Consider the tip above this one, but even more so. Would the twins want to be tied through life as Hope and Faith, or Nicholas and Alexandra, or Lily and Billy (or Lily and Iris)? Too great a similarity (Taylor and Tyler, Christopher and Christine, Sara and Sierra) could affect a twin's sense of individuality and cause endless confusion. If you're going to look for a connection between names, you may want to take your inspiration from two grandparents. For creativity, an anagram might work: Leon and Noel, Amy and May, Dyan and Andy. Check meanings too, and look for common origins. Chantal and Dustin are both derived from the word "stone." You could also base your selections on favourite authors or actors and actresses.

Be cautious about asking opinions

Taste in names is very personal, so it is often better not to ask others what they think of your baby name shortlist. If you do decide to show your choices to the critics, take their advice with a pinch of salt—it's surprising how many otherwise kind and considerate people, on being confronted with a list of a new parent's prospective names, will tactlessly reel off the bad associations the name has for them. ("I hate the name Graham. He was a mean kid from my Grade Two class.") The opinions of older generations will often be skewed to the names that were popular when they were young. Listening to many opinions may eventually yield an average-sounding name, but it may also have less appeal to you.

People will accept it

One final thing to remember. Once you have given your child the name, all the judgments and criticisms rapidly fade away as the name, like the child, becomes its own entity. Friends who told you that Poppy was "just the worst name ever" a few weeks earlier will be leaning over the crib, cooing "Hello, Poppy!" as they try to get your child's attention.

2

The Most Popular Names in Canada

Most Popular Girls' Names in Canada

Rank	Name	Canada Total	Est. Number
1	Emma	1.4711%	2405
2	Emily	1.2651%	2069
3	Sarah	0.8531%	1395
4	Madison	0.8155%	1333
5	Olivia	0.7797%	1275
6	Hannah	0.7780%	1272
7	Jessica	0.5947%	972
8	Grace	0.5624%	920
9	Julia	0.5366%	877
10	Megan	0.5199%	850
11	Abigail	0.5119%	837
12	Lauren	0.5098%	834
13	Rachel	0.4919%	804
14	Isabella	0.4896%	801
15	Samantha	0.4703%	769
16	Paige	0.4582%	749

Most Popular Boys' Names in Canada

Rank	Name	Canada Total	Est. Number
1	Ethan	1.3095%	2248
2	Matthew	1.1484%	1972
3	Joshua	1.1144%	1913
4	Jacob	1.0437%	1792
5	Ryan	0.9447%	1622
6	Nicholas	0.8576%	1472
7	Benjamin	0.8278%	1421
8	Alexander	0.8088%	1389
9	William	0.7927%	1361
10	Michael	0.7660%	1315
11	Daniel	0.7562%	1298
12	Nathan	0.7287%	1251
13	Owen	0.6765%	1161
14	Liam	0.6693%	1149
15	Dylan	0.6678%	1147
16	Tyler	0.6571%	1128

Most Popular Girls' Names in Canada (*cont'd*)					Most Popular Boys' Names in Canada (*cont'd*)			
Rank	Name	Canada Total	Est. Number		Rank	Name	Canada Total	Est. Number
17	Hailey	0.4466%	730		17	Samuel	0.6525%	1120
18	Chloe	0.4452%	728		18	Justin	0.6445%	1106
19	Ashley	0.4375%	715		19	Connor	0.6393%	1098
20	Taylor	0.4353%	712		20	Andrew	0.6240%	1071
21	Victoria	0.4335%	709		21	Noah	0.6114%	1050
22	Alyssa	0.4332%	708		22	Zachary	0.5765%	990
23	Mackenzie	0.4214%	689		23	Logan	0.5656%	971
24	Sydney	0.4203%	687		24	James	0.5440%	934
25	Alexandra	0.3844%	629		25	Aidan	0.5400%	927
26	Nicole	0.3777%	618		26	Evan	0.5357%	920
27	Ella	0.3493%	571		27	Adam	0.5352%	919
28	Sophia	0.3488%	570		28	Lucas	0.5147%	884
29	Jenna	0.3399%	556		29	Joseph	0.4899%	841
30	Maya	0.3335%	545		30	David	0.4886%	839
31	Elizabeth	0.3199%	523		31	Jordan	0.4813%	826
32	Kaitlyn	0.3160%	517		32	Thomas	0.4768%	819
33	Alexis	0.3146%	514		33	Jack	0.4520%	776
34	Kayla	0.3109%	508		34	Cameron	0.4478%	769
35	Brianna	0.3073%	502		35	Anthony	0.4476%	769
36	Rebecca	0.2866%	469		36	Kyle	0.4293%	737
37	Anna	0.2856%	467		37	Christopher	0.4217%	724
38	Sara	0.2813%	460		38	Gabriel	0.3911%	671

Rank	Name	Canada Total	Est. Number
39	Brooke	0.2796%	457
40	Brooklyn	0.2758%	451
41	Noemie	0.2452%	401
42	Jade	0.2400%	392
43	Ava	0.2260%	370
44	Laurence	0.2153%	352
45	Zoe	0.2085%	341
46	Sophie	0.2055%	336
47	Gabrielle	0.2032%	332
48	Rosalie	0.1945%	318
49	Morgan	0.1823%	298
50	Trinity	0.1822%	298
51	Jasmine	0.1803%	295
52	Amy	0.1778%	291
53	Maude	0.1670%	273
54	Megane	0.1615%	264
55	Faith	0.1597%	261
56	Jennifer	0.1574%	257
57	Natalie	0.1565%	256
58	Jordan	0.1562%	255
59	Sierra	0.1556%	254
60	Avery	0.1518%	248

Rank	Name	Canada Total	Est. Number
39	Austin	0.3847%	661
40	Eric	0.3760%	646
41	Cole	0.3640%	625
42	Brandon	0.3539%	608
43	Aiden	0.3198%	549
44	Jeremy	0.3120%	536
45	Carter	0.2987%	513
46	Jayden	0.2706%	465
47	Hunter	0.2615%	449
48	Kaden	0.2610%	448
49	Riley	0.2536%	435
50	Tristan	0.2456%	422
51	Isaac	0.2418%	415
52	Caleb	0.2417%	415
53	Tyson	0.2340%	402
54	John	0.2303%	395
55	Jonathan	0.2294%	394
56	Brayden	0.2273%	390
57	Olivier	0.2252%	387
58	Aaron	0.2252%	387
59	Mathis	0.2245%	385
60	Xavier	0.2239%	384

Name Rankings by Province–Girls

Rank	AB	BC	NB	NS	ON	QC	SK
1	Ava	Emma	Emma	Emma	Emma	Léa	Madison
2	Emma	Emily	Madison	Madison	Emily	Jade	Emma
3	Emily	Olivia	Emily	Olivia	Sarah	Sarah	Emily
4	Hannah	Hannah	Abigail	Emily	Olivia	Noémie	Olivia
5	Madison	Madison	Sarah	Hannah	Madison	Rosalie	Hailey
6	Sarah	Ava	Olivia	Abigail	Hannah	Laurence	Ava
7	Abigail	Sarah	Hannah	Sarah	Julia	Camille	Hannah
8	Olivia	Ella	Taylor	Grace	Jessica	Florence	Brooklyn
9	Grace	Isabella	Jenna	Ava	Lauren	Mégane	Chloe
10	Ella	Grace	Grace	Lauren	Abigail	Coralie	Abigail
11	Hailey	Sophia	Chloé	Chloe	Grace	Megan	Sarah
12	Samantha	Samantha	Paige	Ella	Rachel	Océane	Brooke
13	Chloe	Maya	Jessica	Julia	Isabella	Ariane	Grace
14	Taylor	Abigail	Sophie	Brooke	Victoria	Gabrielle	Elizabeth
15	Brooklyn	Jessica	Chloe	Hailey	Samantha	Audrey	Taylor
16	Elizabeth	Hailey	Hailey	Mackenzie	Megan	Laurie	Samantha
17	Isabella	Chloe	Megan	Samantha	Alyssa	Juliette	Mackenzie
18	Brooke	Megan	Jasmine	Sophie	Ashley	Justine	Avery
19	Sophia	Julia	Mackenzie	Brianna	Nicole	Émilie	Jenna
20	Keira	Lauren	Kayla	Brooklyn	Paige	Élodie	Jordyn
21	Sydney	Rachel	Lauren	n/a	Mackenzie	Marianne	n/a
22	Rachel	Elizabeth	Alyssa	n/a	Alexandra	Chloé	n/a
23	Maya	Sydney	Brianna	n/a	Hailey	Émy	n/a
24	Alexis	Taylor	Gabrielle	n/a	Taylor	Charlotte	n/a
25	Avery	Alyssa	Isabelle	n/a	Sydney	Emma	n/a

Name Rankings by Province–Boys

Rank	AB	BC	NB	NS	ON	QC	SK
1	Ethan	Ethan	Jacob	Jacob	Matthew	Samuel	Ethan
2	Joshua	Joshua	Samuel	Ethan	Ethan	William	Joshua
3	Jacob	Matthew	Nicholas	Alexander	Joshua	Alexis	Matthew
4	Logan	Jacob	Joshua	Logan	Jacob	Gabriel	Carter
5	Matthew	Nathan	Ryan	Jack	Ryan	Félix	Logan
6	Noah	Ryan	Zachary	Joshua	Nicholas	Nathan	Jacob
7	Nathan	Alexander	Ethan	Connor	Michael	Antoine	Ashton
8	Liam	Liam	William	Nicholas	Alexander	Olivier	Liam
9	Carter	Nicholas	Matthew	Noah	Daniel	Thomas	Austin
10	William	Noah	Benjamin	Matthew	Benjamin	Xavier	Owen
11	Alexander	Daniel	Dylan	Nathan	Owen	Justin	Nicholas
12	Evan	Benjamin	Tyler	Ryan	Tyler	Jérémy	Ty
13	Austin	James	Noah	William	William	Mathis	Aiden
14	Owen	William	Brandon	Owen	Andrew	Anthony	Noah
15	Benjamin	Owen	Alex	Benjamin	Nathan	Raphaël	Dylan
16	Lucas	Dylan	Logan	Dylan	Liam	Alexandre	Hunter
17	Cole	Logan	Alexander	Evan	Noah	Zachary	Mason
18	Jack	Evan	Connor	Liam	Dylan	Jacob	Connor
19	Ryan	Tyler	Cole	Cameron	Connor	Vincent	Samuel
20	Tyler	Jack	Justin	Samuel	Justin	Nicholas	Brayden
21	Adam	Samuel	Evan	n/a	Aidan	Émile	n/a
22	Aiden	Lucas	Riley	n/a	Joseph	Benjamin	n/a
23	Connor	Andrew	Liam	n/a	Lucas	Maxime	n/a
24	Riley	Jordan	Austin	n/a	James	Mathieu	n/a
25	Samuel	Connor	Cameron	n/a	Adam	Simon	n/a

A Note on the Statistics

Determining which baby names are the most popular in Canada is surprisingly difficult. Unlike Britain or the United States, Canada has no central registry of births, and the provincial authorities charged with collecting and compiling this information—in most cases the province's department of vital statistics—process the data at different speeds in different provinces.

Some provinces, such as Quebec, British Columbia, and Alberta, provide information for births the previous year, and make most of it available online. Others, like Canada's most populous province, Ontario, are a few years behind in their data. Unfortunately, a few provinces are unable to provide researchers with any information at all. This means that any attempt to provide a recent snapshot of baby names across the country requires a certain amount of extrapolation.

Some provinces provided data for thousands of names, others for only the top 20 in the province. In total, the data we received covers the majority of all births across Canada.

Statistics for "The Most Popular Names in Canada" are based on a single year — the most recent year for which all participating provinces provided data. "Name Rankings by Province" are based on the most current information provided by each reporting province: Alberta (2006), British Columbia (2005), New Brunswick (2003), Nova Scotia (2005), Ontario (2003), Quebec (2005), and Saskatchewan (2005).

3
Baby Names and Canadian Trends

You Say Brianna, I Say Tianna–Canadian vs. U.S. Names

It could be argued that the most distinctively Canadian names are those from Quebec. Quebec has its own naming trends, and it's hardly surprising that many of the names in the Quebec Top 30 don't appear anywhere in the Top 1,000 U.S. names. These include the boys' names Olivier, Mathis, Mathieu, Maxime, Raphaël, Émile, Philippe, and Guillaume; and the girls' names Noémie, Laurence, Ariane, Rosalie, Maude, Mégane, Marianne, and Coralie.

English-Canadian names are less distinct from their American counterparts. As a general rule a baby name that is popular in Canada is likely to be popular in the United States as well. But some names are considerably more popular north of the border.

The English-Canadian names on page 17, which are sorted by their popularity in Canada, are all at least twice as popular among Canadians as Americans. (You can see exactly how many times more popular by looking at the final column.)

When it comes to naming girls, Canadian parents show a preference for T-names—Taryn, Tianna, Teagan, and Taya were all vastly more popular in Canada than in the United States. Ironically, some of the more distinctive Canadian girls' names are those that suggest U.S. locations—such as Brooklyn or Georgia.

Distinctly Canadian boys' names are a more traditional mix. Many reflect a certain ethnic background. Matteo, which is 10 times more popular in Canada than in the United States, is the Italian equivalent of Matthew (the number two boys' name), and seems a logical choice for those in Canada's large Italian-Canadian community. Armaan, which is off the radar in the United States, is a popular Hindi name in this country.

Canadians show a preference for boys' names with Celtic origins (Owen, Liam, Declan). The name Tyson, which is a particular favourite in Western Canada, may be popular largely because of cowboy folk singer Ian Tyson. In the United States, it may be decidedly unpopular because of its association with disgraced boxer Mike Tyson.

Girls' Names: Popularity Comparison–
Canada vs. U.S.

Name	Cdn. Rank	U.S. Rank	How many times more popular in Canada
Paige	16	47	2.07
Brooklyn	26	118	3.38
Maya	34	84	2.19
Sophie	45	151	2.86
Amy	50	119	2.01
Jordyn	52	155	2.53
Hayley	62	174	2.59
Cassidy	67	150	2.08
Natasha	69	320	4.46
Kate	71	161	2.05
Annika	74	283	3.64
Kiara	82	173	2.03
Kyra	88	223	2.47
Georgia	94	371	4.02
Hanna	94	212	2.10
Holly	98	261	2.61
Kendra	110	259	2.39
Taryn	112	452	4.37
Tianna	120	618	6.31
Kiera	130	444	3.69
Halle	130	337	2.71
Katrina	135	274	2.14
Kira	142	286	2.16

Boys' Names: Popularity Comparison–
Canada vs. U.S.

Name	Cdn. Rank	U.S. Rank	How many times more popular in Canada
Owen	11	72	3.31
Liam	13	114	5.06
Lucas	27	71	2.43
Cole	31	69	2.23
Aiden	37	73	2.09
Carter	39	102	2.68
Riley	45	104	2.36
Brayden	48	110	2.47
Ashton	51	101	2.03
Tyson	53	296	8.15
Nolan	60	175	3.30
Ty	63	193	3.47
Levi	80	172	2.19
Kai	88	264	3.80
Brody	89	232	3.16
Keegan	95	260	3.32
Brett	95	217	2.61
Dawson	102	204	2.18
Kieran	103	537	8.84
Quinn	104	290	3.50
Oliver	113	244	2.54
Simon	115	235	2.42
Jakob	119	218	2.05

Girls' Names: Popularity Comparison– Canada vs. U.S. (cont'd)

Name	Cdn. Rank	U.S. Rank	How many times more popular in Canada
Kirsten	142	278	2.09
Camryn	146	310	2.29
Teagan	148	626	5.22
Tessa	148	280	2.01
Brooklynn	152	404	2.99
Anika	156	482	3.49
Kiana	159	331	2.20
Reese	159	309	2.09
Jessie	165	476	3.30
Madeleine	168	324	2.06
Fiona	175	350	2.13
Eden	177	342	2.08
Sasha	182	369	2.17
Tiana	185	400	2.29
Ainsley	191	437	2.37
Tia	197	481	2.57
Cadence	197	474	2.54
Taya	204	942	6.09
Keira	204	622	3.54.

Boys' Names: Popularity Comparison– Canada vs. U.S. (cont'd)

Name	Cdn. Rank	U.S. Rank	How many times more popular in Canada
Rylan	122	425	5.20
Braeden	122	329	3.59
Jaxon	127	284	2.77
Kayden	129	367	4.12
Markus	130	659	9.97
Matteo	139	739	10.83
Hudson	151	391	3.49
Dayton	153	504	4.71
Reid	153	458	4.15
Declan	159	420	3.56
Marshall	159	349	2.73
Armaan	164	*	*
Kaiden	164	368	2.99
Damon	164	298	2.08
Grayson	164	297	2.08
Rowan	172	627	6.20
Morgan	178	362	2.65
Easton	180	490	3.84
Ali	181	344	2.38

* Does not appear in U.S. Top 1,000.

*Where names appear to be tied for a particular ranking, differences in actual numbers were too small to be of statistical significance.

A Different Name: It's Easier Than You Think

Annual "Top 20 Baby Names" show that names like Ethan, Joshua, Matthew, and Jacob currently lead the pack for boys in Canada, while the popularity charts for girls are led by such runaway favourites as Emma, Emily, Hannah, and Madison.

However, there's one interesting trend these Top 20 lists don't show—with each year that passes, fewer children are likely to have *any* of the most popular names.

This shift away from popular names has been going on for some time. Back in 1960, nearly 40% of all boys and about 26% of all girls had Top 20 names. In those days, schools were awash with Daves, Mikes, Marys, Sues, and Lindas.

But the popularity of the most popular names has been steadily dropping. In 1998 in British Columbia, only about 25% of baby boys and 19% of baby girls were given one of the Top 20 names for their sex. And that figure has dropped still further since then. In fact, by 2005, Top 20 names made up less than 19% of all boys' names and only around 14% of all girls' names.

The names we give our children are becoming increasingly diverse. Most parents don't want to give their child a name that will appear on a Top 20 list. Popularity is becoming unpopular.

All of which is good news for parents. It means that if you want to give your child a name that's a bit different, you're in good company. On the other hand, if you're in love with one of the most popular names, you will probably find that the name isn't so popular that it becomes a nuisance. At present, Emma is Canada's runaway favourite name for girls, but, even so, only

1 newborn girl in 80 will receive the name, so the odds are that there won't be another one in her kindergarten class.

With so many unusual names being given, standing out may actually help a child to fit in.

A Sampling of Unusual Names

Alberta's unique names are a fascinating mix of variant spellings, names from various ethnic backgrounds, names from history, surnames, place names, words that have been turned into names, and a smattering of traditional names that have become surprisingly rare. Here's a sample from the many thousands of Alberta's unique names from 2005:

Girls

Acadia, Agnes, Annette, Arizona, Azure, Cidney, Cleopatra, Gail, Gertrude, Hilda, Holland, Jax, Jaymee, Kamilla, MecKenzie, Memphis, Mystery, Orion, Paneet, Paula, Serina, Tacoma, Tate, Trudy, Xiu, Zenith, Zipporah, Zya.

Boys

Abhijeet, Alister, Apollo, Ark, Boris, Bradlee, Brampton, Domonik, Edison, Grey, Hadrian, Hank, Heinrich, Heron, Ivory, Job, Keewatin, Lee, Linus, Mack, McCoy, Noel, Paris, Riel, Sanjay, Spirit, Steel, Thorin, Tobin, Tor, Trice, Wallace.

Want to see more? Check out the detailed online name lists available for Alberta. For a taste of naming trends in French

Canada, look at the equally detailed information available for Quebec.

Alberta:

governmentservices.gov.ab.ca/vs/top10_names.cfm

Quebec:

www.rrq.gouv.qc.ca/en/enfants/banque_prenoms.htm

Names Most Likely to Succeed

One of the most fascinating aspects of name-watching is figuring out which names are on their way up and which are on their way down.

Many of the names in the top spots reached their peak several years ago and have since been slowly declining in popularity. Emma and Emily still held the top spots among girls' names in 2005, but Emma seems to have reached its peak in 2003, and Emily, while it has maintained a hold on its place in the name charts, has been in slow decline since 1998. Other top girls' names that are slipping in the ranks include Hannah, Madison, and Sarah.

The same is true of boys' names. Ethan, Joshua, Matthew, and Jacob have been in the top spots for several years, but all are slowly slipping in popularity, while another red-hot name for boys, Nathan, may have peaked around 2005.

Further down the rankings, though, a number of names have shown steady and impressive growth. It's a good bet that these names—or at least some of them—will be the top-ranked baby names of the future.

Among girls' names, one of the most spectacular risers has been Ava. In 1997, roughly 1 girl in 2,000 was given this name. In 2005, it was closer to 1 in 80—high enough to put it into the Top 10 lists of many provinces. The very newest baby name data from Alberta showed Ava in top place among girls' names; Ava seems poised to become the next Emma or Emily.

Another "fast climber" is the name Isabella and its many variations, including Isabelle and Isabel. If the Isa-somethings were taken as a group, they would top the 2005 name charts—and their popularity is still increasing. The male counterpart to this success story is Kaden—also spelled Kayden and Kaiden—which has been moving briskly up the charts for some years.

Among the boys' names, two of the rising stars include nick-name variations of classic names—Jack and Charlie. Charles is also showing signs of regaining popularity.

Nevaeh ("heaven" backwards) has gained sudden popularity and some media attention in the past few years. It remains to be seen whether Nevaeh will be a new hot name or just a brief fad. While the name's popularity seems to be rising in Canada, in the United States it's in decline, having peaked around 2001.

Following are "fast climbers" among baby names. Not all are yet popular, but it's a good bet that at least some of these will show up in future lists of most popular names.

Girls

Amelia, Angelina, Arianna, Ashlyn, Audrey, Ava, Charlotte, Gracie, Isabel, Isabella, Isabelle, Jaida, Kaylee, Keira, Lily, Lola, Makenna, Maya, Mia, Nevaeh, Ruby, Scarlett, Sienna, Sophia, Stella

Boys

Ayden, Brady, Carter, Charles, Charlie, Cooper, Declan, Evan, Gage, Gavin, Hayden, Jack, Kaden, Kai, Kaleb, Kayden, Landon, Lukas, Max, Oliver, Oscar, Roman, Ryder, Rylan, Ty

Endangered Species

If you want to give a child an unusual name, you don't have to resort to Jazmine or Zion—in fact, Ann or Gary will do the trick. A surprising number of the names many of us think of as commonplace have become surprisingly rare.

In 2005, only five girls received the name Ann in British Columbia, and only two in Alberta, putting the name well below such "exotic" names as Kaydence, Ireland and Meadow. (The variant Anne is more common, but only very slightly.)

Other "endangered species" include Wendy, Joan, Dawn, Vera, and Gail, all of which barely register on current listings. This is surprising in the case of Gail, since the related name Abigail is one of the Top 20 girls' names. Lois, a Top 20 name in the 1920s and 30s, with a respectable presence until the mid-60s, is now almost extinct and doesn't appear on any of the currently available provincial listings. It seems to have dropped off U.S. listings around 1984.

Jane, a name that was once duplicated in most classes, has now fallen into the "rare" category. Even the name Mary, which ranked number one for most of the 20th century, has fallen on hard times and, in much of Canada, languishes below the Top 100, far behind Mackenzie and Trinity.

Among the boys' names that have virtually dropped off the chart in much of Canada are Todd, Lewis, Ralph, Perry, Alfred, Larry, Nigel, Hugh, Randall, Edmund, Eugene, and Howard. Such names as Gary, Neil, Norman, and Stuart (or Stewart) don't fare much better, ranking far below the likes of Phoenix, Payton, and Jace.

One place where many traditional names have maintained their hold is as middle names. For example, in 2003, Nova Scotia parents were fairly well tuned in to national trends, with a similar fondness for Emmas, Madisons, Ethans, and Joshuas. But parents were far more conservative when choosing middle names, with the top choices being Elizabeth, Marie, Dawn Grace, and Ann, even though Ann was used only twice that year as a first name, and Dawn doesn't appear at all.

A similar, if less pronounced disparity exists with boys' names. The runaway top choice for middle names in New Brunswick was James, which registered a modest 53rd place as a first name.

Is It Short for Something?

You love the name Max but hate Maxwell and Maximilian. You've always dreamed of naming your daughter Lola but were disappointed to find out it was the short form of Dolores. Or you thought Kit would be a nice name for a boy but didn't want to call him Christopher and have him end up as Chris.

Parents facing situations like these have two choices. They can either choose the full-length name and try to ensure that the nickname they like is used, or they can make the nickname the child's official name.

On the plus side, using a nickname as an independent name forces the issue of how the child will be addressed. On the downside, with many nicknames you may be condemning the child to a lifetime of being asked what his or her name is short for.

The following are some of the more popular nicknames currently being used as independent names by parents across Canada.

Girls' Name	Canada Ranking	Boys' Name	Canada Ranking
Laurie	82	Jack	33
Kate	97	Ty	79
Abby	147	Alex	85
Molly	155	Jake	105
Gracie	169	Max	145
Jessie	206	Drew	248
Lorie	226	Ben	265
Charlie	369	Josh	277
Ellie	391	Andy	284
Carly	398	Joey	286
Susie	444	Alec	293
Jesse	464	Sam	320
Lola	503	Jamie	360
Drew	504	Zack	364
Elle	504	Jimmy	390

Gender Breakdown of Unisex Names

Name	% Girls	% Boys
Jayden	18	82
Riley	20	80
Jaden	24	76
Micah	25	75
Jordan	28	72
Charlie	29	71
Quinn	31	69
Rowan	31	69
Phoenix	36	64
Jamie	56	44
Dakota	57	43
Morgan	66	34
Reese	68	32
Peyton	71	29
Sage	74	26
Payton	77	23
Avery	78	22
Teagan	81	19
Taylor	85	15

Unisex Names

Common boys' names are sometimes bestowed on girls, although the reverse is less common. In the past, this has tended to mean that names which become popular as girls' names will then lose their popularity among boys. A number of names that we would now consider decidedly female were once all-male names, including Beverly, Carol, Evelyn, Jocelyn, Meredith, Nicole, Shirley, and Shannon.

Today we have a new crop of unisex names. In 2005, Charlie, Quinn, Rowan, and Phoenix were most likely to be boys' names but were also well represented among girls' names, while Jamie, Dakota, Morgan, and Reese were somewhat more likely to be for girls, if by a small margin.

The names at right, taken from 2005 data from Alberta and British Columbia, are all frequently applied to both boys and girls. They're sorted from "maleness" to "femaleness," with those around the middle of the list being the most "unisexual."

Names from the Far North

A great thing about being in a smaller community when you're naming your child is that common or popular names become much more distinctive. Looking at the names in Iqaluit, there is only 1 Ethan registered for the year 2005, whereas his Calgary namesake joins 93 other Ethans to be unleashed on their Board of Education in 2009.

The Iqaluit list also has a number of names that reflect its vibrant aboriginal community. Just like Ethan, out of 148 boys born, there is one Katsuaq and one Saagiaqtuq.

Among baby girls, you're as likely to run into Iqaluit's only Kimberly as you are to meet little Koonoo, and as likely to meet Juniper or Jo as your are to encounter Jennifer and Jessica. That is, if you can make your way past the teeming mobs of tiny Amys, Breannas, and Lilys (2 of each). Other names, like Bertha, Marlene, and Linda, have almost dropped off the map elsewhere in Canada, but they appear on Iqaluit's lists.

Compared to Iqaluit, the baby name trends from the Yukon for 1998–2003 seem downright conventional. For the most part, they aren't too different from the national figures—with one exception. The most popular Yukon boys' name, tied for first place with Matthew and well ahead of Canadian favourites like Ethan, Joshua, or Jacob, was Cole. Is it a coincidence that this is one letter short of *Cold*?

Quebec's Distinctive Names

According to 2005 figures, the most popular name for boys in Quebec is Samuel, followed closely by William. The names that follow—Alexis, Gabriel, and Félix—rank fairly low on lists from other provinces, although the popularity of Gabriel has been slowly increasing in English Canada.

Quebec's girls' names are equally distinct. Of the Top 5 girls' names—Léa, Jade, Sarah, Noémie, Rosalie—only Sarah is popular in Ontario. The remaining names barely register in Ontario or on any other provincial list.

Popular Names for Girls in Quebec (2005)

Rank	Given Name	Frequency
1	Léa	516
2	Jade	361
3	Sarah	336
4	Noémie	322
5	Rosalie	318
6	Laurence	297
7	Camille	291
8	Florence	286
9	Mégane	274
10	Coralie	264
11	Megan	262
12	Océane	257
13	Ariane	250
14	Gabrielle	250
15	Audrey	243
16	Laurie	243
17	Juliette	229
18	Justine	229
19	Émilie	226
20	Élodie	208
21	Marianne	206
22	Chloé	205
23	Émy	200
24	Charlotte	194
25	Emma	194

Popular Names for Boys in Quebec (2005)

Rank	Given Name	Frequency
1	Samuel	814
2	William	807
3	Alexis	602
4	Gabriel	601
5	Félix	577
6	Nathan	570
7	Antoine	566
8	Olivier	565
9	Thomas	562
10	Xavier	543
11	Justin	536
12	Jérémy	504
13	Mathis	492
14	Anthony	459
15	Raphaël	440
16	Alexandre	435
17	Zachary	432
18	Jacob	422
19	Vincent	401
20	Nicolas	397
21	Émile	357
22	Benjamin	328
23	Maxime	306
24	Mathieu	290
25	Simon	270

4
Choosing the Name: Some Personal Stories

Many Canadians were happy to share stories about how they made their child-naming decisions. As well, some adult children shared their experiences of living with—and in some cases surviving—their names. We hope these accounts will offer tips, provide insights, and help parents avoid some common pitfalls.

It Had Better Be a Girl!

My husband, Terry, and I couldn't agree on a boy's name. I wanted Avery—my mother's maiden name and my middle name—but by the time I was ready to use it, the TV show "Murphy Brown" had just used it for Murphy's little boy, so *everyone* was using it. Terry liked the name Dexter. Some of his favourite sports stars were named Dexter, and to him it represented everything macho. To me it was the name of a pet dog or a cartoon character. We did, however, completely agree on a girl's name, Matilda Rosemary—Tillie for short—after Terry's grandmother. She was an amazing woman—strong and quiet, but she loved to laugh.

We were a little anxious when Tillie was born because neither one of us knew if the child would be a boy or a girl; and we still hadn't resolved the problem of a boy's name. We found out what she was when the doctor, who knew our choices for names, started singing "Waltzing Matilda" as he delivered her.

—Susan A.

Beyond the Real Jennifer and Jason

My wife and I were both saddled with unbelievably common names for our generation (Jennifer and Jason), so we wanted a name that was a little unusual.

The inspiration behind the name Evan began back when we had somehow gotten it into our heads that we were going to have a girl, which seems to be what happens when you are going to have a boy, and Jen was idly running through the names of all her favourite classic female authors, looking for a girl's name she liked. But she hated them all—Charlotte, Emily, Jane, Virginia, and so on. Then she thought of the author George Eliot, whose real name was Mary Ann Evans. Jen didn't like Mary or Mary Ann either, but she thought, well, Evan is a nice name if we have a boy.

I went through the same exercise trying to come up with a middle name. One of my favourite authors is Harlan Ellison. I didn't like the way Harlan sort of rhymed with Evan, but it occurred to me that Evan Ellison, along with our surname, had a really nice ring to it. Jennifer agreed; we both liked the way that the "unusualness" of Ellison offset the "normalness" of Evan, and we thought that the "e-literation" of Evan and Ellison

was very pleasing and distinctive. So finally our son had his first and middle names, each of them inspired by an author's last name!

—Jason T.

People We Admire and Love

Audrey was named after the movie star Audrey Hepburn. Karen always admired her for her beauty and spirit (see the lovely *Roman Holiday* sometime) and for her humanitarian work with the United Nations. Karen always just liked the name Audrey, too. Our other daughter, Sara, was named after my late sister, who died in a car accident when she was only 15 years old and I was only 10. I thought I would honour her memory with the naming and, in a spiritual sort of way, give her another chance at life. At first it was awkward calling the little baby Sara because I still thought of my sister every time I heard it or said the name, but eventually she became her own person and I only think of this once in a while. Eric was named after his grandfather, Karen's dad, whom he missed knowing by only months. Karen was pregnant with Eric when her dad died. Her dad was William Eric Bricker Shelby and we named our boy Eric Bricker, sort of taking the middle.

—Gary P.

Spelling Matters

My name, Eoin (pronounced like the Welsh "Owen"), is an old Irish name—roughly equivalent to John. I have a brother named Liam and a sister named Siobhan, and growing up in the late 50s and early 60s, we might as well have been using the symbol that Prince adopted, such was the confusion our foreign names engendered. One teacher dubbed my brother Lyman. That morphed into Lemon, which is his nickname to this day. These days, with Liam Neeson of movie fame and Liam Gallagher of Oasis, my brother's name has become more mainstream. It cracked the Top 10 in Alberta last year at number seven.

My sister, Siobhan, has gone through every possible permutation including Sheboygan. My favourite was Sh'boom.

As for me, Eoin was a tough one for folks to get a handle on—Edin, Odin, Evan, Erin, Orin, Ian . . . the list is endless. A music teacher sealed the deal when he looked at something I had signed Eoin K. and asked, "Who is Oink?" That nickname stuck, and it's still my nickname with some of my friends. It's a little easier to take at 50 than it was at 15. And in Ireland, it's great to be somewhere people don't stumble over your name. I've been in a room with four Eoins. None beside me had ever encountered any confusion or teasing.

—Eoin K.

No Pressure, Though

I would like to be able to weave some marvellously wild tale about how we came up with our kids' names, but the truth is we simply bought a name book and spent weeks or months (I forget now) flipping pages. It was easy for us both to agree on the names we both hated—there were plenty of those—but for almost every name one of us liked, inevitably, the other

> "My sister, Siobhan, has gone through every possible permutation including Sheboygan. My favourite was Sh'boom."

would sneer, and on we'd go. Classic names seemed to be more our style. I hated the trendy media types, as everyone was using them. Imagine the look on a teacher's face today as 15 girls raise their hands when Brittany and Ashley are called during attendance.

Matthew is one of the most popular names, but we liked it and it stuck. No religious link was involved, however. Justin's middle name is Richard, after my father.

Only a parent could appreciate how much responsibility it is to choose a name that will forever identify this new life form. I remember feeling that we had to do this well, as we would be measured at some point based on our decision. Neither child has complained, so I guess we did all right.

—Paul G.

Sibling Rivalry

When our daughter Claire was 19 months old, we welcomed twin girls to the family. (Claire was chosen as a name because we thought it was beautiful, but for no other particular reason than that.)

Our first twin is named Hannah Margaret. The second twin is named Lauren Blanche. Both Margaret and Blanche are names that come from the grandmothers. In fact, both of my grandmothers are named Blanche. When my grandmother Blanche C. heard that we had named Lauren this, she said, "Why would you give that poor baby such a terrible name?" I absolutely love the name and so do the twins. It has become such an issue in our house that we try not to say the name Blanche. In fact,

"Who knew that
the one name
everybody
questioned
would become
the favourite
family name?"

whenever one of them hears the name Blanche, we end up with a screaming fight. Both girls insist that they are Blanche. On several occasions we have ended up with crying girls saying, "I'm Blanche. No . . . I'm the real Blanche . . ." Who knew that the one name everybody questioned would become the favourite family name?

—Julie G.

You Can Ruin a Good Thing

It came as quite a surprise to us during the ultrasound when we found out we were having a boy. After three beautiful girls, we assumed we would have a fourth girl to add to the family; when we found out it would be a boy, it led to many baby-naming problems. We so clearly had several girls' names to use but were absolutely baffled about a boy's name. Two weeks before the baby was born, we finally decided on Nathan. I preferred the name Nate. I lovingly rubbed my belly for the final weeks, calling our baby by name.

But unfortunately for me, my husband is a fan of rap music. Apparently there is a rapper named Nate Dog. My husband, Tony, decided that this would be a fun name to call our baby. So for the last week of my pregnancy, Tony kept saying to the baby, "Yo, Nate Dog, what's up? Nate Dog, Nate Dog, Nate Dog . . ."

Needless to say, minutes after our son was born I informed my husband that the baby was no longer going to be Nathan and we needed to come up with a name. He exclaimed, "You can't do that." I had to. The name had been ruined for me. Nate

Dog was all I could see as I looked at this beautiful baby. Forty-eight hours later, as we were being discharged from the hospital, we finally agreed on the name Trevor Anthony. We have absolutely no regrets with such a great choice.

—Julie G.

Two Great Flavours Rolled into One

I named my third daughter Emily for the odd reason that I liked/wanted the name Amelia, but Steve had never heard of the name. I grew up in an Italian neighbourhood with lots of Amelias. Steve was from Anglo Beaconsfield in Montreal and was all for Emma. Emily was our compromise.

—Maureen S.

I Am Not a Number

I was one of many Lindas in my Grade Two class at Brookhaven Public School in 1951. The teacher, Miss Money, had difficulty keeping the Lindas straight in her mind so she assigned us a number according to our last names. I ended up being Linda number five. That made me angry. Being referred to by a number was really rather dehumanizing, even to my seven-year-old mind. I decided then and there to change my name to Lin. I wonder if that teacher ever thought about what she had done to us with the numbers. This had an impact on me when I had children of my own, and they were given names that were unusual for the time.

—Linda B. (Linda was the number one name in 1951.)

Oliver's Story

Our nine-month-old boy is Oliver Mattawa Baker Benjamin Davis (the poor thing). We had no idea what to call him. I had only girls' names in mind, and his father had no ideas at all. Then about two weeks before I was due, we attended a reading of Canadian author Sandra Birdsell at a local Chapters, here in Ottawa. She read from her new novel, *Children of the Day*. The main character was a fellow named Oliver. Richard and I both looked at each other and, at the exact same time, asked, "What do you think of the name Oliver?" And so it was.

Mattawa is in there because it's the name of the first river we canoe-tripped on together. Baker is his mother's maiden name. Benjamin is my last name, and Davis is Richard's. "Mattawa" raises a lot of eyebrows. Hopefully we haven't burdened the little guy too much!

—Erin B.

Jennifer's Story

The name Jennifer was very popular in the early 1970s. The successful movie *Love Story* opened in 1970, and the lead character was Jennifer. Perhaps that's what inspired so many parents around that time. My mom just liked the name, and it wasn't until I went to school that we realized just how many Jennifers were out there. There was at least one other in my class throughout public and high school. At university there were 5 on my floor in residence and 25 in the building. Unlike Michael or David, both very popular names, Jennifer was the rage of my generation only.

I have to say I now feel no great attachment to my name. Even my middle name—Lynn—is much used with Jennifer.

It was because of my experiences that I wanted a distinctive, unusual name for my daughter. My husband preferred a traditional name. Together we looked through all the baby name books. I wanted Lavender, and my husband liked Heather. Claire and Clara were the final choices (not unusual but hopefully not too common). We settled on Clara, my great-grandmother's name.

We waited till after Clara was born to share the name with family and friends because we didn't want to hear their opinions beforehand. It seems that everyone likes the name, including, most important of all, Clara.

—Jennifer A.

This Is How You Remind Me . . .

My mom is from Wales and left home at 16 to train and then work as a nurse. She travelled extensively throughout the world (Egypt, Australia, America, and Europe), before arriving in North Battleford, Saskatchewan, on "assignment," thinking it would be just another gig. That's where she met my dad. They dated, but he wasn't making a move to get married—so she took a job in British Columbia. She travelled by train and went through Lake Louise. She thought it was the most beautiful place that she had ever seen. She decided if she ever had a girl she would name her Louise. So when my dad eventually got around to proposing and I was finally born, my mom named me Louise. She still thinks Lake Louise is the prettiest place she's ever seen.

—Louise P.

But I Go by My Second Name

I was initially named Patricia, for the flagship *The Patricia* of the RCYC (Royal Canadian Yacht Club in Toronto). Then, when I was one month old, my parents played the family card and went for Ann, after my two grandmothers. Smart. I've been Ann ever since. The two names are confusing only at official functions. Funnily enough *The Patricia* was decommissioned, and in the 60s it sank. Just like the name.

—(Patricia) Ann L.

A Piece of Home: Transplanted Culture

My husband and I are from Kenya. Our daughter's name, Makena, is a Kikuyu (my tribe) name, meaning "joyful or cheerful person." I picked the name because it has a nice ring to it. I believe strongly that names are meaningful, and the idea of a joyful daughter appealed to me. Most people in Canada don't realize the name is Kenyan and tend to write it McKenna, as if it were Scottish. My son Jerome has the middle name Thayu (thigh-yoh), also Kikuyu. It means "peace." Most North Americans find it hard to pronounce. Kikuyus always name their children after the father's parents first and then the mother's, but although I used my cultural background to choose my children's names, I didn't feel constrained by that custom.

—Loise G.

"Our daughter's name, Makena, is a Kikuyu name, meaning 'joyful or cheerful person.'"

Watch Those Initials!

My husband, Jeff, and I named our girls Tayla Danielle and Kira Lynn. We tried to get original names. I thought I had made up Tayla, but after she was born I checked online and saw that it's popular in Australia. We went with Danielle because it went nicely with Tayla and our last name, and my husband has a thing for Jack Daniels. (It's a good thing we didn't have a boy!) I thought Kira was unusual, and then again, after her birth, noticed many Kiras, but at least the spelling seems different. Jeff's mom's middle name is Katherine, but the KKK initials stopped us with that one!

—Cheryl K.

Just Look at the Numbers!

We chose our son's name, Taylor Adam, because it represents his maternal and paternal grandmothers' maiden names. So there was a family connection, which is important to our Irish/Scottish roots. We wanted to avoid the generational "hand-me-down" names like George and went for something a little different but not "way out there." The name had a good flow, and numerologically it means "number one—will be successful."

The downside to the name, Taylor plus Adam plus our last name, is that they are all first names, which sometimes causes confusion. Also, 22 years ago the name Taylor was very rare, but now it's popular and often assumed to be a girl's name.

—Hazel D.

You Take the High Road

In Highland dancing, the music played for the sword dance is called "Gillie Callum." My mother has a picture with that title, swords, and a pair of dance shoes. Because Highland dancing is such a big thing in our family, and we have a Scottish background, I thought Callum Gilbert was a great name (and it does suit our son). His middle name is my mother's maiden name.

—Kerry S.

Iceland Gets the Cold Shoulder

When our first child, a boy, was born, we agreed on a first name but were stuck over middle names. We chose Nicholas for a first name because it was biblical. (We hadn't a clue that it was also rather trendy—we were desperately trying to avoid that!) But we agreed he was never going to be Nick. He was to be addressed only as Nicholas. Now he signs his name Nick. And, yes, we call him Nick too.

My family background is Icelandic. For Nicholas, I suggested the middle names Helgi Finnbogi (HEL-gee Fin-BOY-ya), after my grandfather. My wife didn't like the names. She was willing to consider Finn as a compromise, but to me that sounded more Irish than Icelandic. We ended up using the middle names Brian Timothy.

When our first daughter came along, my wife wanted to name her Arwen. She thought it was beautiful. I thought that it would sound like it was invented by a couple of Dungeons and Dragons geeks and would subject her to endless taunting. So we named her Natalie Jane. Then the Lord of the Rings movies came out, and it turned out that Natalie loved the name Arwen and wished we had given her that name.

When our next daughter was on the verge of arriving, I tried again to inject some Icelandic nomenclature into the family. I suggested the names Sigrithur, after my great-aunt, who was the first female medical doctor in Western Canada, or Haldora, after my grandmother. Both names were vetoed because of their "Norse coarseness," and we ended up calling our daughter Amy Caroline, because Amy is a pretty name, and Caroline, the diminutive of Carol, was after her maternal Grammie, Carol.

—Richard B.

Name on, Macduff!

My dad's name was Donald MacDonald. He was a handsome fellow, and the girls used to flock around him and tease him. When they were studying *Macbeth* in high school, the girls started calling my dad Macduff MacDonald, after the character Macduff in the play. They thought that was pretty funny! But the nickname stuck, and over the years he was called Duffy MacDonald.

When he married my mother, they had seven children and gave most of them names starting with a D—Dennis, Dale, Doreen, Diane. By the time I came along, as number seven, they decided that I would be "Little Duffy," although they gave me a few other names too. (Donald Bruce Duff MacDonald is the full name.)

When I got into my early 20s, I decided that "Little Duffy"

"Then the Lord of the Rings movies came out, and it turned out that Natalie loved the name Arwen and wished we had given her that name."

could just be Duff. I'm an actor now, and I like having a name that comes from one of the greatest plays of all time.

—Duff MacD.

I Hate Seymour!

I was born in the old Mount Sinai Hospital in Toronto. My mother had just come to Canada from Lithuania. She'd only been in Canada nine months, and she didn't know much about English names. I was supposed to be named after my father's father. So my mother asked the woman in the next bed, "What's a good English name for Shmuel Shimon?" The woman in the next bed said, "Seymour is a great name." So I was called Seymour Simon. Seymour! I hated that name.

On the first day of Grade Three, my new teacher, Mrs. Schultz, was calling attendance. She called each name, and each kid raised a hand. She called Seymour Levitan. I just sat there. So she said, "Is there anyone else whose name I haven't called?" Then I raised my hand and told her, "My name is Steven, and if you call me anything else, I'm not answering." So she crossed out Seymour and wrote in Steven Levitan.

I went by Steve after that, and for years I told my parents I wanted to change my name legally. They said no. So, when I was 18, I went to my parents' lawyer to change my name, Seymour Simon Levitan, to Steven Simon Levitan. I signed the papers. I swore affidavits, etc. But when the papers came back, I realized the lawyer had made a mistake.

My name had been changed to Seymour Steven Levitan.

—Steve L.

Is That Short for Something?

Having gone through my own name issues, choosing the right name for my children was very important. My wife and I both wanted a name that was unusual. When our first daughter was born, I wanted a name that could be male or female. I liked the idea that when she was applying for a job, people wouldn't instantly classify her as a female. This was back in 1986, when sexism was still a big issue.

We had chosen a Hebrew name. My father had just died. He was named Chonon, so we named our daughter Chanit. We just needed an English name that began with *Ch,* as is the custom. So we picked Charlie. Even now, when my daughter meets someone new, she'll say "My name is Charlie." They say, "Charlene? Charlotte?" "No, Charlie." "Is that short for something?" Our second daughter, Michael, gets the same thing. "My name is Michael." "Is that Michel?"

At 10, their names were a source of embarrassment to them. Now they're older, and it's a cool thing.

—Steve L.

> "At 10, their names were a source of embarrassment to them. Now they're older, and it's a cool thing."

A Name, Not a Label

We wanted a unique but not offbeat name for our son—a name, not a label. We liked Griffin for its mythology and connotation. Half-lion, half-eagle, the griffin signifies strength and intelligence. We also liked the way the name sounded with our surname.

As a kid, I was ribbed because of my name. When we narrowed down the choices for our son, it was important to go for a name that wouldn't be easy to rhyme.

> "As a kid, I was ribbed because of my name. When we narrowed down the choices for our son, it was important to go for a name that wouldn't be easy to rhyme."

We had a short list of names and settled on Griffin during the seventh month of pregnancy. We weren't sure how our older relatives would take to the name, but everyone—including Griffin—seems very pleased with the choice. We've yet to meet anyone who shares the name.

—Simon W.

Teachers' Choice

As I recall, there were a few considerations, or rather parameters, that we put in place before the naming process began for our first son.

Being a Libra, I wanted to avoid any perceived favouritism for a particular side of the family (not that anyone would have voiced an opinion openly, coming from a conservative Presbyterian background). That parameter meant choosing a name not used recently on either side. The next consideration was the sound of the name. My husband, an accomplished linguist as well as a musician, was sensitive to the number of syllables in relation to our surname: two syllables in our surname apparently meant that you should have either one or three in the first name; otherwise it would be too "cute." We both wanted strong-sounding names, as we knew in advance that it would be a boy. The stereotype was well in place.

Next came the cultural parameter—strong on both sides—which was Celtic. We then compiled a list of all the male Celtic names found in various books. Some were dismissed as being a bit too odd, especially in their spelling. Since both of us were teachers, we were keenly aware of how time-consuming, and sometimes awkward, it can be if one's name doesn't sound anything like the way it's spelled. The Gaelic tradition excels in this phenomenon.

Our list was narrowing. Next came the significance of the name—its origin. We wanted the name to have been derived from something honourable—a name bearing positive energy and goodness. Out came the name-derivation books. The list was quickly narrowed to a few, and we both agreed on one.

Since he would have my husband's surname, it was quickly decided that he would take my maiden name for his middle name. This procedure is a family tradition. We did first check that the initials weren't some inappropriate acronym.

When the second son announced his arrival, I suggested just one name, and my husband liked it. No research, no lists— but it did meet all the criteria from the first search. (I didn't tell my spouse that it was the name of someone I had a crush on in high school.) Several relatives said the name was a mistake—too similar to the first-born's, as they both started with the same letter. They said the names would be confusing. The relatives proved to be right, and I realize now that's probably one reason people resort to calling their children "sweetie" and "dear." For his middle name, we went one generation back and used my mother's maiden name.

—Nora C.

Brontë, Dickinson, and Carr

Our daughter Emily, now in high school, was named for Emily Brontë and Emily Dickinson and Emily Carr. Her middle names, Hannah and Marie, come from my husband's aunt, who introduced us, and from my father's mother, the only grandmother I got to meet. We were going to call our baby Charlotte (after another Brontë), but my husband, whose background is European, could not pronounce the "r," which came out "ahhh" followed by a kind of choking sound. I was surprised to discover, when Em started school, that I had picked a very common name for her generation, since my reasons had been so personal.

And from our daughter herself: I think Emily is a beautiful name, languid and melodious like water. I am not sure whether I am alone in the feeling, but every time I introduce myself as "Emily" it sounds so foreign to me. I never really understood that. I love the name, but it doesn't really feel like a part of me. In my own mind, I am simply "me," not "Emily."

—Eva S. and Emily

Reflecting on the Future

Our baby is named Jayden, and we adopted him in China. As Christians, we feel blessed to nurture this child who otherwise would have grown up in miserable conditions.

Jayden came from Jadon (Hebrew), which means "God has heard." He is an insignificant person in the Old Testament, yet he is significant in his humble way—being a role model of a spiritual, humble, and hard worker. We wanted to give Jayden his name to reflect both a little of his background and the future of his path.

The sound/spelling played a role in the final decision of

choosing his name. We chose Jay*den* over Jay*don* because it has the last two letters matching our last name. We put "Jay-" over "Ja-" because Jayden looks to us more like a boy's name than, say, Jaden.

Our relatives and friends all think the name is great for its sound (easy for our grandmother to say, for sounds such as "th," "z," "1," and "n" are harder for non-English-speaking Chinese relatives).

His Chinese name is Wai Lun, which means "greatness and harmony within family." At the moment, no one has called him by his Chinese name. Even our 90-year-old grandmother calls him Jayden. I'm sure we'll teach him his Chinese name when he gets older.

—Simon and Elizabeth Y.

I Now Pronounce Me . . .

My father chose my name, Manon, and apparently Mom did not object. The song "Manon, Viens Danser le Ska" had been heard for a few years, and when I was born, everyone was naming their baby girls Manon.

Being Catholic French-Canadians, our family is loaded with middle names. My sister is Marie Annie Céline. Our middle names are chosen after our godparents.

Nobody in my family complains about their names—we can't change them. However, now living in a non-Francophone world, I'm tired of spelling mine. To save time and frustration, I've sometimes used a more common name to introduce myself to strangers. And when I sense I may need to repeat

"And when I sense I may need to repeat and spell my name many times, I've made dinner reservations under a name like Julie or Donna."

and spell my name many times, I've made dinner reservations under a name like Julie or Donna.

My parents' and grandparents' generation named their kids after saints and family members. If I should be blessed with children, I'd want to find a name that is easily pronounced in both English and French.

—Manon D.

Paging Mrs. Hopkins

My parents were in the Canadian diplomatic service, and I was born when they were posted in New Orleans. They had discussed different names for both boys and girls but hadn't come to any decision, thinking they'd have plenty of time to do so after the birth. My father was adamant that if the baby were a girl, she would be named after my mother. My mother had been named after her own mother, Ethel, but was always called by her middle name, Jean, in order to avoid confusion.

The hospital was not a very pleasant place, and my mother was anxious to collect me and go home. But she couldn't check out until she had given me a name and registered it with the hospital. The pressure was on to pick a name. Staff were paging my mother over the intercom: "Dr. Smith, please report to surgery. And, Mrs. Hopkins, have you named that baby yet?" The next time my father poked his head into my mother's hospital room, she said rather desperately, "How about Barbara Jean?" My father agreed, and my mother was dressed and packed up before filling out the necessary forms.

—Barbara C.

5
Who's Who of Canadian First Names

The lists that follow highlight Canadians who've made names for themselves. There are authors, entertainers, sports figures, artists, architects, doctors, activists, educators, inventors, entrepreneurs, designers, journalists, scientists, politicians—and more. You may want to check out these names once you have a short list of your own choices and see who else they belong to in Canada.

Male

This list includes many Canadian hockey legends and Olympic heroes. For a more comprehensive selection, see Chapter 6, "The Top 50 First Names in NHL History."

Abraham Gesner (inventor, kerosene)
Abraham Moses (A.M.) Klein (poet)
Adam Foote (hockey player)
Al MacInnis (hockey player)
Al Purdy (poet)
Al Waxman (actor)
Alan Brown (co-inventor, Pablum)
Alan Scarfe (actor)
Alan Thicke (actor)
Alberto Manguel (author)
Alex Baumann (swimmer)
Alex Colville (artist)
Alex Lifeson (singer, Rush)
Alex Trebek (TV host)
Alexander Brott (composer)
Alexander Graham Bell (inventor, telephone)
Alexander Mackenzie (explorer)
Alexander Mackenzie (prime minister)
Alexander Young (A.Y.) Jackson (artist)
Alfred Fuller (inventor, Fuller brush)
Alistair MacLeod (author)
Andy Creeggan (singer, Barenaked Ladies)
Anthony Sherwood (actor)
Anton Kuerti (pianist)
Archibald G. Huntsman (inventor, frozen fish)

Art Linkletter (TV host)
Arthur Currie (general)
Arthur Erickson (architect)
Arthur Hailey (author)
Arthur Hill (actor)
Arthur Hiller (director)
Arthur Kent (journalist)
Arthur Lismer (artist)
Arthur Meighen (prime minister)
Arthur Schawlow (Nobel Prize winner, physics)
Ashley MacIsaac (fiddler)
Atom Egoyan (director)
Austin Clarke (author)

Barry Morse (actor)
Ben Heppner (singer)
Ben Mulroney (TV host)
Ben Wicks (cartoonist)
Benjamin Darvill (singer, Crash Test Dummies)
Bernie Toorish (singer, Four Lads)
Bert Schneider (boxer)
Bertram Brockhouse (Nobel Prize winner, physics)
bill bissett (poet)
Billy Bishop (aviator)
Billy Van (actor)
Bliss Carman (author)
Bobby Hull (hockey player)
Bobby Orr (hockey player)
Bobby Vinton (singer)
Brad Gushue (curler)
Brad Roberts (Crash Test Dummies)
Brendan Fraser (actor)

Brendan Shanahan (hockey player)
Brent Butt (actor)
Brent Carver (actor)
Brett Hull (hockey player)
Brian Moore (author)
Brian (Martin Brian) Mulroney (prime minister)
Brian Orser (figure skater)
Bruce Cockburn (singer/songwriter)
Bruce Gray (actor)
Bruce Hutchison (author)
Bruce McCulloch (*The Kids in the Hall*)
Bruno Gerussi (actor)
Bruny Surin (track and field athlete)
Bryan Adams (singer/songwriter)
Bryan Trottier (hockey player)
Burton Cummings (singer/songwriter)

Charles Best (insulin co-discoverer)
Charles Joseph (Joe) Clark (prime minister)
Charles Pachter (artist)
Charles Perry (C.P.) Stacey (author)
Charles Tupper (prime minister)
Chris Hadfield (astronaut)
Chris Makepeace (actor)
Chris Potter (actor)
Chris Pronger (hockey player)
Chris Schille (curler)
Christopher Newton (director)
Christopher Plummer (actor)
Christopher Pratt (artist)
Clarence Gagnon (artist)
Clark Blaise (author)
Claude Jutra (director)

Colin Mochrie (actor)
Colm Feore (actor)
Connie Codarini (singer, Four Lads)
Conrad Bain (actor)
Conrad Black (author)
Corey Haim (actor)
Corey Hart (singer/songwriter)
Cornelius Krieghoff (artist)
Craig Dobbin (business)
Curtis Joseph (hockey player)
Cyrus Eaton (industrialist)

Dan Aykroyd (actor)
Dan George (Chief) (actor)
Dan Hill (singer/songwriter)
Dan Roberts (Crash Test Dummies)
Daniel Igali (wrestler)
Daniel Nestor (tennis player)
Daniel Petrie (director)
Dave Broadfoot (comedian)
Dave MacEachern (bobsleigher)
Dave Thomas (actor)
David Adams Richards (author)
David Bergen (author)
David Clayton-Thomas (singer/songwriter)
David Cronenberg (director)
David Foley (*The Kids in the Hall*)
David Hubel (Nobel Prize winner, medicine)
David McTaggart (Greenpeace co-founder)
David Pelletier (figure skater)
David Steinberg (comedian)
David Suzuki (author and environmentalist)
David Thompson (explorer)

Dennis Lee (poet)
Denny Doherty (singer/songwriter)
Denys Arcand (director)
Derrick Campbell (speed skater)
Domenic Troiano (guitarist)
Don Cherry (coach and commentator)
Don Duguid (curler)
Don Francks (actor)
Don Harron (comedian)
Donald Jackson (figure skater)
Donald L. Hings (inventor, Walkie-Talkie)
Donald Sutherland (actor)
Donnelly Rhodes (actor)
Donovan Bailey (track and field athlete)
Doug Anakin (bobsleigher)
Doug Harvey (hockey player)
Doug Henning (magician)
Douglas Campbell (actor)
Douglas Coupland (author)
Douglas Rain (actor)
Duncan McNaughton (track and field athlete)

Earl W. Basom (sculptor)
Earle Birney (poet)
Ed Belfour (hockey player)
Ed Evanko (actor)
Ed Jovanovski (hockey player)
Ed Robertson (singer, Barenaked Ladies)
Eddie Shore (hockey player)
Edgar Bronfman (distillery family)
Edward (Ted) Rogers (Rogers Communications)
Edward Bronfman (distillery family)
Edward Dmytryk (director)

Edward Plunket (E.P.) Taylor (entrepreneur)
Edward Samuel Rogers (inventor, "batteryless" radio)
Edward Schreyer (governor general)
Edwin Holgate (artist)
Edwin J. (E.J.) Pratt (poet)
Eli Mandel (poet)
Emanuel Sandhu (figure skater)
Eric Bédard (speed skater)
Eric Brewer (hockey player)
Eric Lindros (hockey player)
Eric McCormack (actor)
Eric Peterson (actor)
Eugene Levy (actor)

Farley Flex (*Canadian Idol* judge)
Farley Mowat (author)
Ferguson Jenkins (baseball player)
Floyd Chalmers (publisher)
François Drolet (speed skater)
François-Louis Tremblay (speed skater)
Frank Augustyn (dancer)
Frank Busseri (singer, Four Lads)
Frank Gehry (architect)
Frank Johnston (artist)
Frank Stronach (Magna founder)
Frank Shuster (comedian)
Franklin Carmichael (artist)
Fred Davis (TV host)
Fred Ewanuick (actor)
Fred Tisdall (co-inventor, Pablum)
Frederick Banting (insulin co-discoverer)
Frederick Varley (artist)

Gaétan Boucher (speed skater)

Galen Weston (billionaire)

Geddy Lee (singer, Rush)

Gene Lockhart (actor)

George Chuvalo (boxer)

George Dunning (director)

George Knudson (golfer)

George Mercer Dawson (explorer)

George Woodcock (poet)

Georges Vanier (governor general)

Gerhard Herzberg (Nobel Prize winner, chemistry)

Gideon Sundback (inventor, zipper)

Gilles Villeneuve (Formula One driver)

Glenn Ford (actor)

Glenn Goss (curler)

Glenn Gould (pianist)

Glenn Hall (hockey player)

Glenroy Gilbert (track and field athlete)

Gord Sinclair (singer, Tragically Hip)

Gordie Howe (hockey player)

Gordon Downie (singer, Tragically Hip)

Gordon Lightfoot (singer/songwriter)

Gordon Pinsent (actor)

Gordon Sinclair (journalist)

Graeme Gibson (author)

Graham Greene (actor)

Greg Joy (track and field athlete)

Greg Moore (karter)

Guy Lafleur (hockey player)

Guy Lombardo (bandleader)

Hagood Hardy (composer)

Hank Snow (singer)

Harold Russell (actor)

Harold Town (artist)

Harrison McCain (potato magnate)

Harry Somers (composer)

Harry Wasyluk (co-inventor, green garbage bag)

Hart Bochner (actor)

Harvey Atkin (actor)

Hayden Christensen (actor)

Henry Taube (Nobel Prize winner, chemistry)

Henry Woodward (co-inventor, electric light bulb)

Homer Watson (artist)

Horace Gwynne (boxer)

Howie Mandel (comedian)

Hugh Garner (author)

Hugh MacLennan (author)

Hume Cronyn (actor)

Ian Brown (journalist)

Ian Tyson (singer/songwriter)

Irving Layton (poet)

Isaac Brock (general)

Isadore Sharp (hotel-chain founder)

Ivan Reitman (director)

Jack Bush (artist)

Jack Carson (actor)

Jack Chambers (artist)

Jack Diamond (architect)

Jack Hodgins (author)

Jack Shadbolt (artist)

Jack Warner (Warner Bros. co-founder)

Jacques Plante (hockey player)

Jacques Villeneuve (Formula One driver)

Jake Gold (*Canadian Idol* judge)

James Barber (chef)

James Cameron (director)

James Doohan (actor)

James Dunn (financier)

James Edward Harvey (J.E.H.) MacDonald (artist)

James Gosling (inventor, Java language)

James Naismith (inventor, basketball)

James Reaney (author)

Jamie Kennedy (chef)

Jamie Korab (curler)

Jan Rubes (actor)

Jarome Iginla (hockey player)

Jason Priestley (actor)

Jay Silverheels (actor)

Jean Beliveau (hockey player)

Jean Chrétien (prime minister)

Jean Gascon (director)

Jean Vanier (activist)

Jean-Luc Brassard (skier)

Jean-Paul Riopelle (artist)

Jeff Buttle (figure skater)

Jeffrey Simpson (journalist)

Jim Carrey (actor)

Jim Creeggan (singer, Barenaked Ladies)

Jim Day (equestrian)

Jim Elder (equestrian)

Jim Pattison (billionaire)

Jimmy Arnold (singer, Four Lads)

Jimmy Rankin (singer/songwriter)

Joe Clark (prime minister)

Joe Flaherty (actor)

Joe Nieuwendyk (hockey player)

Joe Sakic (hockey player)

Joe Shuster (Superman co-creator)

John A. Macdonald (prime minister)

John Abbott (prime minister)

John Alcorn (singer)

John Arpin (composer)

John Candy (actor)

John Colicos (actor)

John Connon (inventor, panoramic camera)

John Diefenbaker (prime minister)

John Emery (bobsleigher)

John F. Allen (physicist)

John Hirsch (director)

John Ireland (actor)

John Kenneth Galbraith (economist)

John McCrae (soldier and poet)

John Molson (Molson Breweries founder)

John Morris Rankin (singer/songwriter)

John Neville (actor)

John Polanyi (Nobel Prize winner, chemistry)

John Rae (explorer)

John Robert Colombo (author)

John Thompson (prime minister)

John Turner (prime minister)

John Vernon (actor)

Johnny Fay (singer, Tragically Hip)

Johnny Wayne (comedian)

Jonathan Guilmette (speed skater)

Joseph Wiseman (actor)

Joseph-Armand Bombardier (inventor, snowmobile)

Jules Léger (governor general)

Kalan Porter (Canadian Idol)

Keanu Reeves (actor)

Keith Morrison (journalist)

Ken Danby (artist)

Ken Dryden (hockey player)

Ken Read (skier)

Kenneth Colin (K. C.) Irving (industrialist)

Kenneth Thomson (billionaire publisher)

Kevin Hearn (singer, Barenaked Ladies)

Kevin McDonald (*The Kids in the Hall*)

Kevin Zegers (actor)

Kiefer Sutherland (actor)

Kurt Browning (figure skater)

Larry Hanson (co-inventor, green garbage bag)

Lawren Harris (artist)

Len Cariou (actor)

Lennox Lewis (boxer)

Leonard Cohen (singer/poet)

Leslie McFarlane (author)

Leslie Nielsen (actor)

Lester Pearson (prime minister)

Lewis MacKenzie (General)

Lewis Urry (inventor, alkaline battery)

Lloyd Bochner (actor)

Lloyd Eisler (figure skater)

Lloyd Robertson (news anchor)

Lorne Cardinal (actor)

Lorne Greene (actor)

Lorne Michaels (*Saturday Night Live* producer)

Lou Jacobi (actor)

Louis Applebaum (composer)

Louis B. Mayer (MGM co-founder)

Louis Del Grande (actor)

Louis Fréchette (author)

Louis Hémon (author)

Louis Joliet (explorer)

Louis Negin (actor)

Louis Quilico (singer)

Louis St. Laurent (prime minister)

Mack Sennett (director)

Mackenzie Bowell (prime minister)

Malcolm Lowry (author)

Marc Gagnon (speed skater)

Marc Garneau (astronaut)

Marcel Dionne (hockey player)

Mike Bossy (hockey player)

Mario Bernardi (musician)

Mario Lemieux (hockey player)

Mark McCoy (track and field athlete)

Mark McKinney (*The Kids in the Hall*)

Mark Messier (hockey player)

Mark Nichols (curler)

Mark Tewksbury (swimmer)

Marshall McLuhan (communications theorist)

Martin Brodeur (hockey player)

Martin Short (actor)

Mathew Evans (co-inventor, electric light bulb)

Mathieu Turcotte (speed skater)

Matt Cohen (author)

Matt Craven (actor)

Matt Frewer (actor)

Matthew Perry (actor)

Maurice Richard (hockey player)

Maury Chaykin (actor)

Max Braithwaite (author)
Michael Ironside (actor)
Michael J. Fox (actor)
Michael Ondaatje (author)
Michael Ontkean (actor)
Michael Sarrazin (actor)
Michael Smith (chef)
Michael Smith (Nobel Prize winner, chemistry)
Michael Snow (artist)
Michel Tremblay (playwright)
Mike Adam (curler)
Mike Frogley (basketball)
Mike Myers (actor)
Mike Peca (hockey player)
Mike Smith (decathlete)
Mike Weir (golfer)
Milton Acorn (author)
Mitch Dorge (Crash Test Dummies)
Moe Koffman (musician)
Monty Hall (TV host)
Mordecai Richler (author)
Morley Callaghan (author)
Morley Safer (journalist)
Moses Znaimer (television mogul)
Moshe Safdie (architect)
Myron Scholes (Nobel Prize winner, economics)

Nat Taylor (movie theatre mogul)
Ned Hanlan (rower)
Neil Peart (drummer, Rush)
Neil Young (singer/songwriter)
Nicholas Pennell (actor)
Nick Mancuso (actor)

Nino Ricci (author)
Norm MacDonald (comedian)
Norman Bethune (surgeon)
Norman Breakey (inventor, paint roller)
Norman Jewison (director)
Northrop Frye (critic and scholar)
Norval Morrisseau (artist)

Oscar Brand (singer/songwriter)
Oscar Peterson (jazz pianist)
Otto Jelinek (figure skater)
Owen Nolan (hockey player)

Patrick Roy (hockey player)
Paul Anka (singer/songwriter)
Paul Coffey (hockey player)
Paul Desmarais (businessman)
Paul Gross (actor)
Paul Henderson (hockey player)
Paul Kane (artist)
Paul Kariya (hockey player)
Paul Langlois (singer, Tragically Hip)
Paul Martin (prime minister)
Paul Martini (figure skater)
Paul Peel (artist)
Paul Quarrington (author)
Paul Reichmann (businessman)
Paul Shaffer (*Letterman* musical director)
Paul Soles (actor)
Paul Tracy (Indy race-car driver)
Percy Faith (bandleader)
Percy Williams (triathlon)
Peter Aykroyd (actor)

Peter Gzowski (radio show anchor)
Peter Jennings (journalist)
Peter Kirby (bobsleigher)
Peter (P. L.) Robertson (inventor, Robertson screwdriver)
Peter Munk (Barrick Gold founder)
Peter Newman (author)
Phil Esposito (hockey player)
Phil Hartman (actor)
Pierre Berton (author)
Pierre Fritz Lueders (bobsleigher)
Pierre Elliott Trudeau (prime minister)

Raffi (singer)
Ramon Hnatyshyn (governor general)
Randy Bachman (singer/songwriter)
Ray Bourque (hockey player)
Raymond Burr (actor)
Raymond Massey (actor)
Raymond Moriyama (architect)
Reginald Fessenden (inventor, sonar)
Rex Harrington (dancer)
Rex Murphy (journalist)
Rich Little (impressionist)
Richard Bennett (prime minister)
Richard Monette (director)
Richard Taylor (Nobel Prize, physics)
Rick Hansen (Man in Motion)
Rick Mercer (TV host)
Rick Moranis (actor)
Rob Baker (singer, Tragically Hip)
Rob Feenie (chef)
Rob McConnell (musician)

Robbie Roberstson (singer/songwriter)
Robert Bateman (artist)
Robert Blake (hockey player)
Robert Borden (prime minister)
Robert Campeau (financier)
Robert Esmie (track and field athlete)
Robert Farnon (composer)
Robert Foulis (inventor, foghorn)
Robert Fulford (journalist)
Robert Goulet (singer)
Robert MacNeil (journalist)
Robert Thirsk (astronaut)
Robert W. Service (poet)
Robertson Davies (author)
Roch Carrier (author)
Rohinton Mistry (author)
Roland Michener (governor general)
Roméo Dallaire (General)
Roméo LeBlanc (governor general)
Ron Francis (hockey player)
Ron Turcotte (jockey)
Ronnie Hawkins (singer/songwriter)
Ross Rebagliati (skier)
Roy Bonisteel (journalist)
Roy Brown (aviator)
Roy Thomson (publisher)
Rudolph Marcus (Nobel Prize winner, chemistry)
Rudy Wiebe (author)
Rufus Wainwright (singer/songwriter)
Russ Howard (curler)
Ryan Malcolm (Canadian Idol)
Ryan Smyth (hockey player)

Sam McLaughlin (auto manufacturer)
Samuel Bronfman (distillery founder)
Samuel Cunard (Cunard line founder)
Sandford Fleming (inventor, Standard Time zone)
Sandy Hawley (jockey)
Saul Bellow (author)
Saul Rubinek (actor)
Scott Bairstow (actor)
Scott Goodyear (race-car driver)
Scott Niedermayer (hockey player)
Scott Thompson (*The Kids in the Hall*)
Seán Cullen (actor)
Sebastien Lareau (tennis player)
Sidney Altman (Nobel Prize winner, chemistry)
Silver Donald Cameron (author)
Simon Fraser (explorer)
Simon Gagne (hockey player)
Simon McTavish (fur trader)
Simon Whitfield (triathlete)
Sinclair Ross (author)
Stan Mikita (hockey player)
Stan Rogers (musician)
Stephen Harper (prime minister)
Stephen Leacock (humourist)
Stephen Lewis (humanitarian)
Stephen Yan (chef)
Steve Nash (basketball)
Steve Podborski (skier)
Steve Smith (*The Red Green Show*)
Steve Yzerman (hockey player)
Steven MacLean (astronaut)
Steven Page (singer, Barenaked Ladies)
Stuart McLean (storyteller)

Ted Kotcheff (director)
Terry Fox (hero)
Terry Sawchuk (hockey player)
Theo Drake (co-inventor, Pablum)
Theo Fleury (hockey player)
Thomas Ahearn (inventor, electric-cooking range)
Thomas Carroll (inventor, combine harvester)
Thomas Chong (actor)
Thomas E. Ryan (inventor, five-pin bowling)
Thomas Raddall (author)
Tim Horton (hockey player)
Timothy Eaton (department store founder)
Timothy Findley (author)
Toller Cranston (figure skater)
Tom Cochrane (singer/songwriter)
Tom Connors (Stompin') (singer/songwriter)
Tom Gayford (equestrian)
Tom Green (TV host)
Tom Kneebone (actor)
Tom Longboat (track and field athlete)
Tom Patterson (Stratford Festival founder)
Tom Thomson (artist)
Tommy Burns (boxer)
Tommy Douglas (father of Medicare)
Tony Quarrington (musician)
Travis MacRae (singer)
Tyler Stewart (singer, Barenaked Ladies)

Vic Emery (bobsleigher)
Victor Davis (swimmer)
Victor Garber (actor)
Vincent Massey (governor general)

Walter Huston (actor)

Walter Pidgeon (actor)

Wayne Gretzy (hockey player)

Wilder Penfield (neurosurgeon)

Wilfred Bigelow (inventor, pacemaker)

Wilfrid Laurier (prime minister)

William Cornelius Van Horne (railway executive)

William Francis Giauque (Nobel Prize winner, chemistry)

William Gibson (author)

William Hutt (actor)

William Kurulek (artist)

William Lyon Mackenzie King (prime minister)

William Maxwell Aitken (publisher)

William Ormond (W. O.) Mitchell (author)

William Osler (physician)

William Patrick (W. P.) Kinsella (author)

William Shatner (actor)

William Stephenson (World War II spy)

William Vickrey (Nobel Prize winner, economics)

Willian Gibson (author)

Yousuf Karsh (photographer)

Zack Werner (*Canadian Idol* judge)

Female

Abby (Abigail) Hoffman (track and field athlete)

Ada Mackenzie (golfer)

Adele Wiseman (author)

Adrienne Clarkson (governor general)

Agnes Macphail (politician)

Alanis Morissette (singer/songwriter)

Alexa McDonough (politician)

Alexis Smith (actress)

Alice Munro (author)

Alice Wilson (geologist)

Alison Sydor (mountain biker)

Amanda Marshall (singer)

Amanda Plummer (actress)

Amy Sky (singer/songwriter)

Andrea Martin (actress)

Angela Cutrone (speed skater)

Angela Hewitt (pianist)

Ann Blades (illustrator)

Anna Hilliard (physician)

Anna Maria Tremonti (radio host)

Anna McGarrigle (singer/songwriter)

Anna Olson (chef)

Anna Sandor (screenwriter)

Anna Van Der Kamp (rower)

Anne Hébert (author)

Anne Heggtveit (skier)

Anne Murray (singer/songwriter)

Anne Ottenbrite (swimmer)

Anne Wheeler (director)

Annette av Paul (dancer)

Annie Perreault (speed skater)
Ann-Marie MacDonald (author)
Antonine Maillet (author)
Ashevak Kenojuak (artist)
Audrey McLaughlin (politician)
Avril (Kim) Campbell (prime minister)
Avril Lavigne (singer/songwriter)

Barbara Ann Scott (figure skater)
Barbara Astman (photographer)
Barbara Frum (journalist)
Barbara Gowdy (author)
Barbara McDougall (politician)
Barbara Smucker (author)
Barbara Underhill (figure skater)
Barbara Wagner (figure skater)
Beatrice Lillie (actress)
Beckie Scott (skier)
Becky Kellar (hockey player)
Bertha Wilson (judge)
Beth Underhill (equestrian)
Betsey Clifford (skier)
Betty Goodwin (artist)
Betty Oliphant (ballet educator)
Beverley McLachlin (chief justice)
Beverly Boys (diver)
Birute Galdikas (scientist)
Blair Brown (actress)
Blanche van Ginkel (architect)
Bobbie (Fanny) Rosenfeld (track and field athlete)
Bonnie Burnard (author)
Bonnie Sherr Klein (director)
Brenda Taylor (rower)

Bronwyn Drainie (journalist)
Buffy Sainte-Marie (singer/songwriter)

Cairine Wilson (politician)
Camilla Scott (actress)
Carla Macleod (hockey player)
Carling Bassett (tennis player)
Carol Shields (author)
Carole James (politician)
Carole Pope (singer)
Caroline Brunet (kayaker)
Caroline Ouellette (hockey player)
Caroline Rhea (comedian)
Carolyn Waldo (swimmer)
Carrie Derick (botanist)
Carrie-Anne Moss (actress)
Carroll Baker (singer/songwriter)
Cassie Campbell (hockey player)
Catherine Callbeck (politician)
Catherine McKinnon (actress)
Catherine McPherson (pioneer)
Catherine O'Hara (actress)
Catherine Papineau (pioneer)
Catherine Parr Traill (author)
Catherine Priestner-Allinger (speed skater)
Catherine Wisnicki (architect)
Cathleen Morawetz (mathematician)
Cathy Townsend (bowler)
Catriona LeMay Doan (speed skater)
Celia Franca (National Ballet Founder)
Céline Dion (singer)
Chandra Crawford (sprinter)
Chantal Petitclerc (track and field athlete)

Charline Labonte (hockey player)
Charlotte Gray (author)
Charlotte Van Allen (author)
Charlotte Whitton (politician)
Charmaine Crooks (track and field athlete)
Charmion King (actress)
Cheryl Pounder (hockey player)
Christina McCall (journalist)
Cherie Piper (hockey player)
Christine Boudrias (speed skater)
Christine Nordhagen Vierling (wrestler)
Christine Yoshikawa (pianist)
Cindy Klassen (speed skater)
Cindy Nicholas (swimmer)
Claire L'Heureux-Dubé (judge)
Clara Hughes (cyclist, speed skater)
Colleen Dewhurst (actress)
Colleen Sostorics (hockey player)
Constance Beresford-Howe (author)
Cookie Rankin (singer, Rankin Family)
Cynthia Dale (actress)

Danielle Goyette (hockey player)
Daphne Odjig (artist)
Dawn Goss (photographer)
Deanna Brasseur (pilot)
Deanna Durbin (actress)
Debbie Brill (track and field athlete)
Debbie Travis (decorator)
Deborah Grey (politician)
Deepa Mehta (director)
Denise Filiatrault (actress)
Diana Krall (singer/songwriter)

Diana Leblanc (director)
Diane Dufresne (actress)
Diane Dupuy (director)
Diane Francis (journalist)
Diane Jones Konihowski (track and field athlete)
Dinah Christie (singer)
Donna Feore (director)
Dora de Pédery-Hunt (sculptor)
Doreen Kimura (psychologist)
Doris Anderson (journalist)
Doris Giller (journalist)
Dorothea Crittenden (politician)
Dorothy Grant (fashion designer)
Dorothy Livesay (author)

Edith Firth (librarian)
Elaine Tanner (swimmer)
Elizabeth Arden (a.k.a. Florence Nightingale
     Graham) (businesswoman)
Elizabeth Legge (curator)
Elizabeth MacGill (engineer)
Elizabeth Manley (figure skater)
Elizabeth Smart (author)
Ellen Fairclough (politician)
Ellen Reid (singer, Crash Test Dummies)
Emily Carr (artist)
Emily Stowe (physician)
Emily VanCamp (actress)
Emma Robinson (rower)
Erica Durance (actress)
Erika Ritter (playwright)
Esther Hill (architect)
Ethel Blondin-Andrew (politician)

Ethel Catherwood (track and field athlete)
Ethel Wilson (author)
Eva Avila (Canadian Idol)
Eva Tanguay (actress)
Evelyn Hart (dancer)
Evelyn Lau (author)
Evelyn Nelson (mathematician)

Fannie ("Bobbie") Rosenfeld (track and field
    athlete)
Fay Wray (actress)
Fifi D'Orsay (actress)
Fiona MacGillivray (singer)
Fiona Reid (actress)
Flora Eaton (businesswoman)
Flora MacDonald (politician)
Florence Bell (track and field athlete)
Florence Bird (politician)
Florence Carlyle (artist)
Florence Harvey (golfer)
Florence Nightingale Graham (a.k.a. Elizabeth
    Arden)
Florence Wyle (sculptor)
France St. Louis (hockey player)
Frances Hyland (actress)
Frances Loring (sculptor)
Francess Halpenny (editor)

Gabrielle Miller (actress)
Gabrielle Roy (author)
Gail Greenough (equestrian)
Gail Kim (wrestler)

Gale Garnett (singer/songwriter)
Geneviève Bujold (actress)
Geneviève Jeanson (cyclist)
Gillian Apps (hockey player)
Gillian Ferrari (hockey player)
Gina Kingsbury (hockey player)
Ginette Anfousse (illustrator)
Ginette Reno (singer)
Gisele MacKenzie (singer)
Gloria Reuben (actress)
Grace Hartman (activist)
Grace MacInnis (politician)
Gwendolyn MacEwan (poet)

Haley Wickenheiser (hockey player)
Hana Gartner (journalist)
Heather Collins (illustrator)
Heather Mallick (journalist)
Heather Reisman (businesswoman)
Helen Hogg-Priestley (astronomer)
Helen Kelesi (tennis player)
Helen Maksagak (lieutenant governor)
Helen Shaver (actress)
Helen Vanderburg (swimmer)
Helene Winston (actress)
Hilary Corbett (fashion designer)
Hilary Weston (lieutenant goveror)
Holly Cole (singer)

Iona Campagnolo (lieutenant governor)
Ione Christensen (senator)
Irene MacDonald (diver)

Isabel Bassett (journalist)
Isabel McLaughlin (artist)
Isabelle Brasseur (figure skater)
Isabelle Duchesnay (figure skater)

Jackie Burroughs (actress)
Jamie Salé (figure skater)
Jan Betker (curler)
Jane Jacobs (urban activist)
Jane Mallett (actress)
Jane Urquhart (author)
Janet Carnochan (historian)
Janet Lunn (author)
Janet Wright (actress)
Jann Arden (singer/songwriter)
Jayna Hefford (hockey player)
Jayne Eastwood (actress)
Jean Adair (actress)
Jean Augustine (politician)
Jean Little (author)
Jean Wilson (speed skater)
Jeanne Sauvé (governor general)
Jehane Benôit (chef)
Jennifer Botterill (hockey player)
Jennifer Dale (actress)
Jennifer de Silva (director)
Jennifer Heil (skier)
Jennifer Robinson (figure skater)
Jenny Trout (physician)
Jessica Monroe (rower)
Jessica Rakoczy (boxer)
Jessica Steen (actress)

Jessie Gray (surgeon)
Jillian Hennessy (actress)
Joan McCusker (curler)
Joanna Gleason (actress)
Joni Mitchell (singer/songwriter)
Josée Chouinard (figure skater)
Joy Coghill (actress)
Joy Kogawa (author)
Joyce Fairbairn (politician)
Joyce Wieland (artist)
Judith Crawley (director)
Judith Forst (singer)
Judy Cameron (aviator)
Judy LaMarsh (politician)
Judy Rebick (activist)
Judy Sams (golfer)
Julia Levy (microbiologist)
Julie Khaner (actress)
Julie Payette (astronaut)
Juliette (singer)
June Callwood (author)
June Havoc (actress)
June Kander (educator)

Karen Baldwin (Miss Universe)
Karen Clark (swimmer)
Karen Kain (dancer)
Karen Magnussen (figure skater)
Karen Percy (skier)
Kate Aitken (cookbook writer)
Kate Gallant (actress)
Kate McGarrigle (singer/songwriter)

Kate Nelligan (actress)

Kate Reid (actress)

Katherine Acheson (scholar)

Kathleen Heddle (rower)

Kathryn Dawn (k.d.) Lang (singer)

Kathy Kreiner (skier)

Katie Weatherston (hockey player)

Kay Worthington (rower)

Kerrin Lee-Gartner (skier)

Kim Campbell (Avril Kim Campbell) (prime
   minister)

Kim Cattrall (actress)

Kim Ondaatje (artist)

Kim St. Pierre (hockey player)

Kim Stockwood (singer)

Kimberley Glasco (dancer)

Kirsten Barnes (rower)

Lally Cadeau (actress)

Laura Secord (heroine)

Laurie Graham (skier)

Léa Pool (director)

Leah Pells (track and field athlete)

Lela Alene Brooks (speed skater)

Lesley Thompson (rower)

Leslie Cliff (swimmer)

Lilias Torrance Newton (artist)

Lillian Smith (librarian)

Linda Evangelista (supermodel)

Linda Jackson (cyclist)

Linda Thorson (actress)

Liona Boyd (guitarist)

Lisa Bertoncini (archer)

Lise Payette (politician)

Lise Thibault (lieutenant governor)

Lois Marshall (singer)

Lois Maxwell (actress)

Lois Smith (dancer)

Loreena McKennitt (singer)

Lori Ann Munenzer (cyclist)

Lori Dupuis (hockey player)

Lori Fung (gymnist)

Lorna Crozier (poet)

Louise Arbour (judge)

Louise Frechette (ambassador)

Louise Petrie (actress)

Luba Goy (comedian)

Lucille Lessard (archer)

Lucille Wheeler (skier)

Lucy Maude Montgomery (author)

Lyn McLeod (politician)

Lynn Crosbie (author)

Lynn Johnston (cartoonist)

Lynn Verge (politician)

Lynne Griffin (actress)

Madeline Fritz (paleontologist)

Manon Rhéaume (hockey player)

Marcia Gudereit (curler)

Margaret Atwood (author)

Margaret Gibson (author)

Margaret Illmann (dancer)

Margaret Laurence (author)

Margaret MacMillan (author)

Margaret McCain (lieutenant governor)

Margaret Newton (pathologist)

Margie Gillis (dancer)
Margot Kidder (actress)
Maria Jelinek (figure skater)
Marian Engel (author)
Marianne Limpert (swimmer)
Marianne Scott (librarian)
Marie Chouinard (choreographer)
Marie Dressler (actress)
Marie Gay (cartoonist)
Marie Thérèse Casgrain (politician)
Marie-Claire Blais (author)
Marilyn Bell (swimmer)
Marilyn Brooks (fashion designer)
Marilyn Lightstone (actress)
Marion Boyd (politician)
Marion Dewar (politician)
Marion Long (artist)
Marion Reid (lieutenant governor)
Marlene Streit (golfer)
Marnie McBean (rower)
Martha Billes (businesswoman)
Martha Henry (actress)
Mary Pickford (actress)
Mary Pratt (artist)
Mary Walsh (comedian)
Maryse Carmichael (aviator)
Maryse Turcotte (weightlifter)
Maud Menten (scientist)
Maude Abbott (physician)
Maude Barlow (activist)
Maureen Forrester (singer)
Mavis Gallant (author)
Mayann Francis (lieutenant governor)

Mazo de la Roche (author)
Meg Tilly (actress)
Megan Delehanty (rower)
Megan Follows (actress)
Meghan Agosta (hockey player)
Mélanie Turgeon (skier)
Melissa Hayden (dancer)
Melissa O'Neil (Canadian Idol)
Michaëlle Jean (governor general)
Michele Landsberg (journalist)
Michelle Buckingham (judo)
Michelle Cameron (swimmer)
Michelle Latimer (actress)
Michelle Wright (singer)
Miriam Toews (author)
Miriam Waddington (author)
Molly Brant (pioneer)
Monika Deol (journalist)
Monika Schnarre (model)
Monique Bégin (politician)
Monique Frize (engineer)
Monique Leyrac (singer)
Muriel Fergusson (politician)
Myra Freeman (lieutenant governor)
Myriam Bédard (biathlete)
Myrtle Cook (track and field athlete)

Nancy Greene (skier)
Nancy MacBeth (politician)
Nancy Robertson (actress)
Naomi Klein (activist)
Natalie Blebova (Miss Universe)
Natalie Davis (author)

Natasha Henstridge (actress, model)
Nathalie Lambert (speed skater)
Nellie Cournoyea (politician)
Nellie McClung (politician)
Nelly Furtado (singer)
Neve Campbell (actress)
Nia Vardalos (actress)
Noreen Young (puppeteer)
Norma Shearer (actress)

Ofra Harnoy (cellist)
Olivia Poole (inventor, Jolly Jumper)

Pamela Anderson (actress)
Pamela Wallin (journalist)
Pat Mella (politician)
Patricia Beatty (dancer)
Pauline Jewett (educator)
Pauline Johnson (poet)
Pauline McGibbon (lieutenant governor)
Pauline Vaillancourt (singer)
Pauline Vanier (humanitarian)
Pearl McGonigal (lieutenant governor)
Perdita Felicien (track and field athlete)
Petra Burka (figure skater)
Phyllis Dewar (swimmer)
Phyllis Lambert (architect)
Prudence Heward (artist)

Rachel Blanchard (actress)
Rachel McAdams (actress)
Rachel Zimmerman (inventor, computer program)
Rae Dawn Chong (actress)

Rita Johnston (politician)
Rita MacNeil (singer)
Roberta Bondar (astronaut)
Roberta Maxwell (actress)
Rosalie Silberman Abella (judge)
Rose Sheinin (educator)
Rosella Bjornson (aviator)
Rosemary Brown (politician)
Rosemary Forsyth (actress)
Ruby Keeler (actress)
Ruth Collins-Nakai (educator)
Ruth Ohi (author and illustrator)

Sandie Rinaldo (journalist)
Sandra Gwyn (author)
Sandra Lundy (cartoonist)
Sandra Oh (actress)
Sandra Post (golfer)
Sandra Schmirler (curler)
Sandra Shamas (comedian)
Sara Botsford (actress)
Sarah McLachlan (singer/songwriter)
Sarah Polley (actress)
Sarah Vaillancourt (hockey player)
Sass Jordan (*Canadian Idol* judge)
Shania Twain (singer/songwriter)
Shannon Crawford (rower)
Sharon Acker (actress)
Sharon Carstairs (politician)
Sharon Wood (mountaineer)
Sheila Copps (politician)
Sheila Fischman (translator)
Sheila Fraser (politician)

Sheila McCarthy (actress)
Sheila Watson (author)
Shelagh Grant (educator)
Shelagh Rogers (broadcaster)
Sherry Boudreau (body builder)
Sherry Cooper (economist)
Shirley Cheechoo (artist)
Shirley Douglas (actress)
Silken Laumann (rower)
Silvia Pecota (photographer)
Sonja Bata (businesswoman)
Stevie Cameron (journalist)
Sue Holloway (skier)
Sue Johanson (educator)
Susan Aglukark (singer)
Susan Clark (actress)
Susan Musgrave (author)
Susan Swan (author)
Susanna Moodie (author)
Susannah Oland (businesswoman)
Suzanne Tremblay (politician)
Sylvia Fedoruk (lieutenant governor)
Sylvia Tyson (singer/songwriter)
Sylvie Bernier (diver)
Sylvie Burka (speed skater)
Sylvie Daigle (speed skater)
Sylvie Fortier (swimmer)
Sylvie Fréchette (swimmer)

Tanya Dubnicoff (cyclist)
Tara Spencer-Nairn (actress)
Teresa Stratas (singer)
Thelma Finlayson (biologist)
Theresa Anne Luke (rower)
Theresa Sokyrka (singer)
Toya Alexis (singer)

Ursula Franklin (physicist)

Valerie Pringle (journalist)
Vanessa Harwood (dancer)
Vanessa Lengies (actress)
Veronica Tennant (dancer)
Vicki Gabereau (journalist)
Vicki Keith (swimmer)
Vicky Sunohara (hockey player)

Wendy Clay (military leader)
Wendy Crewson (actress)

Yvonne De Carlo (actress)
Yvonne McKague-Housser (artist)

Zahra Kazemi (photographer)

6

The Top 50 First Names
in NHL History

Rank	Name*	Number of players	Rank	Name*	Number of players	Rank	Name*	Number of players
1	Mike	218	18	Ed	64	35	Brad	40
2	Bob/Robert	202	19	Doug	63	36	Jean	39
3	Jim	135	20	Don	63	37	Andrew	39
4	Dave	127	21	Al	63	38	Martin	38
5	John	124	22	Ron	61	39	Jason	37
6	Bill/Will	123	23	Jeff	59	40	Dennis	37
7	Steve	116	24	Pat	56	41	Fred	36
8	Rick/Dick	97	25	Gord	53	42	Eric	36
9	Tom	93	26	Ken	51	43	Norm	34
10	Marc	87	27	Gerry	51	44	Tony	33
11	Pete	85	28	Gary	49	45	Nick	33
12	Chris	84	29	Alex	49	46	Kevin	33
13	Paul	83	30	Scott	45	47	Craig	33
14	Dan	83	31	Frank	44	48	Randy	31
15	Bryan	82	32	Matt	43	49	Charles	31
16	Jack	73	33	Greg	42	50	Tim	30
17	Joe	67	34	George	42			

*"Name"column includes all variations (including European variations, such as Alexei, which is Russian for Alex); the most common version of the name is shown. The cutoff point for the number of recurring names was 30, which means that Wayne and Todd, at 28 each, didn't make this list. Information was extracted from The National Hockey League Official Guide and Record Book 2006.

Interesting Facts

Some of the most popular first names among today's top hockey players and up-and-comers include:

Dan/Daniel/Dany (Boyle, Alfredsson, Briere, Heatley)
Alex/Alexander/Alexei (Steen, Ovechkin, Yashin)
Chris (Drury, Higgins, Pronger)
Eric/Erik (Lindros, Staal, Cole)
Martin/Marty (Brodeur, St. Louis, Turco)
Ryan (Getzlaf, Miller, Smyth)
Thomas/Tomas (Vanek, Vokoun, Kaberle)

All these are among the Top 50 first names in NHL history. (Eric is lowest overall, at 42). Mike (including Michael and Miika)—by far the most popular NHL first name over the years—remains extremely hot (Mike Modano and Mike Richards; Michael Peca and Michael Ryder; and the NHL's top goaltender, Miikka Kiprusoff).

Mike, Bob, Jim, and Dave have been favourite first names in both the hockey and general populations (although the overall popularity of Jim/James has been sliding). But in lists that go back 50 years and more, Steven and Peter—both in hockey's Top 12—have never been in that league among the general population.

Most players like the short form of a name. There are 116 Bills and Billy's but no Williams. (Exception: There are more Martins than Marty's—26 vs. 12.)

Out of all the male first names in the world, it seems that just 50 of them make up more than half (55%, in fact) of all hockey players who ever appeared in the NHL. (There are about 5,800 NHL players in hockey history. The Top 50 names account for an extraordinary 3,200 of them.)

The Top 50 First Names of NHL Players (in alphabetical order)

Al, Alain, Alan, Albert, Allan, Allen, Alyn: 63

Alec, Alek, Aleksander, Aleksey, Ales, Alex, Alexander, Alexei: 49

Andrei, Andrew, Andy: 39

Bill, Billy: 116; Will, Willie, Willy: 7

Bob, Bobby: 147; Rob, Robbie, Robert, Roberto: 55

Brad: 40

Brian, Bryan, Bryon: 82

Chris, Christian, Christer, Christoph, Christopher: 76; Kris, Kristian, Krystofer: 8

Charles, Charley, Charlie, Chuck: 31

Craig: 33

Dan, Daniel, Danny, Dany: 83

Dave, David: 127

Dennis, Denny: 37

Don, Donald: 63

Doug, Douglas: 63

Ed, Eddie, Eddy, Edward: 64

Eric, Erich, Erik: 36

Frank: 44

Fred, Freddy, Frederic, Fredrik: 36

Gary, Garry: 49

George, Georges: 42

Gerry, Gerald: 39; Jerome, Jerry, Jarome, Jaromir: 12

Gord, Gordie, Gordon: 53

Greg, Gregg, Gregory: 42

Jack, Jackie, Jacques: 73

James, Jamie: 27; Jim, Jimmy: 108

Jason: 37

Jean (includes Jean-Claude, Jean-Marc, etc.): 39

Jeff: 54; Geoff: 5

Joe, Joey: 57; José, Josef (no Josephs): 10

John, John, Jon, Jonathan: 124

Ken, Kenny: 51

Kevin: 33

Marc, Marco, Marcus, Mark, Marko, Markus: 87

Martin, Marty: 38

Mathieu, Mats, Matt, Matti, Mattias: 43

Mike: 155; Michael: 8; Michal, Michel: 26;
   Mick, Mickey, Micki, Miika, Miikka,
   Mika, Mikko: 18; Mikael, Mikhael: 11

Nick, Nicklas, Niclas, Nik, Nikita, Niklas,
   Niko, Nikolai, Nikos: 33

Norm, Normand: 34

Pat, Patric, Patrice, Patrick, Patrik, Patsy: 56

Paul: 71; Pavel: 12

Pete, Peter, Petr, Petri, Petteri: 85

Randy: 31

Ric, Rick, Richard: 81; Dick, Dickie, 16

Ron, Ronald, Ronnie: 61

Ryan: 23

Scot, Scott, Scottie, Scotty: 45

Stefan, Stephan, Stephane: 18; Stephen: 6;
   Steve: 87; Steven: 5

Thomas: 10; Thommie, Thommy: 2; Tomas:
   16; Tom: 51; Tomi, Tommi, Tommy: 14

Tim, Timo: 30

Toni, Tony: 33

7
Your Baby's Name and the Stars

Here's a capsule summary of personality traits and qualities associated with each sign of the zodiac. You may want to look for a name that suggests some of the characteristics of the sign your baby will be born under.

Also listed are some well-known people—good people; we've left out the villains—born under each sign. You'll see that there are some common threads here.

And even if you take astrology with a grain of salt, you may spot some names or people who inspire you as you thumb your way down these lists.

A few comments. The signs are sun signs, and you should remember that other planets and the moon also play key roles in each person's astrological chart. But because of the sun's prominence, the traits below should give an idea of the impression your child might make on others.

The dates used for each sign vary slightly, but the ones given in the following pages are fairly standard. Also, the date when your child makes his or her appearance is the one that astrologers use—even if the child is actually due before or after that date and under a different sign.

Aries
March 21–April 20

Top 10 Aries Traits
Adventurous
Ambitious
Decisive
Domineering
Idealistic
Impatient
Independent
Inspiring
Optimistic
Take-charge

Well-known Aries
You'll find songwriters, figure skaters, and ballet dancers among the prominent people born under the sign of the ram.

March 21
Matthew Broderick (1962)
Rosie O'Donnell (1962)

March 22
William Shatner (1931)
Andrew Lloyd Webber
(1948)
Elvis Stojko (1972)
Reese Witherspoon (1976)

March 23
Akira Kurosawa (1910)
Chaka Khan (1953)

March 24
David Suzuki (1936)
Alyson Hannigan (1974)

March 25
Gloria Steinem (1934)
Elton John (1947)
Sarah Jessica Parker (1965)

March 26
Martin Short (1950)
Keira Knightley (1985)

March 27
Jann Arden (1962)
Mariah Carey (1970)

March 28
Karen Kain (1951)
Vince Vaughan (1970)

March 29
John Major (1943)
Lucy Lawless (1968)

March 30
Norman Bethune (1890)
Eric Clapton (1945)
Céline Dion (1968)
Norah Jones (1979)

March 31
Gordie Howe (1928)
Ewan McGregor (1971)

April 1
Sergei Rachmaninoff
(1873)
Toshiro Mifune (1920)

April 2
Shirley Douglas (1934)
Marvin Gaye (1939)

April 3
Jane Goodall (1934)
Alec Baldwin (1958)
Eddie Murphy (1961)

April 4
Maya Angelou (1928)
Karen Magnussen (1952)
Evelyn Hart (1956)

April 5
Bette Davis (1908)
Colin Powell (1937)

April 6
Butch Cassidy (1866)
Marilu Henner (1952)

April 7
Billie Holiday (1915)
Russell Crowe (1964)

April 8
Kofi Annan (1938)
Julian Lennon (1963)

April 9
Hugh Hefner (1926)
Cynthia Nixon (1966)

April 10
Joseph Pulitzer (1847)
Haley Joel Osment (1988)

April 11
Oleg Cassini (1913)
Kelli Garner (1984)

April 12
David Letterman (1947)
Claire Danes (1979)

April 13
Samuel Beckett (1906)
Garry Kasparov (1963)

April 14
Julie Christie (1941)
Brad Garrett (1960)

April 15
Leonardo da Vinci (1452)
Emma Thompson (1959)

April 16
Kareem Abdul-Jabbar
(1947)
Ellen Barkin (1955)

April 17
William Holden (1918)
Jennifer Garner (1972)

April 18
Eric McCormack (1963)
Conan O'Brien (1963)

April 19
Ashley Judd (1968)
Hayden Christensen (1981)
Maria Sharapova (1987)

April 20
Toller Cranston (1949)
Carmen Electra (1972)

Taurus
April 21–May 22

Top 10 Taurus Traits
Cautious
Artistic
Determined
Earthy
Good-natured
Materialistic
Persistent
Possessive
Rigid
Stubborn

Well-known Taureans
The names Barbara (and Barbra), George, Melissa, and Paul, and variations on the name Katherine, are well represented under the sign of the bull.

April 21
Catherine the Great
(1729)
Elizabeth (Queen of the
UK) (1926)
Iggy Pop (1947)

April 22
Betty Page (1923)
Jack Nicholson (1937)

April 23
William Shakespeare
(1564)
Lester B. Pearson (1897)
Sandra Dee (1942)

April 24
William I of Orange
(1533)
Barbra Streisand (1942)

April 25
Edward R. Murrow
(1908)
Melissa Hayden (1923)
Renée Zellweger (1969)

April 26
Carol Burnett (1933)
Jet Li (1963)

April 27
Ulysses S. Grant (1822)
Sheena Easton (1959)

April 28
Harper Lee (1926)
Jay Leno (1950)
Penelope Cruz (1974)

April 29
Jerry Seinfeld (1954)
Daniel Day-Lewis (1957)
Michelle Pfeiffer (1957)
Curtis Joseph (1967)

April 30
Paul Gross (1959)
Stephen Harper (1959)
Kirsten Dunst (1982)

May 1
Judy Collins (1939)
Tim McGraw (1967)

May 2
William Hutt (1920)
Donatella Versace (1955)
David Beckham (1975)

May 3
Dodie Smith (1896)
Doug Henning (1947)

May 4
Audrey Hepburn (1929)
Lance Bass (1979)

May 5
Barbara Wagner (1938)
Michael Palin (1943)

May 6
Willie Mays (1931)
Roma Downey (1960)
George Clooney (1961)

May 7
Gary Cooper (1901)
Eva Peron (1919)

May 8
David Attenborough
(1926)
Melissa Gilbert (1964)
Enrique Iglesias (1975)

May 9
Barbara Ann Scott (1928)
Billy Joel (1949)
Steve Yzerman (1965)

May 10
Barbara Taylor Bradford
(1933)
Paul David Hewson
(Bono) (1960)

May 11
Salvador Dali (1904)
Nancy Greene (1943)

May 12
Katharine Hepburn
(1907)
Mike Weir (1970)

May 13
Bea Arthur (1923)
Dennis Rodman (1961)

May 14
George Lucas (1944)
Cate Blanchett (1969)

May 15
L. Frank Baum (1856)
Madeleine Albright
(1937)
Brian Eno (1948)

May 16
Pierce Brosnan (1953)
Tori Spelling (1973)

May 17
Maureen O'Sullivan
(1911)
Sugar Ray Leonard
(1956)

May 18
Perry Como (1912)
Tina Fey (1970)

May 19
Malcolm X (1925)
Nora Ephron (1941)
Pete Townsend (1945)

May 20
Jimmy Stewart (1908)
Stan Mikita (1940)
Cher (1946)

May 21
Fats Waller (1904)
Fairuza Balk (1974)

May 22
Susan Strasberg (1938)
Morrissey (1959)

Gemini
May 23–June 21

Top 10 Gemini Traits
Adaptable

Curious

Funny

Inquisitive

Intellectual

Reasonable

Restless

Verbally gifted

Versatile

Witty

Well-known Geminis
Gemini is the great communicator of the zodiac, and you'll find this sign includes authors, songwriters, and even a cartoonist.

May 23
Drew Carey (1958)
Jewel (1974)

May 24
Robert Bateman (1930)
Bob Dylan (1941)
Priscilla Presley (1945)

May 25
Ian McKellen (1939)
Mike Myers (1963)
Lauryn Hill (1975)

May 26
Jay Silverheels (1919)
Teresa Stratas (1938)

May 27
Joseph Fiennes (1970)
Lisa "Left Eye" Lopes
    (1971)

May 28
Ian Fleming (1908)
Rita MacNeil (1944)
Lynn Johnston (1947)

May 29
Bob Hope (1903)
Melissa Etheridge (1961)

May 30
Benny Goodman (1909)
Wynonna Judd (1964)

May 31
Brooke Shields (1965)
Colin Farrell (1976)

June 1
Morgan Freeman (1937)
Alanis Morissette (1974)

June 2
June Callwood (1924)
Carol Shields (1935)
Dana Carvey (1955)

June 3
Colleen Dewhurst (1926)
Curtis Mayfield (1942)

June 4
Sandra Post (1948)
Noah Wyle (1971)
Angelina Jolie (1975)

June 5
Richard Scarry (1919)
Laurie Anderson (1947)
"Marky" Mark Wahlberg
    (1971)

June 6
Joy Kogawa (1935)
Bjorn Borg (1956)

June 7
Liam Neeson (1952)
Anna Kournikova (1981)

June 8
Joan Rivers (1933)
Keenen Ivory Wayans
    (1958)

June 9
Michael J. Fox (1961)
Johnny Depp (1963)
Natalie Portman (1981)

June 10
Judy Garland (1922)
Maurice Sendak (1928)
Elizabeth Hurley (1965)

June 11
Jacques Cousteau (1910)
Joshua Jackson (1978)

June 12
Anne Frank (1929)
Jim Nabors (1932)

June 13
Malcolm McDowell
    (1943)
Mary-Kate and Ashley
    Olson (1986)

June 14
Donald Trump (1946)
Steffi Graf (1969)

June 15
Courteney Cox (1964)
Ice Cube (1969)

June 16
Joyce Carol Oates (1938)
Tupac Shakur (1971)

June 17
Igor Stravinsky (1882)
Venus Williams (1980)

June 18
Paul McCartney (1942)
Isabella Rossellini (1952)
Kurt Browning (1966)

June 19
Wallis Simpson (1896)
Pauline Kael (1919)
Salman Rushdie (1947)

June 20
Errol Flynn (1909)
Anne Murray (1945)
Nicole Kidman (1967)

June 21
Jane Russell (1921)
Prince William (1982)

Cancer
June 22–July 22

Top 10 Cancer Traits
Ambitious
Conservative
Emotional
Family-oriented
Focused
Home-oriented
Insecure
Intuitive
Persistent
Sentimental

Well-known Cancerians
Actor Dan Aykroyd, actresses Geneviève Bujold and Pamela Anderson, and Supreme Court Justice Rosalie Abella were all born on Canada Day—July 1.

June 22
Kris Kristofferson (1936)
Meryl Streep (1949)
Cindy Lauper (1953)

June 23
Johannes Gutenberg
 (1400)
June Carter Cash (1929)

June 24
Mick Fleetwood (1942)
Sherry Stringfield (1967)

June 25
George Orwell (1903)
Carly Simon (1945)

June 26
Pearl S. Buck (1892)
Chris O'Donnell (1970)

June 27
Helen Keller (1880)
Tobey Maguire (1975)

June 28
Kathy Bates (1948)
John Cusack (1966)

June 29
Antoine de Saint-Exupéry
 (1900)
Ruth Warrick (1915)
Gary Busey (1944)

June 30
Lena Horne (1917)
Michael Phelps (1985)

July 1
Rosalie Abella (1946)
Dan Aykroyd (1952)
Diana (Princess of Wales)
 (1961)
Pamela Anderson (1967)

July 2
José Canseco (1964)
Evelyn Lau (1971)
Lindsay Lohan (1986)

July 3
Franz Kafka (1883)
Tom Cruise (1962)
Yeardley Smith (1964)

July 4
Ann Landers (1918)
Geraldo Rivera (1943)

July 5
Shirley Knight (1936)
Doug Wilson (1957)

July 6
Frida Kahlo (1907)
Geoffrey Rush (1954)

July 7
Richard Starkey (Ringo
 Starr) (1939)
Michelle Kwan (1980)

July 8
John D. Rockefeller
 (1839)
Anjelica Huston (1951)

July 9
Tom Hanks (1956)
Courtney Love (1964)
Fred Savage (1976)

July 10
Alice Munro (1931)
Arthur Ashe (1943)
Jessica Simpson (1980)

July 11
E.B. White (1899)
Liona Boyd (1949)

July 12
William Osler (1849)
Pierre Berton (1920)
Bill Cosby (1937)
Cheryl Ladd (1951)

July 13
Patrick Stewart (1940)
Harrison Ford (1942)

July 14
Emmeline Pankhurst
 (1857)
Ingmar Bergman (1918)

July 15
Linda Ronstadt (1946)
Brian Austin Green
 (1973)

July 16
Barbara Stanwyck (1907)
Will Ferrell (1967)

July 17
Donald Sutherland
 (1934)
Diahann Carroll (1935)
Camilla Parker Bowles
 (1947)

July 18
Nelson Mandela (1918)
Margaret Laurence
 (1926)

July 19
Atom Egoyan (1960)
Maria Filatova (1961)

July 20
Natalie Wood (1938)
Chris Cornell (1964)

July 21
Janet Reno (1938)
Robin Williams (1952)
Josh Hartnett (1978)

July 22
Rose Kennedy (1890)
Alex Trebek (1940)
Rufus Wainwright (1973)

Leo
July 23–August 22

Top 10 Leo Traits

Attention-loving

Bossy

Determined

Egotistic

Enthusiastic

Friendly

Leadership-oriented

Goal-oriented

Good-natured

Self-confident

Well-known Leos

Many actors and athletes are born under the sign of the lion. The list includes an unusually high number of Oscar winners, along with top tennis stars and figure skaters.

July 23
Stephanie Seymour (1968)
Daniel Radcliffe (1989)

July 24
Amelia Earhart (1897)
Barry Bonds (1964)
Jennifer Lopez (1970)

July 25
Maureen Forrester
    (1930)
Matt LeBlanc (1967)

July 26
Helen Mirren (1945)
Kevin Spacey (1959)
Sandra Bullock (1964)

July 27
Bobby Gentry (1944)
Juliana Hatfield (1967)

July 28
Terry Fox (1958)
Isabelle Brasseur (1970)

July 29
Peter Jennings (1938)
Martina McBride (1966)

July 30
Paul Anka (1941)
Tom Green (1971)
Hilary Swank (1974)

July 31
Sylvie Fortier (1953)
Wesley Snipes (1962)
Joanne Kathleen (J.K.)
    Rowling (1965)

August 1
Jerry Garcia (1942)
Tempestt Bledsoe (1973)

August 2
Myrna Loy (1905)
Peter O'Toole (1932)
Wes Craven (1939)

August 3
Phyllis Dorothy (P. D.)
    James (1920)
Tony Bennett (1926)
Evangeline Lilly (1979)

August 4
Elizabeth (the Queen
    Mother) (1900)
Barack Obama (1961)

August 5
Neil Armstrong (1930)
Loni Anderson (1946)

August 6
Lucille Ball (1911)
Andy Warhol (1928)
Michelle Yeoh (1962)

August 7
Louise Leakey (1903)
Elizabeth Manley (1965)
Charlize Theron (1975)

August 8
Esther Williams (1923)
Ken Dryden (1947)
Roger Federer (1981)

August 9
Sam Elliott (1944)
Gillian Anderson (1968)

August 10
Norma Shearer (1902)
Antonio Banderas (1960)

August 11
Mavis Gallant (1922)
Steve Wozniak (1950)

August 12
Cecil B. DeMille (1881)
Dominique Swain (1980)

August 13
Annie Oakley (1860)
Alfred Hitchcock (1899)
Midori Ito (1969)

August 14
Steve Martin (1945)
Danielle Steel (1947)

August 15
Julia Child (1912)
Ben Affleck (1972)

August 16
Timothy Hutton (1960)
Angela Bassett (1968)

August 17
Mae West (1892)
Robert De Niro (1943)
Sean Penn (1960)

August 18
Shelley Winters (1920)
Christian Slater (1969)

August 19
Coco Chanel (1883)
Kyra Sedgwick (1965)
Matthew Perry (1969)

August 20
Cindy Nicholas (1957)
Fred Durst (1971)

August 21
Kim Cattrall (1956)
Josée Chouinard (1969)

August 22
Dorothy Parker (1893)
Colm Feore (1958)

Virgo
August 23–September 22

Top 10 Virgo Traits
Considerate

Detail-oriented

Inquisitive

Intellectual

Logical

Meticulous

Modest

Practical

Routine-oriented

Self-critical

Well-known Virgos
The Canadians Shania Twain, Eric Lindros, Robertson Davies, and Jason Priestley share a birthday, August 28.

August 23
Barbara Eden (1934)
Kobe Bryant (1978)

August 24
Marlee Matlin (1965)
Dave Chappelle (1973)

August 25
Elvis Costello (1954)
Tim Burton (1958)
Claudia Schiffer (1970)

August 26
Barbara Ehrenreich
    (1941)
Rick Hansen (1957)

August 27
Lyndon B. Johnson
    (1908)
Mother Teresa (1910)
Sarah Chalke (1976)

August 28
Robertson Davies (1913)
Shania Twain (1965)
Jason Priestley (1969)
Eric Lindros (1973)

August 29
Ingrid Bergman (1915)
Charlie "Bird" Parker
    (1920)
Michael Jackson (1958)

August 30
Mary Wollstonecraft
    Shelley (1797)
Andy Roddick (1982)

August 31
Jean Béliveau (1931)
Scott Niedermayer
    (1973)

September 1
Lily Tomlin (1939)
Barry Gibb (1946)
Gloria Estefan (1957)

September 2
Keanu Reeves (1964)
Faith Hill (1967)

September 3
Helen Wagner (1918)
Charlie Sheen (1965)

September 4
Richard Wright (1908)
Beyoncé Knowles (1981)

September 5
Cathy Guisewite (1959)
Dweezil Zappa (1969)

September 6
Roger Waters (1943)
Michaëlle Jean (1957)
Rosie Perez (1964)

September 7
Grandma Moses (1860)
Adam Sandler (1966)

September 8
Sid Caesar (1922)
Barbara Frum (1937)
Alecia Moore (Pink)
    (1979)

September 9
Otis Redding (1941)
Michelle Williams (1980)

September 10
Arnold Palmer (1929)
Margaret Trudeau (1948)

September 11
William Sydney Porter
    (O. Henry) (1862)
Virginia Madsen (1961)
Harry Connick Jr. (1967)

September 12
Michael Ondaatje (1943)
Rachel Ward (1957)

September 13
Laura Secord (1775)
David Clayton-Thomas
    (1941)

September 14
Ivan Pavlov (1849)
Alice Stone Blackwell
    (1857)
Callum Keith Rennie
    (1960)

September 15
Fay Wray (1907)
Harry (Prince Harry)
    (1984)

September 16
Jennifer Tilly (1961)
Marc Anthony (1968)
Alexis Bledel (1982)

September 17
Anne Bancroft (1931)
John Ritter (1948)

September 18
Greta Garbo (1905)
Frankie Avalon (1939)
Lance Armstrong (1971)

September 19
Sylvia Tyson (1940)
Jeremy Irons (1948)
Kevin Zegers (1984)

September 20
Sophia Loren (1934)
Guy Lafleur (1951)

September 21
Leonard Cohen (1934)
Faith Hill (1967)

September 22
Tommy Lasorda (1927)
Scott Baio (1961)
Bonnie Hunt (1964)

Libra
September 23–October 22

Top 10 Libra Traits
Action-oriented
Affectionate
Artistic
Diplomatic
Idealistic
Indecisive
Luxury-loving
Peace-loving
Stylish
Versatile

Well-known Libras
Libra is known for versatility. This list includes a pair of great hockey players (Patrick Roy and Mario Lemieux, both born on October 5, 1965), two statesmen (Pierre Elliott Trudeau and Tommy Douglas), and an astronaut (Julie Payette).

September 23
John Coltrane (1926)
Mary Kay Place (1947)
Bruce Springsteen (1949)

September 24
F. Scott Fitzgerald (1896)
Jim Henson (1936)
Linda McCartney (1941)

September 25
Glenn Gould (1932)
Michael Douglas (1944)
Catherine Zeta-Jones
    (1969)

September 26
Thomas Stearns (T. S.)
    Eliot (1888)
Olivia Newton-John
    (1948)

September 27
Randy Bachman (1943)
Avril Lavigne (1984)

September 28
Ed Sullivan (1901)
Gwyneth Paltrow (1987)
Hilary Duff (1987)

September 29
Gene Autry (1907)
Madeline Kahn (1942)

September 30
Eric Stoltz (1961)
Jenna Elfman (1971)
Kieran Culkin (1982)

October 1
Julie Andrews (1935)
Randy Quaid (1950)

October 2
Groucho Marx (1890)
Kelly Ripa (1970)

October 3
Stevie Ray Vaughan
    (1954)
Neve Campbell (1973)
Ashlee Simpson (1984)

October 4
Buster Keaton (1895)
Alicia Silverstone (1976)

October 5
Patrick Roy (1965)
Mario Lemieux (1965)
Kate Winslet (1975)

October 6
Thor Heyerdahl (1914)
Elisabeth Shue (1963)

October 7
Bishop Desmond Tutu
    (1931)
Thom Yorke (1968)
Rachel McAdams (1976)

October 8
Robert Lawrence (R. L.)
    Stine (1943)
Sigourney Weaver (1949)
Matt Damon (1970)

October 9
Sharon Osbourne (1952)
Tony Shalhoub (1953)

October 10
Thelonius Monk (1917)
Karen Percy (1966)

October 11
Eleanor Roosevelt (1884)
Luke Perry (1966)

October 12
Dorothy Livesay (1909)
Hugh Jackman (1968)
Kirk Cameron (1970)

October 13
Marie Osmond (1959)
Sacha Baron Cohen
    (1971)

October 14
Edward Estlin (e. e.)
    cummings (1894)
Natalie Maines (1974)

October 15
John Kenneth Galbraith
    (1908)
Sarah Ferguson (1959)

October 16
Oscar Wilde (1854)
Angela Lansbury (1925)

October 17
Margot Kidder (1948)
Rick Mercer (1969)
Marshall Mathers
    (Eminem) (1972)

October 18
Pierre Elliott Trudeau
    (1919)
Dawn Wells (1938)

October 19
Marilyn Bell (1957)
Evander Holyfield (1962)

October 20
Tommy Douglas (1904)
Viggo Mortensen (1958)
Julie Payette (1963)

October 21
Samuel Taylor Coleridge
    (1772)
Dizzy Gillespie (1917)
Carrie Fisher (1956)

October 22
Catherine Deneuve
    (1943)
Brian Boitano (1963)

Scorpio
October 23–November 21

Top 10 Scorpio Traits
Competitive

Determined

Fair

Intense

Intuitive

Investigative

Loyal

Persuasive

Secretive

Subtle

Well-known Scorpios
Bryan Adams, Gordon Lightfoot, Neil Young, Bonnie Raitt, Diana Krall, Joan Sutherland, k.d. lang, and Petula Clark are those who bring music to the scorpion's sign.

October 23
Sarah Bernhardt (1844)
Johnny Carson (1925)
Ang Lee (1954)

October 24
Kevin Kline (1947)
Monica (1980)

October 25
Pablo Picasso (1881)
Minnie Pearl (1912)

October 26
Mahalia Jackson (1911)
Hillary Rodham Clinton
   (1947)
Cary Elwes (1962)

October 27
Emily Post (1872)
Dylan Thomas (1914)
John Cleese (1939)

October 28
Bill Gates (1955)
Julia Roberts (1967)

October 29
Fanny Brice (1891)
Richard Dreyfuss (1947)
Winona Ryder (1971)

October 30
Fyodor Dostoevsky
   (1821)
Grace Slick (1939)

October 31
Dale Evans (1912)
John Candy (1950)

November 1
Victoria de los Angeles
   (1923)
Lyle Lovett (1957)

November 2
Burt Lancaster (1913)
Kathryn Dawn (k.d.)
   lang (1961)

November 3
Kate Capshaw (1953)
Dennis Miller (1953)

November 4
Kathy McMullen (1949)
Ralph Macchio (1962)
Corey Schwab (1970)

November 5
Vivien Leigh (1913)
Bryan Adams (1959)

November 6
Sally Field (1946)
Ethan Hawke (1970)

November 7
Billy Graham (1918)
Joan Sutherland (1926)
Joni Mitchell (1943)

November 8
Milton Bradley (1836)
Bonnie Raitt (1949)

November 9
Hedy Lamarr (1913)
Nick Lachey (1973)

November 10
Neil Gaiman (1960)
Brittany Murphy (1977)

November 11
Demi Moore (1962)
Leonardo DiCaprio
   (1974)

November 12
Grace Kelly (1929)
Neil Young (1945)
David Schwimmer
   (1966)

November 13
Robert Louis Stevenson
   (1850)
Whoopi Goldberg (1955)

November 14
Frederick Banting (1891)
Charles (Prince Charles)
   (1948)
Silken Laumann (1964)

November 15
Petula Clark (1932)
Sam Waterston (1940)
Helen Kelesi (1969)

November 16
Chinua Achebe (1930)
Diana Krall (1964)

November 17
Gordon Lightfoot (1938)
Maria Jelinek (1942)
Lorne Michaels (1944)

November 18
Margaret Atwood (1939)
Owen Wilson (1968)

November 19
Dick Cavett (1936)
Jodie Foster (1962)

November 20
Dick Smothers (1939)
Bo Derek (1956)

November 21
Marlo Thomas (1938)
Goldie Hawn (1945)
Ken Griffey, Jr. (1969)

Sagittarius
November 22–December 22

Top 10 Sagittarius Traits
Curious
Entertaining
Freedom-loving
Funny
Generous
Intellectual
Open-minded
Optimistic
Risk-taking
Sociable

Well-known Sagittarians
Kiefer Sutherland is among the prominent Canadians born under the sign of the archer. His dad, actor Donald Sutherland, was born under the sign of the crab; his mom, actress Shirley Douglas, is an Aries; and his grandfather, Tommy Douglas—the father of Medicare—was a Libra.

November 22
Jamie Lee Curtis (1938)
David Pelletier (1974)
Scarlett Johansson (1984)

November 23
Billy the Kid (1859)
Bruce Hornsby (1954)
Myriam Boileau (1977)

November 24
Bat Masterson (1853)
Katherine Heigl (1978)

November 25
Joe DiMaggio (1914)
Jill Hennessy (1968)

November 26
Charles Schulz (1922)
Tina Turner (1939)
Robert Goulet (1949)

November 27
Gail Sheehy (1937)
Jimi Hendrix (1942)

November 28
Nancy Mitford (1904)
Paul Shaffer (1949)
Jon Stewart (1965)

November 29
Louisa May Alcott (1832)
Howie Mandel (1955)

November 30
Lucy Maud Montgomery
    (1874)
Ben Stiller (1965)
Sandra Oh (1971)

December 1
Woody Allen (1935)
Bette Midler (1945)

December 2
Gianni Versace (1946)
Nelly Furtado (1978)
Britney Spears (1981)

December 3
Joseph Conrad (1857)
Julianne Moore (1960)
Brendan Fraser (1968)

December 4
Anna McGarrigle (1944)
Roberta Bondar (1945)
Jeff Bridges (1949)

December 5
Walt Disney (1901)
Joan Didion (1934)
Frankie Muniz (1985)

December 6
Joyce Kilmer (1886)
Dave Brubeck (1920)

December 7
Ellen Burstyn (1932)
Eugene Levy (1946)
Larry Bird (1956)

December 8
Sammy Davis, Jr. (1925)
Kim Basinger (1953)
Teri Hatcher (1964)

December 9
Kirk Douglas (1916)
Judy Dench (1934)
Felicity Huffman (1962)

December 10
Emily Dickinson (1830)
Kenneth Branagh (1960)

December 11
John Kerry (1943)
Carolyn Waldo (1964)

December 12
Frank Sinatra (1915)
Mayim Bialik (1975)

December 13
Emily Carr (1871)
Christopher Plummer
    (1929)

December 14
Patty Duke (1946)
Michael Owen (1979)

December 15
Cindy Birdsong (1939)
Don Johnson (1949)

December 16
Margaret Mead (1901)
Benjamin Bratt (1963)

December 17
Ford Madox Ford (1873)
Milla Jovovich (1975)

December 18
Steven Spielberg (1946)
Brian Orser (1961)
Christina Aguilera (1980)

December 19
Jessica Steen (1965)
Jake Gyllenhaal (1980)

December 20
Maud Gonne (1865)
Billy Bragg (1957)

December 21
Ray Romano (1957)
Florence Griffith Joyner
    (1959)
Kiefer Sutherland (1966)

December 22
Diane Sawyer (1945)
Maurice Gibb (1949)
Robin Gibb (1949)

Capricorn
December 23–January 20

Top 10 Capricorn Traits
Ambitious
Businesslike
Cautious
Grounded
Loyal
Materialistic
Peace-loving
Routine-minded
Sensitive
Shy

Well-known Capricorns
Like its symbol, the goat, Capricorn represents climbing, striving, and ambition. Rags-to-riches author Horatio Alger, shipping mogul Aristotle Onassis, and Canada's beauty mogul, Elizabeth Arden, were all born under this sign.

December 23
Susan Lucci (1946)
Corey Haim (1971)

December 24
Ava Gardner (1922)
Ricky Martin (1971)

December 25
Cab Calloway (1907)
Barbara Mandrell (1948)
Sissy Spacek (1949)

December 26
Henry Miller (1891)
Carlton Fisk (1947)

December 27
Marlene Dietrich (1901)
Gérard Depardieu (1948)

December 28
Maggie Smith (1934)
Denzel Washington
    (1954)

December 29
Mary Tyler Moore (1936)
Ted Danson (1947)
Jude Law (1972)

December 30
Stephen Leacock (1869)
Kristin Kreuk (1982)

December 31
Burton Cummings
    (1947)
Bebe Neuwirth (1958)
Val Kilmer (1959)

January 1
Paul Revere (1735)
Jerome David (J. D.)
    Salinger (1919)
Naomi Judd (1946)

January 2
Taye Diggs (1971)
Kate Bosworth (1982)

January 3
Bobby Hull (1939)
Victoria Principal (1950)

January 4
Jane Wyman (1914)
Matt Frewer (1958)
Michael Stipe (1960)

January 5
Diane Keaton (1946)
Marilyn Manson (1969)

January 6
Joan of Arc (1412)
Bonnie Franklin (1944)
Rowan Atkinson (1955)

January 7
Katie Couric (1957)
Nicolas Cage (1964)

January 8
Elvis Presley (1935)
Shirley Bassey (1937)
David Bowie (1949)

January 9
Joan Baez (1941)
Jimmy Page (1944)

January 10
Rod Stewart (1945)
George Foreman (1949)
Pat Benetar (1953)

January 11
Jean Chrétien (1934)
Amanda Peet (1972)

January 12
Jack London (1876)
Kirstie Alley (1955)

January 13
Julia Louis-Dreyfus
    (1961)
Orlando Bloom (1977)

January 14
Faye Dunaway (1941)
Jason Bateman (1969)

January 15
Dr. Martin Luther King,
    Jr. (1929)
Veronica Tennant (1946)
Andrea Martin (1947)

January 16
Ethel Merman (1909)
John Carpenter (1948)
Kate Moss (1974)

January 17
Eartha Kitt (1927)
Jim Carrey (1962)

January 18
Mark Messier (1961)
Sarah Polley (1979)

January 19
Tippi Hedren (1931)
Janis Joplin (1943)
Robert Palmer (1949)

January 20
George Burns (1896)
Bill Maher (1956)
Melissa Rivers (1968)

Aquarius
January 21–February 19

Top 10 Aquarius Traits
Creative
Funny
Idea-oriented
Independent
Individualistic
Innovative
Peace-loving
Philosophical
Sociable
Unpredictable

Well-known Aquarians
Aquarius is a musical sign that's represented by a range of singers, among them Stompin' Tom Connors, Sheryl Crow, and Placido Domingo.

January 21
Telly Savalas (1924)
Geena Davis (1956)

January 22
Mike Bossy (1957)
Diane Lane (1965)

January 23
Jeanne Moreau (1928)
Rutger Hauer (1944)
Tiffani-Amber Thiessen
    (1974)

January 24
Neil Diamond (1941)
Mischa Barton (1986)

January 25
Robert Burns (1759)
Alicia Keys (1981)

January 26
Paul Newman (1925)
Ellen DeGeneres (1958)
Wayne Gretzky (1961)

January 27
Wolfgang Amadeus
    Mozart (1756)
Donna Reed (1921)
Bridget Fonda (1964)

January 28
Sarah McLachlan (1968)
Elijah Wood (1981)

January 29
Tom Selleck (1945)
Oprah Winfrey (1954)

January 30
Vanessa Redgrave (1937)
Phil Collins (1951)
Christian Bale (1974)

January 31
Minnie Driver (1971)
Justin Timberlake (1981)

February 1
Rick James (1948)
Lisa Marie Presley (1968)

February 2
James Joyce (1882)
Farrah Fawcett (1947)

February 3
Gertrude Stein (1874)
Joey Bishop (1918)
Morgan Fairchild (1950)

February 4
Charles Lindbergh (1902)
Rosa Parks (1913)

February 5
Don Cherry (1934)
Barbara Hershey (1948)

February 6
Zsa Zsa Gabor (1917)
Kate McGarrigle (1946)

February 7
Laura Ingalls Wilder
    (1867)
Chris Rock (1966)
Ashton Kutcher (1978)

February 8
Lana Turner (1921)
Gary Coleman (1968)

February 9
Tom (Stompin' Tom)
    Connors (1936)
Joe Pesci (1944)
Carole King (1948)

February 10
Bertolt Brecht (1898)
Laura Dern (1967)

February 11
Leslie Nielsen (1926)
Abby Hoffman (1947)
Jennifer Aniston (1969)

February 12
Franco Zeffirelli (1923)
Christina Ricci (1980)

February 13
Stockard Channing
    (1944)
Peter Gabriel (1950)

February 14
Jack Benny (1894)
Meg Tilly (1960)

February 15
Susan B. Anthony (1820)
Jane Seymour (1951)
Matt Groening (1954)

February 16
Patty Andrews (1920)
LeVar Burton (1957)
John McEnroe (1959)

February 17
Martha Henry (1938)
Michael Jordan (1963)

February 18
John Travolta (1954)
Matt Dillon (1964)
Molly Ringwald (1968)

February 19
Jeff Daniels (1955)
Haylie Duff (1985)

Pisces
February 20- March 20

Top 10 Pisces Traits
Caring
Considerate
Emotional
Imaginative
Moody
Poetic
Popular
Sensitive
Spiritual
Unpredictable

Well-known Pisces
It's no surprise that swimmer Elaine Tanner was born under the sign of the fish. Pisces is also the sign of poets, among them Elizabeth Barrett Browning, Irving Layton, and Dr. Seuss (a.k.a. Theodore Geisel).

February 20
Buffy Sainte-Marie (1941)
Andrew Shue (1967)

February 21
Ryan Smyth (1976)
Jennifer Love Hewitt
   (1979)
Charlotte Church (1986)

February 22
Elaine Tanner (1951)
Vijay Singh (1963)
Drew Barrymore (1975)

February 23
Peter Fonda (1939)
Dakota Fanning (1994)

February 24
Steven Jobs (1955)
Kristin Davis (1965)

February 25
Sally Jessy Raphael
   (1935)
George Harrison (1943)
Sean Astin (1971)

February 26
Michael Bolton (1953)
Erykah Badu (1972)

February 27
John Steinbeck (1902)
Elizabeth Taylor (1932)

February 28
Frank Gehry (1929)
Bernadette Peters (1948)
Eric Lindros (1973)

February 29
Dinah Shore (1916)
Antonio Sabato, Jr.
   (1972)

March 1
Glen Miller (1904)
Ron Howard (1954)

March 2
Theodore Geisel (Dr.
   Seuss) (1904)
Karen Carpenter (1950)

March 3
Alexander Graham Bell
   (1847)
Jackie Joyner-Kersee
   (1962)

March 4
Antonio Vivaldi (1978)
Patricia Heaton (1958)

March 5
Andy Gibb (1958)
Niki Taylor (1975)

March 6
Elizabeth Barrett
   Browning (1806)
Shaquille O'Neal (1972)

March 7
Willard Scott (1934)
Tammy Faye Bakker
   (1942)
Diane Jones Konihowski
   (1951)

March 8
Aidan Quinn (1959)
Kathy Ireland (1963)

March 9
Bobby Fischer (1943)
Glenn Close (1947)
Juliette Binoche (1964)

March 10
Chuck Norris (1940)
Debbie Brill (1953)

March 11
Rupert Murdoch (1931)
Thora Birch (1982)

March 12
Irving Layton (1912)
Liza Minnelli (1946)
Susan Musgrave (1951)

March 13
Neil Sedaka (1939)
Dana Delany (1956)

March 14
Albert Einstein (1879)
Billy Crystal (1947)
Megan Follows (1968)

March 15
Mary Pratt (1935)
Sly Stone (1944)
Eva Longoria (1975)

March 16
Victor Garber (1949)
Kate Nelligan (1950)

March 17
Kurt Russell (1951)
Mia Hamm (1972)

March 18
John Updike (1932)
Vanessa Williams (1963)

March 19
Wyatt Earp (1848)
Glenn Close (1947)

March 20
Bobby Orr (1948)
Holly Hunter (1958)

8
Registering the Birth of Your Baby

In Canada, the registration of your baby's birth is documented by the provincial Vital Statistics agencies. If the birth isn't registered, you cannot obtain a birth certificate or health card. In most cases, you should receive these registration forms right after the birth of your baby, either through the hospital or your midwife. On the other hand, if your baby was born while you were hiking up Sulphur Mountain or camping in the Gaspé, you might want to contact the offices below.

The registration process is fairly straightforward, but each province has its own quirks and rules to abide by, so we suggest you contact the Vital Statistics Office in your area or check out its online services. A myriad of post-natal frustrations can be caused by the use of unusual ink colours, correction fluid, illegible script, and deadlines, so carefully read the instructions they give you.

Even if you fill out the forms perfectly, mistakes occasionally slip through. If you find that your darling Chloe has ended up as Chlop, or Bruno has been labelled a girl, try to be patient and pleasant when you deal with the overworked Vital Statistics personnel. They're probably as sleep-deprived as you are.

The following section provides basic information, including listed available addresses and phone numbers, for Vital Statistics offices.

Alberta

The birth registration form should be left with the hospital where the child was born, so that the document can be forwarded from there to Vital Statistics. The birth registration must be sent to the Vital Statistics Office within 10 days of the date of the child's birth. *Only under special circumstances can the parent(s) mail this registration directly to Vital Statistics.* If you want to ask any questions, you can call Government Services at (780) 427-7013.

Alberta Registries Vital Statistics
Box 2023
Edmonton, AB
T5J 4W7
Tel: (780) 427-7013 (recording)
www.servicealberta.gov.ab.ca/ra/ran.cfm

British Columbia

To register a child's birth, complete and return the Registration of Live Birth form to the Vital Statistics Agency within 30 days of the date of birth. This form is contained in the birth package given to parents during their stay in the hospital. It is also available at any Vital Statistics Office.

Vital Statistics Agency
818 Fort Street
PO Box 9657, STN PROV GOVT
Victoria, BC
V8W 9P3
Tel (general inquiries): (250) 952-2681
Fax: (250) 952-2527
Ordering by credit card: (250) 952-2557
Fax: (250) 952-2182
www.vs.gov.bc.ca

Business Hours:
Monday–Friday, 8:30 a.m.–4:30 p.m.

In Victoria:
818 Fort Street
Fax: (250) 952-2527

In Vancouver:
605 Robson Street, Room 250
Fax: (604) 660-2645

In Kelowna:
1475 Ellis Street, Room 101
Fax: (250) 712-7598

In Prince George:
433 Queensway Street
Fax: (250) 565-7106

Manitoba

Manitoba Vital Statistics
254 Portage Avenue
Winnipeg, MB
R3C 0B6
Tel: (204) 945-3701
Toll free in Manitoba:
1-800-282-8069, extension 3701
Fax: (204) 948-3128
E-mail:vitalstats@gov.mb.ca
www.gov.mb.ca/cca/vital

Business Hours:
Monday–Friday, 8:30 a.m.–4:30 p.m.

New Brunswick

The document used to record the birth of
your baby is called the Registration of Birth,
Form C-1. It has to be filled out within 14
days of the birth of the child.

In New Brunswick, the birth registration form must be completed before you
leave the hospital. The Government of New
Brunswick has the rules all nicely laid out in
its Vital Statistics "Birth Registration Guide"
at the Web address below.

Vital Statistics Office
Service New Brunswick
PO Box 1998
Fredericton, NB
E3B 5G4

Or:

Service New Brunswick
435 King Street, Suite 203
Fredericton, NB
E3B 1E5
Tel: (506) 453-2385
Fax: (506) 453-3245
www.snb.ca/e/1000/1000-01/e/
namebaby-e.asp

Newfoundland and Labrador

Vital Statistics
Government Service Centre
Department of Government Services
5 Mews Place
PO Box 8700
St. John's, NL
A1B 4J6
E-mail: info@gov.nl.ca

You may also apply in person at the following government service centres:

Clarenville: 2 Masonic Terrace
Corner Brook: The Noton Building,
   1 Riverside Drive
Gander: McCurdy Complex, Markham Place
Grand Bank: Buffett Building, Main Street
Grand Falls-Windsor: 9 Queensway
Happy Valley-Goose Bay: Thomas Building,
   13 Churchill Street
Harbour Grace: Conception Bay Highway
Labrador City: 118 Humphrey Road,
   Bruno Plaza
St. Anthony: Viking Mall
St. John's: 5 Mews Place
Stephenville: 35 Alabama Drive

Northwest Territories

Registrar-General of Vital Statistics
Department of Health and Social Services
Government of Northwest Territories
Bag #9
Inuvik NT
X0E 0T0
Tel: (867) 777-7420
Toll free: 1-800-661-0830
Fax: (867) 777-3197
Forms available at:
www.hlthss.gov.nt.ca/content/Publications/
Forms/Certificates/ApplicationCertificate
Eng.pdf

Nova Scotia

The Live Birth Registration form must be received by the Vital Statistics Office within 30 days. It is usually submitted by the local division registrar at the hospital. Please note that for this province the receipt of the registration form is *not* acknowledged by the Vital Statistics Office. The instruction page also includes the ominous statement "additional forms may be required."

Vital Statistics Office
PO Box 157
Halifax, NS
B3J 2M9
Tel: (902) 424-4381
Toll free: 1-877-848-2578
Fax: (902) 424-0678
E-mail: vstat@gov.ns.ca
www.gov.ns.ca/snsmr/vstat

Counter service:
1690 Hollis Street
Ground floor, Joseph Howe Building
Halifax, NS

Business Hours:
Monday–Friday, 8:30 a.m.–4:30 p.m.

Nunavut

Nunavut Health & Social Services
Bag #3
Rankin Inlet, NU
X0C 0G0
Tel: (867) 645-8001
Toll free: 1-888-252-9869
Fax: (867) 645-8092

Department of Health and Social Services
Iqaluit
Tel: (867) 975-5700
Fax: (867) 975-5705

Ontario

In Ontario, you must fill out the Statement of Live Birth form (from the hospital or midwife), and then forward it to the division of the Registrar General in your local municipality. Getting through by phone is difficult if you call the main line for the Registrar General, but your own municipality will help you find the division office nearest you.

If a doctor or a midwife was not present at the birth, the mother must submit a form and letters from two people who have knowledge of the birth. The people who submit the declarations must state that they have knowledge of the mother's identity, the mother's pregnancy and delivery, the place of birth, and the sex and weight of the child. The form is available at local Registry Services offices.

For more information:
Tel: (416) 392-7036
www.serviceontario.ca

Office of the Registrar General
PO Box 4600
189 Red River Road
Thunder Bay, ON
P7B 6L8
Tel: 1-800-461-2156 or (416) 325-8305
Fax: (807) 343-7459

For the Toronto area:
City of Toronto Registry Services Office
City Clerk's Office, Elections and Registry
    Services section
100 Queen Street West
Toronto, ON
M5H 2N2
Tel: (416) 392-7036
E-mail: registryservices@toronto.ca
www.toronto.ca/registry-services/
birth.htm

Business Hours:
Monday–Friday, 8:30 a.m.–4:15 p.m.

Prince Edward Island

The child must be registered with Vital Statistics within 30 days of the birth.

Vital Statistics Office
126 Douses Road
Montague, PE
C0A 1R0
Tel: (902) 838-0880
Toll free: 1-877-320-1253
Fax: (902) 838-0883
www.gov.pe.ca/vitalstatistics/index.php3

Charlottetown:
16 Garfield Street
Charlottetown, PE
C1A 6A5

Quebec

The child's birth must be registered within 30 days. There is an Attestation of Birth form as well as a Declaration of Birth form to fill out.

The province has a few interesting recommendations: You should give no more than four first names. A surname may not contain a number or an initial letter. Also, you should be aware that *"The Registrar of Civil Status may ask you to choose a different name from the one you have given your child only if they feel it will cause the child damage by inviting ridicule."*

Civil Registration
Le Directeur de l'état civil
2535 Boulevard Laurier
Québec (Québec)
G1V 5C5
Tel: 1-800-567-3900 (from within Quebec)
(418) 643-3900 (from outside Quebec)
Fax: (418) 646-3255
www.etatcivil.gouv.qc.ca/English/
birth.htm
www.etatcivil.gouv.qc.ca/Naissance.htm

Saskatchewan

By law, the birth of every child in Saskatchewan must be registered with Vital Statistics within 15 days of the birth. The hospital (or midwife/attendant) will send the Registration of Live Birth form to the office of Vital Statistics. The hospital will *strongly* recommend that you fill out the form before leaving.

Saskatchewan Health
Vital Statistics
100-1942 Hamilton Street
Regina, SK
S4P 4W2
Tel: (306) 787-3092
Toll free within Saskatchewan:
1-800-458-1179
Fax: (306) 787-2288
Read the rules for registering a name online at: www.health.gov.sk.ca/ps_birth_registration.html

Yukon Territory

Births must be registered within 30 days. A list of instructions that is easy to follow appears at the Web address given below.

Vital Statistics
Health and Social Services
PO Box 2703
Whitehorse, YT
Y1A 2C6
Tel: (867) 667-5207
Toll free in Yukon only:
1-800-661-0408, extension 5207
Fax: (867) 393-6486
www.hss.gov.yk.ca/programs/vitalstats/birth

Walk-in and Courier
4th Floor, 204 Lambert Street
Whitehorse, YT
Y1A 3T2

Girls' Names A–Z

A

Abigail
From the Hebrew, meaning "father rejoiced." It was the name of one of King David's wives and was much used in England during the 16th and 17th centuries when many Old Testament names were popular. It was so popular for working-class women that it degenerated into a term for a lady's maid and so became unfashionable; but it is now one of the Top 20 names for girls in Canada. Other forms include: **Abagael, Abbie, Abb(e)y, Abiga(i)l, Abigall, Gael, Gail, Gale, Gayel, Gayl(e)**.

Abira
From the Hebrew word meaning "strong" or "heroic."

Abra
The feminine form of **Abraham**, Hebrew for "Father of many." Also Arabic for "example, lesson."

Ada
A name that started life as a short form for **Adela, Adelaide,** and **Adeline,** and so means "noble." Other forms include: **Adan, Adda, Addy, Ad(d)i, Aida(h)**.

Adah
Derived from the Hebrew for "ornament" or "brightness."

Adela
From the Old German, meaning "noble." It died out but was later revived and became fashionable in the French form **Adèle**. **Addie** or **Addy** is used as a short form for the names derived from this root (see also

Adelaide and **Adeline**). Adela can also be spelled **Adella**, which gives us the name **Della**, now more popular than its source.

Adelaide
Derived from the Old German words meaning "noble and kind." Adelaide, the capital city of South Australia, was named after this popular queen. It can be shortened to **Ada, Addie,** and **Addy**. **Alida** is a Hungarian short form. **Heidi** is the popular German form; other variants include: **Adalia, Addison, Adel, Adelaida, Adélaïde, Adelheid, Adelina**.

Adeline
Like **Adelaide**, this name is derived from the Old German for "noble." It was first cited in England in the Domesday

Book and was common during the Middle Ages. After that it disappeared until the Victorian Gothic revival. It is best known from the song "Sweet Adeline." **Ada** is sometimes used as a short form. **Alina** and **Aline**, now used as separate names, were also once short forms.

Adrienne

The French feminine form of **Adrian**, from the Latin, meaning "man from Adria," and a form of the name of the Roman Emperor Hadrian, who built the wall across northern England. It has been used since Roman times; a St. Adrian was the first British martyr in the fourth century. Variants include: **Adria, Adrian, Adrian(n)a, Adrianne, Adrien, Adrienne, Adrina, Hadria**.

Afra *see* **Aphra**

Afua

From the Ghanaian, meaning "born on a Friday."

Agatha

From the Greek for "good woman," this was the name of a third-century martyr and saint. The short form is **Aggie**.

Agnes

From the Greek, meaning "pure." There was an early Christian martyr called Agnes, whose symbol is a lamb, since the name also sounds very like the Latin *agnus*, "lamb." Agnes was popular in Scotland, where it also became **Nessie** and **Nessa**. In Wales it became **Nest** and **Nesta**. **Agneta** is the Swedish form and **Inez** is the anglicized form of the Spanish **Inés**. Other variants include: **Aggi(e), Agna, Agnesa, Aigneis, Anaïs, Annice, An(n)is, Annais, Annys, Ina, Una(h), Ynes, Ynez**.

Ailsa

From the Scottish island, Ailsa Craig. First used in Scotland, where it can also be a short form of **Alice**.

Aimée

French form of **Amy**, meaning "beloved" (see also **Esmé**).

Ainsley

A place and surname used as a first name, this comes from the Old English and probably means "lonely clearing." It can also be spelled **Ainslee, Ainsleigh, Ansley, Ainslie, Aynslee, Aynsley**.

Aisha

From the Arabic, meaning "alive and well" or "prospering," originally borne by the third (and favourite) wife of the Prophet Muhammad. The name is found in many forms, including **Aiesha, Aishah, Asia, Ay(i)sha, Ayshia, Ieasha, Ie(e)sha,** and **Isha**. H. Rider Haggard used the form **Ayesha** in his novel *She*, where the meaning was given as "she who must be obeyed."

Aisling

The most common form of a name also found as **Aislinn, Isleen,** and the phonetic **Ashling**. It is an old Irish name meaning "a dream, vision."

Alana

The feminine form of **Alan**, an old Celtic name of unknown meaning. It may also be Gaelic for "bright one." The short form,

Lana, was made popular by actress Lana Turner. Alana is also spelled **Allana, Alanah,** and **Alanna,** and in the United States has developed the form **Alaina** or **Alayna**. Other forms include: **Alanis, Alina, Allene**.

Alberta
Feminine form of **Albert**, an Old German name meaning "noble and bright." Albert became so popular after the marriage of Queen Victoria to Prince Albert of Saxe-Coburg that it became over-used and so went out of fashion. The province of Alberta is named after their fourth child, Louise Alberta. **Bert** and **Bertie** are short forms. Variants include: **Alba, Albertina, Albertine**.

Albina
From the Latin *Albanus*, meaning "white," and the feminine form of **Alban**. Variants include **Alba, Albinia, Alva, Alvina, Aubine**.

Aledwen
The feminine form of **Aled**, the name of a Welsh river used as a first name.

Alegria
Spanish for "happiness, joy." Other spellings include **Alagria, Allegria**.

Alessandra *see* **Sandra**

Alethea, Aletia *see* **Althea**

Alexandra
The feminine form of **Alexander**, from the Greek meaning "defender of men." **Sandra** was originally an Italian form but has become established as a name in its own right. It shares pet and short forms with Alexander, along with **Alix** or **Alyx** (also from **Alice**) and **Alexa** (see also **Alexis**). **Alejo, Alessandra, Alex, Alexandria, Alexandrina,** and **Alexio** are also found.

Alexis
From the Greek word meaning "helper" or "defender," Alexis is the name of one of the great saints of the Orthodox church. Originally a man's name, it is now more frequently used for women. Alternative forms are **Alexa** and **Alexia** and short forms such as **Lexi(e)** and even **Lexus**.

Alfreda
From the Old English, meaning "elf-strength," it is also used as a female version of **Alfred**, although Alfreda comes from a slightly different name. Alternative forms are **Aelfreda, Alfi(e), Elfrida, Elva, Fr(i)eda**.

Alice
From the Old German word for "nobility." It originally had the form **Adelice** or **Adelise**. A number of forms remained popular from the Middle Ages until the 17th century, when it went out of favour. It was revived again in the 19th century together with the variant **Alicia**. Nowadays these have developed additional forms such as **Allice, Allyce** and **Alyssa, Alysia, Alis(s)a, Alisha**, or even **Elis(s)a** or **Elys(s)a**, although these are also short forms of **Elizabeth**. **Alison** is a variant. **Alys** is the Welsh form and Irish forms are **Alis, Ailis,** or the phonetic **Ailish**. **Ali, Allie,** and **Alley** are used as short forms, while **Alix** and **Alyx** can be used either as forms of Alice or **Alexandra**.

Alida *see* **Adelaide**

Alika
Nigerian, meaning "a beautiful girl."

Alina
Slavic form of **Helen**, which is from the Greek meaning "light." Other forms include **Aleen, Alena, Aline, Alyne, Leena(h), Lyna(h)**.

Alis, Alisa, Alisha *see* **Alice**

Alison
Originally a diminutive of **Alice** that was adopted in the 13th century, this was soon treated as a separate name. It was at one time a particularly Scottish name. Short forms include those used for Alice and **Elsie**. **Allison** and **Al(l)yson** are standard forms in the United States.

Aliyyah
The feminine form of **Ali**, a popular Arabic name meaning "exalted, noble," and as one of the terms used of Allah, invokes God's protection for the child. Aliyyah is also found as

Aliyah, Alia(h), and **Alya** and in the Swahili form **Aaliyah**, popularized by the singer Aaliyah Houston (1974–2001). Ali is also a short form of names such as **Alice, Alison**, or **Alastair**.

Allegra
An Italian word meaning "cheerful, lively," given by the poet Lord Byron to his daughter and still used occasionally as a result.

Allice, Allie, Allyce *see* **Alice, Alison**

Alma
There are many opinions about the origin of this name. It could be derived from the Hebrew word for "maiden," the Latin for "kind" or the Italian for "soul." Most importantly, the name became very popular after the Battle of Alma during the Crimean War, and is still found occasionally.

Alondra
Alondra is the Spanish for "lark." It is a common American place name, but more importantly

in the 1990s it was the name of a successful Mexican-made television series, named after its heroine.

Aloys
The feminine form of **Aloysius**, which is the Latin form of **Aloys**, an old Provençal form of **Louis**. There was a popular Spanish saint of this name in the 16th century and Roman Catholics continue to use the name in the U.K. Aloys, or **Aloyse**, is a possible source of **Eloise**.

Althea
From the Greek for "wholesome," this was the Greek name for the marsh mallow plant, still used as a healing herb. It seems to have been introduced to England with various other classical names during the Stuart period, and appeared in the charming lyric by Richard Lovelace "To Althea from Prison." The similar-sounding **Alethea** (**Alet(h)ia**) comes from the Greek for "truth."

Alvina
The rare feminine form of **Alvin** from two Old English

names, **Alwine**, "friend of all" and **Athelwine**, "noble friend."

Alysia

From the Greek, meaning "entrancing."

Alyssa

From the Greek, meaning "rational." Other forms include **Al(l)issa, Alysa, Ilyssa**.

Amabel

From the Latin, meaning "lovable." It has been in use in England in various forms since the 12th century. The short form **Mabel** became established as an independent name at an early date.

Amanda

From the Latin for "deserving love." It appears first in Restoration plays, where many classical or pseudo-classical names were introduced or fabricated. It has remained in use since then and is still popular. **Mandy** is a short form also used as a name in its own right. **Amandine** is a French form of the name which has been popular in France in recent

years. It was brought to the attention of English speakers when the actor John Malkovich chose it for his daughter.

Amaryllis

Originally from Greek, probably meaning "sparkling," and used by Greek poets as a name for a country girl. It served the same purpose for Latin poets and was introduced to Britain via English poetry in the 17th century.

Amber

The name of the gemstone, now used as a first name. It was not used before the 20th century.

Ambrin

From the Arabic for "ambergris," a substance renowned for its sweet odour. It can also be spelled **Ambreen**.

Ambrosine

A rare feminine form. From the male **Ambrose**, from the Greek for "divine."

Amelia

From an Old German name possibly meaning "work," its form is perhaps influenced by

Emilia (*see* **Emily**). **Amalia, Amalie, Amaline**, and **Amalita** are forms of the name. It can be shortened to **Milly**.

Amina

The feminine form of **Amin**, Arabic for "honest," "trustworthy," or "reliable." Amina has always been much used in honour of Amina bint-Wahab, mother of the Prophet Muhammad. It is sometimes spelled **A(a)mena** or **Aaminah**. **Iman**, "faith, belief," comes from the same root. The model who uses this name has made it widely known, and it sometimes appears as **Imani** or **Imana**.

Aminta, Amynta *see* **Araminta**

Amrit

In the Vedic epics of the Hindus, this Sanskrit name refers to immortality or that which confers it, such as the "water of life, soma juice, nectar, [or] ambrosia." Amrit can be used for both sexes, although the form **Amrita** can also be used for a girl.

Amy
From the French, meaning "beloved." Sir Walter Scott's novel *Kenilworth*, about Amy Robsart, the tragic wife of the Earl of Leicester, made the name fashionable in the 19th century, and it has been popular again in recent years. **Aimée** is the French original of this name, which can also be found in forms such as **Aime(e)**, **Ami(e),** and **Amye**.

Anaïs
A French name that comes from the Greek word for "fruitful."

Ananda
The feminine form of **Anand** from the Sanskrit for "happiness," "joy," or "bliss." It is the name of a god in the Veda, sacred book of the Hindus. Variants include **Anandamayi** ("full of joy"), **Anandi,** and **Anandini** ("joyful").

Anastasia
From the Greek, meaning "resurrection." The name of a 4th-century saint and martyr, it became fashionable in England in the 13th century, though it was usually abbreviated to **Anstey** or **Anstice**, which mainly survive today as surnames. It has always been very popular in Russia, perhaps referring to a daughter of the last Tsar of Russia, called Anastasia, who is said to have escaped from the massacre in which the rest of her family died in 1918. **Stacey** and **Tansy** started as short forms of this name. **Nastasia** is a Russian short form and the emerging name **Tassia** (**Taja, Tasia**) is probably a shortening of this.

Andrea
Feminine form of **Andrew** (from the Greek for "manly"). Andrew is the name of the Apostle who is patron saint of Scotland, Russia, and Greece, and first appears in England in the Domesday Book. The Italian form, Andrea, is actually a boy's name in Italy but is used as a girl's name in Britain. The French boy's form, **André**, is likewise sometimes used for girls, although the more correct form **Andrée** is also used. Other feminine forms include **Andrene, Andrena,** and **Andreana**, while **Andra** is both a traditional Scottish form of the boy's name and used for girls.

Aneka, Aneke, An(n)ika see **Anne**

Angela
From the Latin *angelus* originally derived from the Greek word meaning "messenger," hence our word "angel." It is shortened to **Angel** and **Angie**. Other forms of the name include the French **Angelique**, and elaborations such as **Angelica, Angelia, Angeline,** and **Angelina**, as well as spellings with a "j" instead of a "g."

Angelina see **Angela**

Angharad
A Welsh name meaning "much loved." It is an important name in early Welsh literature and has been in use since at least the ninth century. The stress is on the second syllable.

Anila
The feminine form of **Anil** derived from the Sanskrit

meaning "air" or "wind," also the name of the wind-god in the Hindu Vedic epics.

Anisha
A Sanskrit name, one of the thousand borne by the Hindu god Vishnu. Its meaning is possibly "without a master."

Anita, **Ann**, **Anna** *see* **Anne**

Annabel
Together with **Annabelle** or **Annabella**, this is probably from the Latin *amabilis* meaning "lovable," a variant of **Amabel**. It is found in Scotland earlier than **Anne**, so it is unlikely to be a form of that name, though it is now sometimes thought of as a compound of **Anna** and the Latin *bella* meaning "beautiful." Diminutives include **Bel** and **Belle**.

Anne
From the Hebrew **Hannah**, meaning "God has favoured me." The French form Anne or **Ann**, traditionally the name of the mother of the Virgin Mary, was introduced into Britain in

the 13th century and the name has enjoyed great popularity since. Anne is currently slightly more popular than Ann, but the form **Anna** is now much more popular than either. Short forms include **Nan, Nanette, Nana, Nancy,** and **Annie**, as well as the variants **Anita, Annette,** and **Anona** (although this, with its short form **Nona**, can be Welsh in origin). Ann(e) has often formed part of compounds such as **Mary Ann(e)** or **Annalise**. **Anneke** is the Dutch short form, more often spelled **Anneka** in Britain to reflect the Dutch pronunciation; **Aneke, Aneka,** and **An(n)ika** are also found. **Anya** is from the Spanish pronunciation of the name and **Anouk** is a Russian form.

Annes, Annice, Annis *see* **Agnes**

Annette, Annie, Anona *see* **Anne**

An(n)ora *see* **Honoria**

Anstice *see* **Anastasia**

Anthea
From the Greek *antheos*, meaning "flowery." This name seems to have been introduced by the pastoral poets of the 17th century and it has been in use ever since, although it was not until the 20th century that it became very widely known.

Antonia
A Roman family name from the male **Ant(h)ony**. Its most famous member was Marcus Antonius, the Mark Antony of Shakespeare's *Julius Caesar* and *Antony and Cleopatra*. The name was very popular in the Middle Ages as a result of the influence of St. Antony the Great and St. Antony of Padua. The alternative and more common spelling Anthony, for males, was introduced after the Renaissance, when it was incorrectly thought that the name was derived from the Greek *anthos* meaning "flower," as in Anthea. The usual short form for both males and females is **Tony**, which is also used for the French **Antoinette**. Feminine short forms **Toni** and **Tonya** are

also found, and **Toinette, Net,** and **Nettie** are short forms of Antoinette.

Anusha
The name of a star in Hindu astrology.

Anya *see* **Anne**

Aoife *see* **Eve**

Aphra
From the Hebrew word for "dust." It is best known from the novelist, playwright, and spy Mrs. Aphra Behn (1644–89), said to have been the first woman in England to earn her living as a writer. It is also spelled **Afra**.

Apple
This name came to public attention when it was chosen by Gwyneth Paltrow and Chris Martin for their baby girl. The name is by no means unique —they named her after Martin's agent's daughter, and the publicity the choice generated turned up quite a number of other bearers—but is certainly unusual. Almost any fruit can be found used occasionally as a first name, even raspberry, but the most likely ones are **Peaches** (as in the case of Bob Geldof's daughter) and **Berry**. There is a distinguished Japanese novelist called Banana Yoshimoto.

April *see* **Avril**

Arabella
A possible variant of **Amabel**, though it could be derived from the Latin for "obliging." It used to be a predominantly Scottish name, particularly in the forms **Arabel** and **Arabelle**. It can be shortened to **Bel(le)** and **Bella**.

Araminta
This name appears to have been invented by Sir John Vanbrugh (1644–1726) to use in one of his plays. It may have been influenced by **Aminta** or **Amynta**, an ancient Greek name meaning "protector." They all share the short forms **Minta** and **Minty**.

Ariane
The French form of an ancient Greek name meaning "the very holy one," which probably originally belonged to a goddess. In Greek mythology **Ariadne** was the daughter of King Minos of Crete and helped Theseus to escape from the labyrinth. **Arian(n)a** is an Italian form of the name. Other forms include **Ariadna, Adrianna, Arijona**.

Ariel
The name Ariel has two different origins. The masculine form is a Hebrew name, traditionally said to mean "lion of God." As a girl's name it has been popular ever since it was used as the heroine's name in Disney's *Little Mermaid* film and TV series. This name, which is also found in forms such as **Arial** and **Arielle**, presumably owes at least something to Ariel, the airy spirit in Shakespeare's play *The Tempest*.

Arlene
Arlene, **Arleen,** or **Arline** is a modern name that probably comes from the final sounds of such names as **Charlene** or **Marlene**.

Aruna

The feminine form of **Arun**, an Indian name from the Sanskrit for "reddish brown," a colour associated with the dawn. It became the name of the mythical personification of the dawn, charioteer of the sun. An alternative spelling is **Arumina**.

Asha

An Indian name from the Sanskrit for "hope, desire, aspiration."

Ashanti

The name of a Ghanaian people. It is often shortened to **Shanti (Shante**, **Shaunti)**.

Ashley

A place and surname, from the Old English meaning "ash field," which has become very popular as a first name. Other forms include **Ashlee**, and the more common form **Ashleigh**. A variant is **Ashly(n)n**.

Ashlyn

Gaelic for "dream," but possibly a combination of **Ashley** and **Lynn**. Also spelled **Ashlynn**.

Ashton

A surname meaning "ash farm" that is used as a first name for both boys and girls.

Asma

From the Arabic for "more eminent" or "more prestigious." Asma was the daughter of the caliph Abu-Bakr. She courageously helped the Prophet and her father escape from Mecca when their lives were threatened.

Assisi

Assisi (sometimes Asisi), is, like Florence and Sienna, an Italian town famous for its Renaissance art. It was given publicity when chosen by Jade Jagger for her daughter.

Astrid

From the Old German words meaning "god" and "beauty." The name of the wife of St. Olaf of Norway, it has long been popular in Scandinavia.

Athene

This is the name of the Greek goddess of war, crafts, and wisdom. In Britain, it has been used occasionally as a girl's name, as has the Latin form of the name, **Athena**. The Roman equivalent, **Minerva**, is also found.

Athol

Athol or **Atholl** is the Scottish place name, used as a first name for both sexes. The place name means "New Ireland."

Aubrey

From the Old German, meaning "elf ruler." Originally used in the masculine, in medieval romance the diminutive **Auberon** was used and Shakespeare adopted it as **Oberon** in *A Midsummer Night's Dream*. The German form, **Alberic**, developed first into Albery and later into Aubrey. Aubrey is now used as a girl's name in some countries.

Audrey

A shortened form of **Etheldreda**, Old English for "noble strength" and one of the sources of **Ethel**. St. Etheldreda was a seventh-century Anglo-Saxon princess who founded at

Ely a religious house which later developed into the cathedral that now stands on the site. She was a popular saint and many churches are still dedicated to her.

Augusta

From the Latin for "venerable." The masculine form **Augustus** was a title given to the first Roman Emperor. **Augustine**, the name of two important saints, one of whom converted the English to Christianity, is another form of the name, the feminine form of which is **Augustina**. **Gus** and **Gussie** are short forms.

Aurelia

The feminine form of **Aurelius** from the Latin, meaning "golden." It has been used since the 17th century, and recently a short form, **Auriol, Auriel, Oriel** or **Oriole**, has shown some popularity.

Aurora see Dawn

Autumn

From the Latin for the season.

Ava

Possibly from the Latin, meaning "like a bird," it was made famous by the film star Ava Gardner, and has recently been the choice of a number of American celebrities for their daughters. It is quickly growing in popularity in Canada too and became the number one choice for girls in Alberta in 2006.

Aveline see Evelyn

Avril

French for **April**. The name has been popular for centuries, mainly for girls born in that month.

Ayesha, Ayisha, Aysha see Aisha

Azima(h)

This Arabic name means "determined."

Aziza

From the Arabic *azizi*, meaning "beloved." **Azeeza** is a common alternative spelling.

B

Babette see Barbara, Elizabeth

Bailey

Originally an English surname, which comes from the job of steward or bailiff of an estate. It metamorphosed into a first name in the 19th century.

Bala

An Indian name, from the Sanskrit for "young child."

Barbara

From the Greek *barbaros*, meaning "strange" or "foreign," and associated with St. Barbara, a 3rd-century martyr. The name was little used after the Reformation, but in the 20th century it became popular again. Abbreviations include **Bab(s), Barbie**, and sometimes **Bobbi**. The variant form **Barbra** was publicised by the singer Barbra Streisand. **Babette** is a French form of the name.

Barrie
The English form of a variety of Celtic names, most prominently **Bairre**, a short form of the Irish **Finbarr (Finnbar, Fionnbharr)** meaning "fair-haired."

Bathsheba
This name derives from Hebrew words that mean "daughter of opulence." In the Old Testament Bathsheba was the beautiful wife of Uriah and was seduced by King David, who arranged to have Uriah die during a battle. Bathsheba married David and became the mother of Solomon. The name was formerly used in Cornwall in the form **Bersaba**, and appears also in its short form **Sheba**. Bathsheba Everdene is a central character in Thomas Hardy's *Far From the Madding Crowd*.

Beatrice
From the Latin **Beatrix**, meaning "bringer of happiness." It has strong literary associations. Dante's Beatrice is probably best known, but Shakespeare also used the name in *Much Ado About Nothing*.

Recently, both forms of the name have shown signs of returning to popularity, no doubt helped by the publicity given to it as the name of one of the Duke and Duchess of York's daughters. Short forms include **Bea** or **Bee, Beata, Beatty, Triss,** and **Trixie**. There is also a Welsh variant, **Bettrys**, and a Spanish form **Beatriz**.

Becky *see* **Rebecca**

Bel *see* **Annabel, Arabella, Belinda, Isabel**

Belinda
From an Old German name, the latter part of which means "a snake" (see **Linda**). The first part of the name is obscure but is commonly thought of as representing the French "fair." Its popular use began in the 18th century when it was used in plays by Congreve and Vanbrugh and in Pope's poem *The Rape of the Lock*. Short forms include **Bel** and all forms of Linda.

Bella, Belle *see* **Annabel, Arabella, Isabel**

Benedicta
The feminine form of **Benedict** from the Latin *benedictus*, meaning "blessed," and most familiar as the name of St. Benedict, founder of the Benedictine Order. Variants include **Benedetta** and **Benita**.

Berenice
From the Greek Pherenice, meaning "bringer of victory." It was spread by the imperial conquests of Alexander the Great over Europe and Asia. It was especially popular in Egypt, during the period of Macedonian rule, and its use spread also to the family of Herod of Judea. **Bernice** is a modern form of the name, and **Bunny** is sometimes used as a short form (see also **Veronica**).

Bernadette
The feminine form of **Bernard**. Its use has spread due to the fame of St. Bernadette of Lourdes, who lived in the mid-19th century and whose visions started the pilgrimages of healing to that town. The Italian **Bernardetta** has been shortened to **Detta**, which can be used as an

independent name. **Bernadine** is another form of the name, and **Bernie** the short form.

Bertha

From the Old German word *beraht*, meaning "bright." The first famous English Bertha was the wife of King Ethelbert of Kent who welcomed St. Augustine to England on his mission of conversion. In the Middle Ages both Bertha and **Berta** were popular, and the name has been regularly used ever since, although it is uncommon now.

Beryl

From the gemstone, whose name is related to the Arabic for "crystal." It appeared in the 19th century and was popular in the early part of the 20th century.

Bess, Bessie, Beth *see* **Elizabeth**

Betha *see* **Bethia**

Bethany

A popular name taken from a New Testament place name, the village where Lazarus lived. The short form **Bethan** is used independently and is also a short form of **Elizabeth**, which has spread from Wales.

Bethia

Bethia or **Bethea** can be interpreted in three different ways. It can be thought of as a short form of **Elizabeth**, as a use of the Old Testament place name Bethia, or as an English version of a Gaelic name also found as **Betha**, meaning "life."

Betsy, Bettina, Betty *see* **Elizabeth**

Bettrys *see* **Beatrice**

Beverl(e)y

From an Old English surname meaning "of the beaver-meadow." **Bev** is a short form.

Bharati

A Hindu name identified with the goddess of speech and learning.

Bhavini

A Hindu name meaning "illustrious, beautiful," a term for the goddess Parvati, wife of the god Siva.

Bhavna

An Indian name, from the Sanskrit meaning "wish," "desire," or "thought." The form **Bhavana** is also used.

Bianca *see* **Blanche**

Bidelia, Biddy *see* **Bridget**

Billie, Billy

This short form of the boy's name **William** is being used increasingly as a girl's name particularly in America, often in combinations to produce names such as **Billie Jean** or **Billy Joe**.

Birgitta *see* **Bridget**

Blake

A surname, from the Old English, meaning "black, dark-complexioned," used as a first name.

Blanche

A French name meaning "white" or "fair-skinned." The Spanish and Italian form **Bianca** was used by Shakespeare and is now rather more popular than the older form.

Blodwen
From the Welsh for "white flower." It is rarely found outside Wales. **Blodeuwedd**, "flower form," is the name of a beautiful but unfaithful woman in Welsh medieval romance, while **Blodyn** or **Blodeyn** is the more simple "flower."

Blossom *see* **Fleur**

Bobbi(e), Bobby
These short forms of **Robert(a)** and **Barbara** are used as names in their own right, and in combinations such as **Bobby Joe**.

Bonnie, Bonny
A Scottish word for "pretty" used as a name. Like many modern names, it probably owes its spread to its appearance in *Gone with the Wind*.

Brandy
A popular name in the 1980s, it is also found spelled **Brandi(e)** and **Brandee**, and probably serves as a feminine form of **Brandon**.

Brannan *see* **Brenna**

Breanna
This new name can either be seen as a blend of the names **Bree** (a short form of **Bridget**) and **Anna**, or as a development of **Brianna**, a feminine form of **Brian**. It is also used in the form **Breanne** and found in spellings such as **Breeanna** and **Brieanne**.

Bree *see* **Bridget**

Bren *see* **Brenna**

Brenda
Probably a feminine form of the Norse name **Brand**, meaning "a sword," found in the Shetlands. It was used by Walter Scott in his novel *The Pirate*. However, in practice, it has been used more frequently as a feminine form of **Brendan**.

Brenna
A modern feminine form of **Brennan**, a short form of the Irish name **Bren**, probably means "tear, sorrow." Since the earliest records this name and

Bran, "raven," and its short form **Brannan** have regularly been confused, and it is not always possible to tell which form of the name has come from which source.

Brianna
A feminine form of the Celtic name **Brian**, the origin of which is obscure, though it may be derived from words meaning "hill" or "strength." It was known mainly in Celtic areas until the Norman Conquest, when it was introduced to England. Brian Boru was a famous Irish King of the 11th century, who defeated the invading Vikings. The name continued to be popular in England until Tudor times, but after that it disappeared until it was reintroduced from Ireland in the 18th century. **Bryan(n)a, Brianne,** and **Bryanne** are variants, as is **Bryony**.

Bridget
Brigit was the ancient Irish goddess of poetry whose name meant "strength." Her name was borne by fifth-century St. Brigit of Kildare, the most revered of

the Irish female saints. The Irish name also appears in the forms **Bri(d)gid** and **Bride** (which reflects the Irish pronunciation of the name, with a long "ee" sound and no "g"), with the diminutives **Bridie, Biddy, Bree** (now sometimes **Brea**), and the older elaboration **Bidelia. Brigidine** is a variant chosen by Sinead O'Connor for her child. There is also a Swedish saint **Birgitta** or **Brigitta** whose feast day falls on the same day as St. Brigit's, and her name has influenced the most common English form of the name, Bridget. **Britt** is a short form of the Swedish name.

Brigid, Brigit, Brigitta *see* **Bridget**

Briony *see* **Bryony**

Britney *see* **Brittany**

Britt *see* **Bridget**

Brittany
This French place name began to be used as a name for American girls in the 1960s. The sound of the name rather than its meaning seems to be important, as it also occurs as **Britanee, Britani, Britney** (made famous by Britney Spears), and **Brittney**.

Bronwen
From the Welsh words meaning "white breast." This name has long been popular in Wales, where it has strong associations with ancient legend.

Brooke
The surname meaning "a brook," used as a first name, made famous by the actress Brooke Shields. The American place name **Brooklyn**, most famously used in the U.K. for a boy, Brooklyn Beckham, is more often used for girls and is treated as if a blend of **Brooke** and **Lyn** in forms such as **Brooklynne**.

Bryony
Bryony, or **Briony**, is the name of the climbing hedge plant. It is a rather insignificant plant, although it has pretty berries, and the name probably owes its popularity to the fact that it can be used as a female equivalent to **Brian**.

Bunty
This was a traditional name for a pet lamb, which came into use for girls after 1911, when it was featured in a very successful play called *Bunty Pulls the Strings*. However, it is used more commonly as a nickname.

C

Caddy *see* **Caroline**

Cahal *see* **Carol**

Caitlin
This, like **Kathleen**, is an Irish form of **Katharine**. The Irish pronounce it with the sound of "cat," but the American pronunciation is reflected in the spelling **Katelynn**. Forms such as **Caitlyn(n), Kaitlyn,** and **Katlin** are also found.

Calista
From the Greek, meaning "most beautiful." A name made more popular by the actress Calista Flockhart.

Callie

Callie or **Cally** was originally a short form of several names, but is now used as a name in its own right. It is an old short form of **Caroline**, or it can come from any name beginning Cal-, particularly those containing the Greek element for "beautiful," such as **Calliope**, "beautiful face," the name of the ancient Greek muse of epic poetry. It is also found spelled **Kally** or **Kalli(e)**.

Cameron

From the Gaelic, meaning "crooked nose," this is the name of a Scottish clan. Its popularity as a boy's name has spread from Scotland. It is now being used for girls as well.

Camilla

A name from Roman legend. Camilla was Queen of the Volsci, a great warrior and exceptionally swift runner. The name may be Etruscan and possibly means "one who helps at sacrifices." **Camille** is the French form, which can be used for either sex, and **Milla,** **Milly,** and **Millie** are used as short forms.

Candice, Candace

This is an ancient title of the Queen of Ethiopia. It is also spelled **Candis; Candy** is a short form.

Candida

From the Latin, meaning "white." The name was not used in Britain until the early 20th century and its introduction was probably due to G.B. Shaw's play, *Candida*.

Candis, Candy *see* Candice

Cara

This Italian word meaning "dear" came into use as a first name only in the 20th century and is often spelled **Kara** in the United States. Short forms, used as names in their own right, include **Carissa,** **Carita,** and particularly **Carina** or **Karina**. These are found in a number of variant forms such as **Karissa, Karena, Caryssa,** and **Charissa**, and it is not always easy to tell when parents are using forms of Cara, **Karen,** or **Charis**.

Carla

The German feminine form of **Charles**. The name has been in general use in America for a century, and from there spread to Britain. Carla or **Karla** and Carlie or **Carly** can also be found as forms of the names found under **Caroline**.

Carlyn *see* Caroline

Carmel

From the Hebrew, meaning "garden," and the name of a mountain famous for its lush vegetation near the city of Haifa in Israel. St. Louis founded the church and convent on this mountain, which, as legend has it, the Virgin Mary and infant Jesus often visited. **Carmen** is the Spanish form of the name, **Carmela** the Italian, and **Carmelita** and **Carmelina** short forms. Carmen is also the Latin word for "song," and some people like to think of it in this sense, hence such modern coinages as **Carmina**, the Latin for "songs."

Carol

The feminine forms of this name, which include **Carole, Carola,** and **Caryl**, were originally short forms of **Caroline** or **Carolina** but are now popular names in their own right.

Caroline, Carolyn

These names come from **Carolina**, the Italian feminine form of **Carlo**. The name was introduced into Britain from southern Germany by Queen Caroline of Brandenburg-Anspach, wife of George II. Both forms have been used steadily since the 18th century. Derivatives are **Carla, Carlyn, Carol, Carola, Carole**. Abbreviations include **Carrie, Caddy, Caro**, and **Lyn**.

Caron see **Karen**

Carrie see **Caroline**

Carwen, Carwyn see **Ceri**

Casey

This comes from an Irish surname meaning "vigilant in war." It can also be a form of the Polish name **Casimir**, "proclamation of peace," which has a feminine form **Casimira**. The name takes various forms, often spelled with a "K."

Cassandra

In Greek literature this was the name of a prophetess and princess of Troy. She foretold the truth, but was never believed. The name first became popular in the Middle Ages and has continued in use ever since. It is shortened to **Cassie** and **Cass** and sometimes **Sandra** or **Sandy**. Cass also occurs as a masculine name, when it may come from an Irish name meaning "curly-haired."

Cassia see **Kezia(h)**

Cassidy

This is an Irish surname, of unknown meaning, used as a first name. **Cassie**, also used as a name in its own right, is a short form it shares with **Cassandra**. It is occasionally used for boys.

Catharine, Catherine, Cathleen, Cathy see **Katharine**

Catriona

A Gaelic form of **Katharine**. It was the title of a book by Robert Louis Stevenson and became very popular in the 19th century as a result of this. **Catrina, Katrina,** and **Katrine** are other forms of the name, and it becomes **Catrin** in Welsh. **Riona** is an Irish short form.

Cecily see **Cecilia**

Cecilia

The female version of **Cecil**. It was the name of a second-century martyr and saint, the patroness of music. Variant forms are **Cicely, Cecily, Sisley, Cecil**, and the French **Cecile** (used for boys and girls in France). The popular shortened form **Celia** (which can also be derived from another Roman name, **Coelia**) probably came into fashion as a result of the Celia in Shakespeare's play *As You Like It*. Other abbreviated forms are **Sis(sy)** and **Ciss(y)** (see also **Sheila**).

Celeste
From the Latin, meaning "heavenly." Short forms, used as names in their own right, are **Celestine**, **Celestina**, and **Celesta**.

Celia *see* **Cecilia**

Celina, **Céline** *see* **Selina**

Ceri
A popular Welsh name, sometimes spelled **Keri** to reflect its pronunciation with a hard "c." It comes from the Welsh word for "love" as do the names **Cerian**, **Cerys** or **Carys** (chosen by Catherine Zeta Jones and Michael Douglas) and **Cari**. **Carwen** is "fair love" and has a masculine form, **Carwyn** (see also **Kerry**).

Ceridwen
This name probably comes from the Welsh words for "poetry" and "white, blessed." It was the name of a Celtic goddess who was said to inspire poetry and was the mother of the great poet **Taliesin** ("radiant brow"). It is pronounced with a hard "c" and is generally confined to Wales.

Cerys *see* **Ceri**

Chandra
An Indian name from the Sanskrit meaning "the moon." In the Hindu religion, the moon is a god rather than a goddess, but the name Chandra is nevertheless a popular one for girls. The variant **Chander** is often used for boys while **Chandrakala**, "moonbeams," can be used for girls.

Chandrakanta
From the Sanskrit for "loved by the moon," referring to a mythical jewel mentioned in classical Hindu texts, supposedly formed by the moon's rays. It is also the name of a white water-lily that blossoms at night.

Chanel
The name of this famous French perfume has been taken up as a girl's name in recent years. The perfume was named after Gabrielle "Coco" Chanel, whose family name derives from an Old French word meaning "wine jar," indicating an ancestral connection with the wine trade.

Chanel is frequently spelled phonetically, taking such forms as **Shan(n)el** and **Shanell(e)**. **Chanelle** is also used.

Chantal
This is a French name that has only been in use since the beginning of the 20th century. It was the surname, meaning "stone," of the 16th-century saint Jeanne-Françoise de Chantal. Variants include **Chantalle** and **Chantel(l)e**. It is pronounced, and sometimes spelled, with a "sh" sound at the beginning.

Charis
From the Greek, meaning "grace." The "Ch" is pronounced as a "K." It was first used as a first name in the 17th century, although in the 16th century the poet Edmund Spenser in the *Faerie Queen* used the form **Charissa**. **Chrissa** can be a short form of this or belong under the **Christine** group of names. There is some overlap between the names under **Ceri**, **Cara**, and Charis as they are pronounced so similarly.

Charity
From the Latin *caritas*, meaning
"Christian love." Translated
into English as charity, it was
adopted when it became the
custom for Puritans to name
childen after the Christian
virtues. The name Charity was
shortened to **Cherry** and is the
source of this name. Another
abbreviation is **Chattie**, used
also for **Charlotte**.

Charlene
A 20th-century, feminine
form of **Charles**. It may owe
something to **Charline**, a
Dutch form of **Charlotte**.
Charleen and **Sharlene** are
also used (see also **Arlene**).

Charlotte
The French feminine form of
Charles. It was introduced
into Britain from France in the
early 17th century. Goethe's
heroine from the romantic
novel *The Sorrows of Werther*, and
Princess Charlotte, daughter
of George IV, increased its
popularity. Abbreviations are
Lottie, Lotty, Totty, Charlie,
and **Chattie**, and spellings
such as **Sharlott** have been

recorded. It has been one of the
most popular girls' names for a
number of years. **Carlotta** is
the Italian form.

Charmaine
A 20th-century name of rather
obscure origin. It may well be a
form of **Charmian**, from the
Greek, meaning "joy." This was
the name of one of Cleopatra's
attendants in Shakespeare's
Antony and Cleopatra. Strictly
speaking, Charmian should be
pronounced with a hard "c," but
the "sh" pronunciation is also
found. Charmaine is sometimes
spelled **Sharmaine**.

Charulata
A Hindu name meaning
"beautiful."

Chastity
Latin for "purity." In 1969 the
singer Cher and her husband
Sonny Bono named their
daughter Chastity.

Chattie *see* **Charity,
Charlotte**

Chelsea
This name of a fashionable part

of London, which originally
indicated a "landing place (on
the River Thames) for chalk
or limestone," is also a place
name in Australia, where its
use as a girl's name seems to
have begun. The name was
introduced to America by a
character in the film *On Golden
Pond*, and its popularity was
secured by the widespread
publicity it received through
Chelsea Clinton, daughter of
U.S. President Bill Clinton,
who was named after a
Joni Mitchell song. Spelling
variants such as **Chelsi(e)** and
Chelsey are also found.

Cheralyn, Cherilyn *see*
Cheryl

Cherie
The French word for "darling."
The forms **Cheri, Sherry,
Sheree**, and **Sherrie** are
phonetic spellings. **Cher** can
be the French for "dear" or a
short form of **Cheryl**. **Cherise**
can be regarded either as a
development of Cherie or as a
form of **Charisse**, the French
form of **Charis**.

Cherry *see* **Charity**

Cheryl
This is probably a development of the name **Cherry** (see **Charity**). Other forms of the name are **Cheralyn**, **Cherilyn**, **Sheril** and **Sheryl**, and **Cher** can be a short form (see also **Cherie**). These names came into general use only in the 1940s but rapidly became popular.

Cheyenne
A Native American name, Cheyenne was first launched as a boy's name in a TV series of that name in the United States in the late-1950s. Pronunciation of the name as **Shyann**, in which form it is also found, possibly linked it in parents' minds with the name **Anne**, suggesting its use for girls.

Cheyna *see* **Shaina**

China *see* **Chyna**

Chintana
An Indian name meaning "meditation." The form **Chintanika** is also used.

Chloe, Chloë
From the Greek, meaning "a green shoot," a name given to the goddess Demeter who protected the green fields. It was a popular name in classical literature, which was picked up by the Elizabethan poets. It is very popular at the moment. **Chloris**, "greenish," is another name from Greek myth and was again associated with fertility. It is sometimes spelled **Cloris**, to reflect the pronunciation of these names with a hard "c."

Chris, Chrissie, Chrissy *see* **Christabel, Christine**

Chrissa *see* **Charis, Christine**

Christabel
This name was first used in Britain in the 16th century and is thought to be a combination of "Christ" and the Latin *bella* to mean "beautiful Christian." It is also spelled **Christobel** and abbreviated forms are **Chris(sy)**, **Chrissie**, or **Christie**.

Christel, Christen *see* **Christine**

Christian
This name has been used for both sexes in Britain since the 13th century. It became more popular after its use by Bunyan for the hero of *Pilgrim's Progress*, but has never been as common as the feminine form, **Christine**, although it is currently enjoying some popularity.

Christie *see* **Christabel**

Christine
The most common of the many girls' names meaning "a Christian." **Christen** is probably the oldest form, followed by **Christiana**. Others are **Christina**, **Christian(n)e**, a feminine form of **Christian**, the Welsh form **Crystin**, and spellings such as **Krystyna**, **Kristin(a)**, and **Krista**. The German form, **Christel**, may have helped the development of the name **Crystal**. Short forms are **Chrissie**, **Chrissy**, and **Chris** and further variants will be found under the Scottish short form, **Kirsty**. **Chrissa**, **Chryssa**, or **Kryssa** can be thought of either as a part of

this group or as a short form of **Charissa** (see **Charis**).

Chyna

Based on the place name **China**, the name is particularly associated with the singer **Chynna** Philips, while the form Chyna is associated in the United States with a woman wrestler.

Ciara

A feminine form of **Kieran** and a name that is increasing in popularity in Canada (see also **Sierra**).

Cicely *see* **Cecilia**

Ciera *see* **Sierra**

Cindy

A short form of names such as **Lucinda** and **Cynthia**, now used as an independent name. It is also spelled **Cindi(e)**.

Ciss, Cissy *see* **Cecilia**

Clare, Claire

From the Latin, meaning "clear, famous." The religious order of the Sisters of St. Clara or "Poor Clares," founded in the 13th century, was probably responsible for the rapid spread of the name throughout Europe. Among the many derivatives are **Claribel** and **Clarinda**, which can be shortened to **Clarrie**.

Clarissa

From the Latin, meaning "brightest, most famous." It was made popular in the 18th century by Samuel Richardson's novel *Clarissa Harlowe*. **Clarice** is an older form of the name. They share the abbreviation **Clarrie** with **Clara**.

Claudia

From the Roman name **Claudius**, itself derived from the Latin, meaning "lame." In homage to the Emperor Claudius, who was ruler when Britain was conquered by the Romans, the name was used in that country in the 1st and 2nd centuries. Its use soon lapsed in Britain though not in France, where it is spelled **Claude** and used for either sex. It was from the French that it was revived in Britain in the 16th century by the Scottish family of Hamilton. A derivative is **Claudian**, and the short form **Claudie** can be found. The feminine form, Claudia, is at the moment the more popular. Two French diminutives are also used: **Claudette** and **Claudine**, a name made famous by the novels of **Colette**.

Clementina, Clementine

The feminine form of **Clement**, from the Latin, meaning "mild, merciful." Clement was the name of an early saint and of several popes. Abbreviated forms are **Clem** and **Clemmie**, which are shared with the feminine forms Clementina and Clementine. Clementine was originally a German form, fashionable during the 19th century. **Clemency** is also used.

Cleo

A shortened form of **Cleopatra**, from the Greek meaning "glory of her father." The famous Egyptian queen of this name died in 30 B.C., and it did not take long for her name to become a byword for sexual allure and tragic love. The form **Clio** is, strictly speaking, the name of the Greek Muse of history.

Clodagh

The name of a river in Ireland. It was first used in the 20th century as a first name by the Marquis of Waterford for his daughter. Its use has now spread beyond Ireland.

Cloris see Chloe

Clover

This is the flower name used as a first name. Its spread may have been helped by its use for a character in the *Katy* books by Susan Coolidge. Names such as **Clova** can be interpreted either as a re-spelling of Clover or as a feminine form of **Clovis**.

Codie, Cody

Cody is said to be an Irish surname meaning "descendant of a helpful person." It has been popular in the United States, where it is also a place name and well known as the surname of the Wild West hero, Buffalo Bill Cody. Codey and spellings with

"K" have also been recorded. Codi(e) is the spelling most often used for girls.

Colette

From a French diminutive of **Nicola**. It was the name of the 15th-century reformer of the "Poor Clares" religious order. The name is best known in this country as the pen-name of a 20th-century French writer. It is also spelled **Collette**.

Colleen

The Irish word for "girl" used as a first name.

Collette see Colette

Constance

Constance and its Latin form, **Constantia**, mean "constancy." It became popular in many parts of Christendom after Constantine the Great ordered the toleration of Christianity in the Roman Empire, A.D. 313. It was introduced into England at the time of the Norman Conquest. The form **Constancy** was used by the Puritans in the 17th century while **Constantia** became

popular in the 18th century. **Constantina** is another form of the name. Constance has been out of fashion since the early 20th century, but there has recently been an increase in its use. Its abbreviation is **Connie**.

Cora see Corinna

Coralie

The French form of **Coral**, this name reflects the beauty and value of the substance and is popular in Quebec.

Cordelia

This name first appeared as **Cordeilla** in the 16th-century chronicles of Holinshed, from which Shakespeare altered the name to Cordelia for his play *King Lear*. The name is probably a form of **Cordula**, the name of one of the virgins martyred with St. Ursula. It probably comes from the Latin word for "heart."

Corey

This is an Irish surname of unknown meaning which has come to be used as a first name. It is also spelled **Cory**, and in forms such as **Cori** or **Corrie** has been used especially in combination with other names. Spellings beginning with "K," particularly Kori, are also found.

Corinna

This name and **Cora** both come from the Greek word *kore* meaning "girl" or "maiden," a name given to the goddess **Persephone** who was associated with the coming of spring. The appearance of the name in Ovid's love poetry probably inspired its use among some 17th-century poets, particularly Herrick. The French form **Corinne** is also used. **Corin**, much used in poetry as the name for a love-sick shepherd, is the masculine form of the name, although it is occasionally also used for girls.

Cornelia

The feminine form of **Cornelius** from the Latin *cornu,* meaning "a horn." These were the masculine and feminine forms of the name of a famous Roman clan. Its abbreviated forms are **Corn(e)y** and **Cornie**.

Corrie, Cory *see* **Corey**

Courtney

An aristocratic surname used as a first name. It comes from **Courtnay**, a French place name, although the name is often interpreted as coming from *court nez*, the French for "short nose." It is currently more used for girls than for boys.

Cressida

Cressida comes from a misreading of the name **Briseida**, "daughter of Brisis," who appears in Homer's account of the Trojan War. In the 14th century, the Italian writer Boccaccio used the name, and it was adapted by Chaucer in his verse-novel *Troilus and Criseyde*, the story of Troilus's undying love for the fair Cressida, set against the background of the Trojan War. Shakespeare changed the name to Cressida for his version of the story. Despite the fictional character's faithlessness in love, the name has recently become quite popular in Britain. An abbreviated form is **Cressy**.

Cruz

This name, the Spanish word for "cross," got a lot of publicity when it was chosen by David and Victoria Beckham for their third son. Although there were reports in the press that it was a girl's name, it has always been used for both sexes and is increasingly popular as a boy's name.

Crystal

While this looks like, and is no doubt mainly used as, another jewel name (see also **Amber, Jade**), the spread of this name may have been helped by **Christel**, the German form of **Christine**. Crystal is also spelled **Chrystal** and the form **Krystal** has become known through the TV series *Dynasty*.

Crystin *see* **Christine**

Cynthia

One of the titles of the Greek goddess Artemis (see **Diana**), Cynthia means "of Mount Cynthus," reputedly one of her favourite places. It first became known as a name through its use by the Latin poet Propertius, and it was later popular among

Elizabethan poets. Mrs. Gaskell's character in her novel *Wives and Daughters* brought it back into favour during the late 19th century. Short forms include **Cindy** or **Cindi(e)**, and the rarer **Cimmie**.

D

Daisy
This probably started out as a 19th-century pet name for **Margaret**, a pun on *marguerite*, the French word for daisy. However, there is no reason why it should not have come into use as a simple flower name, and few people today would use it otherwise.

Dakota
Native American, meaning "friend" or "ally."

Dale
The Old English for "valley." At first more common as a girl's name, it is now more frequently used for boys.

Damaris
The Greek name in the New Testament of an Athenian woman converted by St. Paul. This led to its adoption by Puritans in the 17th century. It is probably a form of a Greek name meaning "heifer."

Damhnait *see* **Devnet**

Dana
Either a Scandinavian girl's form of **Daniel**, or, in Ireland, can be taken from the pagan fertility goddess, Dana or **Ana**.

Danica, Danika
Of Slavic origin, meaning "the morning star." Although the name **Star** is not popular, different languages base names on the word. **Stella** is a name from the Latin for "star."

Danielle
The feminine form of **Daniel**, meaning "God has judged," also the Hebrew name of an Old Testament prophet. It was found in England before the Norman Conquest, but only among priests and monks. It became more widespread in the 13th and 14th centuries. In Ireland and Wales it is often found as a version of the Irish **Domhnall** and Welsh **Deiniol**, meaning "attractive, charming." For girls, **Danielle** is the most common form, but **Daniel(l)a** and **Danette** are also used.

Daphne
From the Greek for "bay tree, laurel." In classical mythology, it was the name of a nymph who the god Apollo loved. She called on the gods for help to escape his attentions and was changed by them into a laurel. The name was a traditional name for dogs until the end of the 19th century, when it became quite common as a girl's name.

Dara
This is an Irish name, a shortened form of Mac Dara, "son of the oak," the name of a popular Connemara saint. It is also spelled **Darragh**. Although traditionally a boy's name, it is now also used for girls.

Darcey
Darcey can be either from a French surname meaning someone from a place called Arcy, hence the form d'Arcy,

or an Irish surname meaning "descendant of the dark one."

Daria

The feminine form of **Darius**, the name of the sixth-century B.C. king of the Persians who was defeated by the Athenians at Marathon. The name means "protector."

Darian, Darien *see* Dorian

Darlene

This appears to be a relatively modern invention, made up of the first syllable of one of the names beginning "Dar-," or perhaps from "darling," with the "-ene" ending that is popular with newly created names such as **Charlene** and **Raelene**.

Darrel(l)

Also spelled **Dar(r)yl**, this is another surname used as a first name. In this case the surname comes from a French village, the village name meaning "courtyard, open space." Originally mainly a boy's name, its spread as a girl's name may owe something to Enid Blyton's use of her second

husband's surname, Darrell, for the heroine of her *Malory Towers* school stories.

Davida, Davina

These Scottish feminine forms of **David** are found from the 17th century but were not much used until the 20th century, when they started to become more popular. They are sometimes shortened to **Vida** and **Vina**, and **Davita** and **Davinia** are also found.

Dawn

This name came into use in the late 19th century. **Aurora**, the name of the Greek goddess of dawn, had been in vogue slightly earlier and the English translation was probably a literary invention.

Deborah

A Hebrew name meaning "bee," and the name of a prophetess and poet in the Old Testament. It was first used by Puritans in the 17th century. **Debbie** or **Debby** is a common abbreviation, which is sometimes used independently. **Debra** is a modern spelling of the name.

Dee

This is usually a nickname, given to anyone with a name beginning with the letter "D," but is occasionally found as a given name. Compounds such as **Deedee** also occur.

Deepika

An Indian name from the Sanskrit meaning "little lamp." It is one of the descriptive names applied to Kama, god of love.

Deirdre

The Irish name of a character in Irish and Scottish legend, possibly meaning "raging" or "sorrowful." In Irish legend, Deirdre was the most beautiful woman in Ireland.

Deja

This new name is something of a mystery. It has been linked to the French word *déjà*, "already," as in *déjà vu*, but this seems unlikely. A more likely source is the character of Dejah Thoris, the beautiful princess in Edgar Rice Burroughs' *Barsoom* novels. Spellings include **Dejah, Dasha,** and **Dasia**.

Delia
This name is derived from Delos, the legendary birthplace of the Greek moon goddess Artemis (see **Diana**) and a name sometimes given to her. It was popular with pastoral poets in the 17th and 18th centuries.

Delilah
This is the name borne by the well-known biblical character who betrayed Samson to the Philistines. It derives from a Hebrew name meaning "coquette" or "flirt." It was also the title of a song popularized by Tom Jones, but this failed to persuade many parents to make use of it.

Della
Originally a short form of **Adela**, this is now well established as a name in its own right.

Denise
The feminine form of **Denis**, a development of the name of Dionysos, the Greek god of wine and revelry. Denis or **Dennis** is the French form and the name of the patron saint of France. It occurs in England from the 12th century on. In Ireland it has long been used as a substitute for the Irish **Donnchadh**. **Den** and **Denny** are short forms. **Dionne** can either come from Dionysos or be a separate name from the same root, connected with the word for "a god," while **Dione** can be thought of either as a variant of Dionne, or as the name of another character from Greek mythology whose name means "divine queen." These are growing in popularity.

Dervla
This is the phonetic form of **Deirbhaile**, an old Irish name that means "daughter of the poet." It is best known through the travel writer Dervla Murphy. It also occurs as **Dervila**, reflecting the Irish pronunciation. The similar-looking **Dearbhail**, which can be anglicized **Derval(ia)**, meaning "daughter of Fal" (a figure in Irish legend), is also popular at the moment in Ireland.

Désirée
A French name meaning "desired." It has been in use since the beginning of the Christian era in the Latin form **Desideria**, originally for a long-awaited, much-desired child.

Destiny
An American name meaning "one's fate."

Detta *see* **Bernadette**

Devnet
This is the anglicized spelling of the Irish name **Damhnait**, the name of an early Irish martyr meaning "fawn, little deer." An older form is **Dymp(h)na**.

Devon
A county in England. The alternative spelling **Devin** is more common for boys, and forms such as **DaVon** are also found.

Dhanishta
An Indian name that derives from the Sanskrit for "star."

Diana
The Latin name of the Roman goddess, equivalent to the Greek **Artemis**. She was associated with the moon

and virginity. She was also the goddess of hunting and protector of wild animals. Its use as a first name dates from the Renaissance, when the French form **Diane** is also first found. **Di** is the most common short form, as seen in the popular nickname for the late Princess of Wales. Despite her immense popularity the name is not widely used, although it was given to rather more babies than usual in the months following her death in 1997. The actress **Deanna** Durbin introduced a different form of the name, and the form **Deanne** is also found, while Diane has developed forms such as **Dianne** and **Dyan(ne)**. **Dinah** is a separate name.

Didi, **Didier** *see* **Désirée**

Dido

Dido, possibly meaning "maiden," was the name of the wise and cunnning Queen of Carthage, who, in Roman myth, fell in love with the wandering **Aeneus**. When he left to found the Roman nation on the orders of the gods, she killed herself in despair. The singer who has made the name famous in modern times was born Florian Cloud De Bounevialle, but was given Dido as a family nickname when small.

Dilys

From the Welsh, meaning "perfect, genuine." The name became current in Wales in the 19th century, and is now no longer confined to Wales. **Dilly** is a short form.

Dinah

From the Hebrew, meaning "lawsuit" or "judged." It was the name of one of Jacob's daughters in the Old Testament. It came into use in the 17th century and was a favourite name in the 19th century, when it was often confused with **Diana**. Nowadays it is often spelled **Dina**.

Divya

An Indian name from the Sanskrit for "divine lustre."

Dolores

This name was originally a short form of the Spanish *Maria de los Dolores*, or "Mary of the Sorrows," after the feast of the "Seven Sorrows of Our Lady." Spain uses other names from titles of the Virgin: **Mercedes** (Our Lady of the Mercies) and **Montserrat**, from Our Lady of Montserrat, a famous monastery. Dolores became popular in North America in about 1930. Short forms are **Lo(la)**, and **Lolita**.

Dominique

The French feminine form from the Latin *dominicus,* meaning "of the Lord." It probably became more widespread on account of St. Dominic, founder of the Order of Preachers known as the Black Friars early in the 13th century. Until this century it was almost exclusively a Roman Catholic name but is now widely used. Dominique is now the most popular form for girls, although **Dominica**, the original Latin feminine form, is sometimes used.

Donata

This name is far more often used than its male equivalent, **Donatus** or **Donat**, both Latin for "given [by God]." The

Old French equivalent was **Dieudonné(e)**, which is still very occasionally found.

Donella
Various forms of the name **Donald** (meaning "world mighty") were coined in Scotland to turn Donald into a girl's name, of which Donalda and Donella have been the most common.

Donna
This is the Italian word for "lady." It became popular as a first name in the 20th century, particularly in North America. **Madonna**, "My Lady," used of the Virgin Mary, in use in the United States by the 1930s, comes from the same word.

Dora
Originally this name was a short form of **Dorothy** and **Theodora**, but it is now a name in its own right. It came into use at the beginning of the 19th century. A short form is **Dorrie**, shared with other names like **Doreen** and **Doris**. **Dorinda** was an 18th-century elaboration of the name.

Dorcas see **Tabitha**

Doreen
From the Irish **Doireann**, a name sometimes found in English spelling as **Dorren**. Its origin is rather obscure, but in Irish mythology it is the name of at least two supernatural beings. A short form is **Dorrie**, and the name can also be spelled **Dorinne**.

Dorian
The ancient Greek people known as Dorians came from Doris in the north, but later dominated southern Greece. The best-known group were the Spartans. The word was introduced as a first name in Oscar Wilde's *The Picture of Dorian Gray* (1891). Like so many boys' names, it is now used as a girl's name as well. It is now also spelled **Dorianne** and **Doriana**.

Dorinda see **Dora**

Dorinne see **Doreen**

Doris
The name of a sea nymph in Greek mythology, possibly meaning "bountiful," and also a term for a woman member of the Dorian people of Greece. In classical literature it was used as a poetic name for a lovely woman. It came into common use at the end of the 19th century and was popular into the 1930s. A short form is **Dorrie**.

Dorothy
From the Greek, meaning "gift of God." The name is found in Britain from the end of the 15th century and has been in use ever since. In the 16th century, it was abbreviated to **Doll(y)**, and was so popular that the toy became known as a doll, Doll being such a likely name for a baby. In Scottish dialect, a doll is sometimes called a **Dorrity**. Later short forms are **Dora, Dot(tie), Dodo, Dodie**, and **Thea**. Variants include **Dorot(h)ea, Dorothé, Doroteia**, and **Dorota**.

Dorren see **Doreen**

Dorrie see **Dora, Doreen, Doris**

Dorrity, Dot, Dottie *see* **Dorothy**

Drew
From the Old German **Drogo**, meaning "to carry" or "to bear," a name that was brought to Britain by the Normans and later became a surname. This surname, which like any other can also be used as a first name, may also come from two other sources: as a short form of the masculine **Andrew**, probably the most common form of Drew as a first name, and from an old French word for "lover." Parents wishing to use this name may take their choice. It has recently been used occasionally for girls.

Drusilla
A feminine form of the Latin **Drusus**, a Roman family name, possibly meaning "firm." It occurs in the New Testament and was adopted in the 17th century by the Puritans. It is still used occasionally, mainly in North America.

Dulcie
Dulcie is a name coined in the 19th century from the Latin *dulcis*, meaning "sweet." There was an earlier name, **Dulcibella** ("fair and sweet"). Dulcie was very popular in the early years of the 20th century, but now has an old-fashioned ring to it.

Durga
The name of the Hindu goddess, the wife of **Shiva**, when depicted in her terrifying form. Durga is from a Sanskrit word for "inaccessible."

E

Eartha
From the Old English *eorthe*, meaning "earth." A famous modern example is the singer and actress Eartha Kitt, but the name is rare outside the southern United States, where **Ertha** and **Erthel** are also found.

Ebony
The name of an intensely black wood that symbolizes blackness, Ebony began to be used by parents in the 1970s. It reached a peak of popularity in the 1980s after the song "Ebony and Ivory" by Paul McCartney and Stevie Wonder, but then began to fade. Its other spellings include **Ebbony, Eboney, Eboni(e)**, and **Ebonnee**.

Edith
From the Old English name **Eadgyth**, meaning "fortunate war." There were at least two English saints of that name in the 10th century. The name survived the Norman Conquest and was probably adopted by the Normans and used to replace several English names. Edith was in use throughout the Middle Ages, after which it became rather rare, but it returned to favour in the 19th and early 20th centuries. Often shortened to **Edie**, it has a rare form, **Editha**.

Edna
One source of this name may be **Edana**, a feminine form of the Irish name **Edan**, meaning "fire." It has also been connected with a shortened form of **Edwina**, via **Edina**. In addition the name occurs twice in the Apocrypha

and its Hebrew meaning is probably "rejuvenation."

Edwina
The 19th-century feminine form of **Edwin**, from the Old English meaning "fortunate friend." Edwin was the first Christian king of Northumbria, in the 7th century. The name survived the Norman Conquest and became popular in the 18th century.

Effie *see* **Euphemia**

Eileen
An Irish development of **Evelyn**. Like other Irish names, it spread throughout Britain at the beginning of the 20th century. **Eily** is a short form. It is not uncommon to find it spelled **Aileen**.

Eilis, Ailis
In theory the name Eilis, sometimes spelled **Eil(l)ish** to reflect its pronunciation, is an Irish form of **Elizabeth**, and Ailis (**Ailish**) an Irish form of **Alice**, but in practice many users do not distinguish between the two.

Eithne
A name prominent in Irish legend and history, being used by a goddess, a number of queens and no less than nine saints. It means "kernel," which in old Irish poetry is a term of praise. Modern variants include **Ethne, Ethna**, and the phonetic **Enya**.

Ekata
An Indian name from the Sanskrit meaning "unity."

Elaine
An Old French form of **Helen**, which occurs in medieval literature. It came into general use through the popularity of Tennyson's *Idylls of the King* (1859), which is based on Malory's *Morte d'Arthur* and which includes the story of *Lancelot and Elaine*. There is also a Welsh name **Elain**, meaning "fawn."

Eleanor
Eleanor and **Elinor** are French forms of **Helen** that have been used in Britain since the Middle Ages. **Eleanora**, the Italian form that gives us **Leonora**, is also found, as is **Elena**. Eleanor is shortened to **Ellie** (currently very popular as a given name), **Ella, Ellen, Nell**, and **Nora**.

Elizabeth, Elisabeth
From the Hebrew *Elisheba*, meaning "oath of God" or "God has sworn." The present form developed from the Greek **Elisabet** through the Latin **Elisabetha** to Elizabeth. In Britain the "z" form is usual, but otherwise the "s" is used, for in the Authorized Version of the New Testament, the name is spelled Elisabeth. It was first used by members of the Eastern Church, then found its way across Europe to France, where it developed the form **Isabel(le)**. This was also the usual medieval form in England. Elizabeth became common about the end of the 15th century, and its later popularity in England stemmed from the long reign of Elizabeth I. Among the many short forms are: **Bess(ie), Betsy, Betty, Beth** (with **Bethan** in Wales), **Buffy, Eliza, Liz(zy), Liza,**

Libby and the Scottish **Elspeth, Elspie,** and **Elsie,** which are now used independently. The German **Elsa, Elissa** (see also **Alice**), **Lisa,** or **Liese(l),** the Italian **Bettina,** and the French **Élizabeth, Elise, Lisette,** and **Babette,** are also used.

Elke

A German short form of the name **Alice**. It is found in a slightly different form used by the singer **Elkie** Brooks.

Ella

A name used by the Normans probably derived from the Old German **Alia,** meaning "all." It can also be a short form of **Isabella** (see **Isabel**), **Ellen,** or **Eleanor** and is currently an increasingly popular choice for parents, as is **Luella**. The real name of the Australian model **Elle** Macpherson, who has brought this form of the name to popular attention, is Eleanor.

Ellen

An older English form of **Helen,** now used independently, and also a short form of **Eleanor**.

In the past it has been especially popular in Scotland and Ireland and is now showing signs of wider popularity.

Ellie see Eleanor

Eloise

Currently, the more popular version of the name known to history as **Heloise**. Abelard and Heloise were two famous and tragic 12th-century lovers, and Heloise was renowned for her beauty, intellect, and faithfulness in love. The name can be spelled **Heloïse** or **Eloïse** and sometimes occurs as **Eloisa**. Experts do not agree on its origins: some say it is an Old German name perhaps meaning "helmet power"; others say it comes from the same source as **Lewis** by way of an old southern French name **Aloys** or **Aloyse**.

Elsa, Elsie

One source of Elsa is the Old German for "noble one," but both names are also used as abbreviations of **Elizabeth,** and Elsie is sometimes a short form

of **Alison**. Elsie was originally Scottish and is the more common form in Britain. Elsa is the heroine in Wagner's opera *Lohengrin,* which made the name popular in the 19th century.

Elspeth, Elspie see Elizabeth

Elvira

A Spanish name, probably introduced by the conquering Visigoths in the Dark Ages. Its meaning is not clear. It has been used occasionally since the beginning of the 19th century. It is perhaps best known as the name of the ghost in Noël Coward's play *Blithe Spirit* and from the 1967 film *Elvira Madigan*.

Emer

Emer (pronounced with a long "ee" at the beginning) is currently one of the more popular Celtic names in Ireland. In legend it was the name of the woman loved by Cuchulainn, the great hero of the Ulster cycle of legends. She is described as having the following six desirable gifts: those of beauty, voice, sweet speech, skill with the needle, wisdom, and chastity. It is occasionally found as **Emir**.

Emerald *see* **Esmeralda**

Emily
From the Latin **Aemilius**, the name of a Roman family. Boccaccio, the 14th-century Italian writer, used **Emilia**, popularizing this form in the Middle Ages, and Chaucer borrowed it in the form **Emelye**. The name has been used since then. In the 19th century it was sometimes shortened to **Emma**. **Milly** is a short form. **Emmeline** and **Émilie** are French forms.

Emma
A shortened form of Old German compound names beginning *ermen* meaning "universal," as in the name **Ermyntrude**, "universal strength." It was introduced to England by Emma, daughter of Richard I, Duke of Normandy. The English form was **Em(m)**, and this was used until the mid-18th century, when the original

form was revived. Jane Austen's novel *Emma* (1816) has also been influential. Today, Emma is the most popular girls' name in most provinces in Canada. **Emmy** is a short form, and Emma is also used as a short form of **Emily**.

Emmeline *see* **Emily**

Ena
This name can come from a number of sources. It can be a short form of any name ending with "-ina" or "-ena," or an English form of **Eithne**, but its popularity in the 19th century came from affection for Queen Victoria's daughter, Princess Ena, who became Queen of Spain. Her name came from neither of these sources, but was due to a misreading of her intended name "**Eva**" at her christening, when the priest read the handwritten "v" as an "n."

Enid
This is a Welsh name, meaning "life, soul," which came into use in England in the 19th century

through Tennyson's Arthurian poem "Geraint and Enid" in *Idylls of the King* (1859).

Erica
Erica, the feminine form, is now sometimes identified with the Latin botanical name for heather. Both forms are sometimes spelled with a "k" instead of "c." A short form is **Ricky**.

Erin
From the Gaelic *Eireann*, a poetical name for Ireland. It is a modern name, particularly popular in the United States and Australia. Kim Bassinger and Alec Baldwin chose the name **Ireland** for their daughter.

Esmé
Probably from the French for "esteemed," this is now usually treated as a form of the French **Aimée**, meaning "beloved" (see **Amy**). It passed from France to Scotland in the 16th century, and then much later to England. It is now more often used as a girl's name, in which case it can also take the forms **Esmée** and **Esma**.

Esmeralda

The Spanish for "emerald." The 19th-century French writer Victor Hugo introduced it when he used it for the heroine in his novel *The Hunchback of Notre Dame*. The English form **Emerald** is also found, as is the form **Esmeraldah**.

Esther

In the Old Testament, this name is the Persian equivalent of a Hebrew word meaning "myrtle." It was frequently used in the form **Hester** and appears in England in the 17th century, adopted by the Puritans. It can also be spelled **Ester**. Shortened forms include **Ess(y)** and **Ess**, with Hester becoming **Hetty**.

Etain

In Irish legend, "The Wooing of Etain" is the story of the love of the fairy Princess Etain of the Fair Hair for a mortal man. This tale was retold in an opera called *The Immortal Hour* first performed in 1914. The opera was a great success at the time and led to a use of the name outside Ireland. In Ireland the name is usually **Etan** or **Eadan** and pronounced "ad-an."

Ethel

Not originally an independent name, but developed in the 19th century as a shortening of various Anglo-Saxon names beginning with the root "Ethel-," from *aethel*, meaning "noble" (see **Audrey**).

Etheldreda *see* **Audrey**

Ethna, Ethne *see* **Eithne**

Etta, Ettie *see* **Henrietta**

Eugenie

The French feminine form of **Eugene**, from the Greek meaning "well-born." Eugenie came into use from the French Empress Eugénie (1826–1920) who spent the last 50 years of her life in England. **Eugenia** is also used.

Eunice

From the Greek, meaning "happy victory." The name is mentioned in the New Testament and was adopted by the Puritans in the 17th century. In Greek it is pronounced as three syllables, with a hard "c" and the final "e" sounded, but modern users soften the "c" if they use the three-syllable pronunciation or more often use the pronunciation indicated by the phonetic spelling **Unice**.

Euphemia

From the Greek, meaning "fair speech" or, by implication, "silence." It occurs as **Eufemia** and **Euphemie** from the 12th century. Later it became confined to Scotland, where it is still found, usually abbreviated to **Effie** (very popular at the beginning of the 20th century), **Eppie** or, occasionally, **Fay** or **Phoebe**.

Evangeline

From the Greek, meaning "bringer of good news," the same word that gives us "evangelist." It was first introduced by Longfellow for his poem "Evangeline" (1847) and still tends to have a rather literary flavour. **Evangelina** is also found.

Eve

From the Hebrew, meaning "life," and in the Old Testament this is the name of the first woman. **Eva** is the Latin form, Eve the English. It was in use in Britain in the Middle Ages, when Old Testament names were not generally popular. In Ireland it was used as a substitute for the earlier Gaelic **Aoife** (pronounced "ee-fa"), meaning "radiant," currently a very popular name. The short form of Eve is **Evie** and **Evita** is a Spanish short form (see also **Zoe**).

Evelyn

When the Normans conquered Ireland, they brought with them a girl's name **Aveline**, meaning "wished for (child)." It was adopted by the Irish in the form **Eibhlin** (pronounced either with the "bh" as a "v" or silent, giving **Eileen**), which in turn was anglicized **Eveline** or **Eveleen** and later developed forms such as **Evaline, Evelena**, and **Evelina**. It was also adopted as a surname, usually spelled Evelyn, and around the 17th century the surname started to be used for boys. The boy's form is usually spelled Evelyn; all spellings are used for girls.

F

Fahimah

A name from the Arabic for "discerning" or "intelligent."

Faith

One of the Christian virtues used as names after the Reformation. It was formerly used for both sexes, but is now primarily a girl's name. **Fay(e)** or **Fae** is a short form.

Fallon

This is an English form of the Irish surname "O Fallamhain," or "leader." It became popular as a first name after a character in the TV series *Dynasty*.

Fanny *see* **Frances, Myfanwy**

Farah

From the Arabic, meaning "joy, cheerfulness." **Farrah** is also found. American actress Farrah Fawcett claimed that her parents were unaware that Farah existed when they invented her first name. **Farhanah** is from the Arabic, for "joyful."

Fatima

This is an Arabic name that means either "chaste" or "motherly." It was the name of the Prophet Muhammad's favourite daughter, the only one of his children to have children of her own. It is also occasionally used in a Christian context in honour of Our Lady of Fatima.

Faustine

Fausta and **Faustus** were names given to his twin children by the ancient Roman dictator Sulla. The names mean "fortunate" and Sulla had always considered himself particularly blessed with good luck, taking the nickname **Felix**. Faustine is the French form of the name. Although the two girls' names are sometimes used, the legend of Dr. Faustus, who sells his soul to the Devil, has made it difficult to use the male variation.

Fawn
The word for a young deer used as a first name.

Fay
A short form of both **Faith** and **Euphemia**, and also an old form of the word "faith." In addition it is an old version of the French word for "fairy" found in the name of the Arthurian enchantress Morgana le Fay. It was in use by 1872, at least in fiction. It is also spelled **Faye**.

Felicia
The feminine form of **Felix**, from the Latin, meaning "happy, lucky." Felicia has a long history of use and was also very popular in the Middle Ages. **Felice** was a variant form.

Felicity
From the Latin *felicitas*, meaning "happiness." It was the name of two saints and was used by the Puritans in the 17th century.

Fenella
A Gaelic name meaning "white-shouldered." The name became known in Britain in the 19th century as a result of Sir

Walter Scott's novel *Peveril of the Peak*. The Irish form of the name is **Finola** or **Fionnuala** (pronounced "Fin-noola"), which can be shortened to **Nola** or **Nuala**, a popular choice in Ireland.

Fern
The plant name used as a first name.

Ffion
Ffion is the Welsh word for the foxglove flower, and a word used in poetry to describe the cheek of a beautiful girl.

Fiona
From Gaelic, meaning "fair, white." It was first used in the 19th century by William Sharp as a pen name (Fiona Macleod). He modelled it on the Irish man's name **Fionn** or **Finn**. It was long thought of as a particularly Scottish name, but is now used throughout the English-speaking world. **Fi** is the short form.

Flavia
A Roman family name, which probably meant something like

"golden or tawny-haired." **Fulvia** has much the same meaning.

Fleur
The French word for "flower." It was first used as a name in the 20th century, in John Galsworthy's series of novels, *The Forsyte Saga*. The English equivalents **Flower** and **Blossom** are also found. (See also **Flora**).

Flo, Floy *see* **Florence**

Flora
From the Latin, meaning "flower." Flora was the Roman goddess of flowers and the spring. The male equivalent names **Florent** and **Florian** are also used.

Florence
From the Latin name **Florentius**, derived from the word meaning "blooming." In the Middle Ages, Florence was used as often for men as for women. Florence Nightingale was named after the town in Italy where she was born, and her fame popularized the name in the 19th century. Abbreviated forms

are **Florrie, Flossie, Floy**, and **Flo**.

Frances
This name derives from **Francesca**, the feminine form of the Italian **Francesco**. It was first used in Italy in the 13th century, about the same time as the French form **Françoise** began to appear. **Francine** is another French form. **Frances** was not used in Britain until the 15th century, and it became popular with the English aristocracy at the time of the Tudors. The short forms are **Fanny, Fran(cie)**, and **Frankie**.

Frederica
The feminine form of **Frederick**, from the Old German, meaning "peaceful ruler." Common abbreviations are **Fred(die)** and **Freddy**, also used as independent names. The feminine form is the origin of the names **Freda, Frida**, or **Frieda** (the last two influenced by the German form, **Friede**).

Freya
The name of the ancient Norse goddess of beauty, love, and fertility. It can also be found as **Frea** or spelled the Swedish way **Freja**. The name became better known through the indomitable travel writer Freya Stark (1893–1993).

Fulvia see **Flavia**

G

Gabrielle
The feminine form of **Gabriel**, from Hebrew, containing the elements "God," "man," and "strength," and possibly implying the phrase "strong man of God" or "God is my strength." In St. Luke's Gospel, Gabriel is the Archangel who announces to Mary that she is to bear the baby Jesus. Gabrielle, a French form, or the Italian **Gabriella**, are much more common. A short form is **Gaby**.

Gaenor, Gaynor see **Jennifer**

Gaia
In Greek myth **Gaea** or Gaia is the earth goddess, the universal mother, probably once the most important divinity. Her name is occasionally found used as a first name, usually with "green" or feminist overtones.

Gail
Originally a short form of **Abigail**, now widely used as a name in its own right. The spellings **Gale** and **Gayle** are also found.

Gauri
This name is from the Sanskrit for "white" and was applied to the wife of the Hindu god **Shiva** when she had acquired a fair complexion after meditating in the snows of the Himalayas.

Gay(e)
This name is simply the adjective meaning happy and lively, and its use dates from the 20th century.

Gayle see **Gail**

Geena see **Gina**

Geeta see **Gita**

Gemma
The Italian word for "gem." Its

modern use is probably due in part to the Italian saint Gemma Galgani (1875–1903), canonized in 1940. Rare before the 1980s, it then became one of the most popular names in the country. It is also spelled **Jemma**.

Genevieve

A French name possibly meaning "lady of the people." It is found in Latin records as **Genovera** and **Genoveva**. St. Genevieve is the patron saint of Paris; she saved the city from the Huns in the 5th century by cool thinking, courage, and prayer. The name has been used in Britain since the 19th century. French short forms are **Gina, Ginette,** and **Veva**.

Georgina

Georgina and **Georgia**, the most common feminine forms of **George**. Other feminine forms of George are **Georgette** and **Georgine**.

Geraldine

Geraldine started life as a poetic nickname used by the 16th-century Earl of Surrey, in a poem praising the beauty of Lady Elizabeth Fitzgerald. Geraldine therefore means "one of the Fitzgeralds." It shares the short forms **Ger(ry)** and **Jerry** with **Gerald**.

Germaine

Several early saints bore this name, which probably indicated someone who came from Germany. Germaine is little used in English-speaking countries, but it has been made well known by the writer and academic Germaine Greer.

Gertrude

From the Old German for "strong spear." The name came to Britain in the Middle Ages from the Netherlands, where a saint of that name was popular. It was much used in the 19th and earlier 20th centuries, but is not often chosen by parents now. Short forms are **Gert(ie)**, and **Trudi(e)** or **Trudy** come from a German short form of the name.

Ghislaine

This is an Old French name, related to **Giselle** and meaning "pledge, hostage." It has only come to be used in Britain comparatively recently. It is also found in the forms **Ghislane** and **Ghislain**, although in France this last form is used for boys. It is pronounced with a hard "g" and the "s" is silent.

Gianna

A short form of the Italian name **Giovanna**, feminine of **Giovanni**, or **John**. Other short forms of Giovanna include **Gina, Giannina**, and **Vanna**.

Gigi

This name became well known in 1958, when the novel *Gigi* by the French writer Colette was made into a successful musical film. In the book Gigi is the short form of **Gilberte**, the French feminine form of **Gilbert**.

Gillian

This name, which is an English rendering of the Latin name **Juliana**, was so common in the Middle Ages that its short form, **Gill**, was used as a general term for a girl, as **Jack** was for a man. It was revived in the

20th century and once again became very popular. A variant form is **Jillian**, and **Jill**, the abbreviated form, is now given as an independent name. **Jilly** is also found.

Gina
A short form of such names as **Georgina** and **Regina** (see **Queenie**), now used as an independent name. In France, Gina and **Ginette** are short forms of **Genevieve**, and it is also a short form of the Italian **Gianna**. **Geena** is also found.

Ginette *see* **Genevieve, Gina**

Gini, Ginny *see* **Virginia**

Giovanna *see* **Gianna**

Giselle
From the Old German, meaning a "pledge" or "hostage." **Gisèle** has for a long time been a common French name, and the English form Giselle and the latinized **Gisela** have been used in Britain (see also **Ghislaine**).

Gita
An Indian name from the Sanskrit, meaning "song." **Geeta** is a popular alternative spelling.

Giulia, Giulietta *see* **Julia**

Gladys
This is the anglicized form of **Gwladys**, which means "ruler." It is recorded in Wales as early as the 5th century, but only moved into the mainstream of names in the 19th century. In the earlier part of the 20th century it was very popular, but in recent decades it has become less fashionable. It is often shortened to **Glad**.

Glenda
This is a Welsh name meaning "holy and good."

Glenna
Feminine form of **Glen**, the Celtic word for "a valley." In the last 40 years they have become popular names throughout the English-speaking world. Other spellings include **Glenne** and **Glyn**.

Glenys
From the Welsh, meaning "holy." It is spelled in a variety of ways, including **Glen(n)is, Glennys**, and **Glenice** (see also **Glynis**).

Gloria
This is Latin for "glory" or "fame." The name seems to have been coined by George Bernard Shaw (1889) in his play *You Never Can Tell*. It was very common in the first half of the 20th century.

Glynis
From the Welsh for "a little valley," and thus related to **Glen** and **Glyn**. It can be spelled **Glinys** and is often confused with **Glenys**.

Govindi
This Indian name is similar to **Gopal**, deriving from the Sanskrit words which mean "cow-finding," a reference to a cowherd, but the 12th-century *Song of Govind* associated the name firmly with Krishna.

Grace
One of the most popular girls' names in Canada, Grace existed as **Gracia**, the Latin form, in the Middle Ages but did not become common until the Puritans adopted Grace along

with other Christian qualities as a name. The short form **Gracie** is sometimes given as a separate name, and forms from other languages, such as **Gracia, Graciela, Gratia**, and **Grazia** are also found.

Grainne, Grania
In Irish and Scottish legend, Grainne was a princess betrothed to **Finn**, the famous chieftain. However, Grainne preferred **Dermot** and eloped with him. The story of Finn's pursuit of the couple and Grainne's suicide after Finn brought about Dermot's death is an important subject in Irish literature. Grania is the anglicized form of the name, reflecting the pronunciation "grahn-ya."

Greta
A Swedish abbreviation of **Margaret**. It was rarely used until the 20th century, when the fame of the film actress Greta Garbo led to some parents using it. **Gretel** and **Gretchen** are the German forms.

Griselda
The meaning of this old Germanic name is disputed, but it may mean "grey battle-maiden." Chaucer told the story of "Patient Griselda" in the *Canterbury Tales*, which encouraged its use by parents who wanted meek and virtuous daughters. **Grizel** is an old Scottish form which is little used nowadays, and **Zelda** started as a short form.

Guendolen *see* **Gwendolyn**

Guenevere, Guinevere *see* **Jennifer**

Gulab
A Hindu flower name, from the Sanskrit for "rose."

Gwen
The short form of several names, such as **Gwendolyn**, which come from the Welsh word meaning "white." Gwen and **Gwenda** (a short form, which can also mean "fair and good") are now used as separate names.

Gwendolyn, Gwendolen, Guendolen
From the Welsh, meaning "white circle," probably a reference to the ancient moon-goddess. The name occurs frequently in Welsh legend. Its wide range of spellings also include **Gwendoline** and **Gwendolyne**. It was a popular name at the beginning of the century, but is not much used now.

Gwyneth
From the Welsh, meaning either "fair maiden" or "happiness." **Gwyn** is the short form.

H

Hailey, Haley
From a surname meaning "hay field." This name came into use in the 1960s, after the success of the film actress, **Hayley** Mills, and has since become very popular. It is spelled in many different ways including **Hailee** and **Haylie** and is occasionally used for boys.

Hana
Hana is from the Arabic, for "bliss" or "happiness." **Haniyya**, meaning "joyful, delighted," and

Hanan, "tenderness, affection," come from the same root.

Hannah
From the Hebrew, meaning "God has favoured me." In the Old Testament it was the name of Samuel's mother. The Greek form of this, **Anna** (see **Anne**), was used at first.

Harriet
From the Greek, meaning "lady of the hearth." Short forms are **Hattie** or **Hatty**.

Harsha
A Hindu name derived from the Sanskrit for "happiness."

Hayden
This appears to be a form of **Haydn**, a name used in honour of the Austrian composer Franz Josef Haydn. As a first name, it is also spelled **Haydon**. The surname Haydn in its turn derives from the Old German word for "heathen." Once restricted to boys, it is now also used for girls and its popularity is spreading.

Hazel
One of the plant names adopted as a girl's name in the 19th century.

Heather
This is one of several plant names first used in the 19th century. **Heath**, another name for the same plant, is also used for both sexes.

Heidi
This name is a short form of the German version of **Adelaide** meaning "noble and kind." It has come into use in the English-speaking world thanks to the popularity of Johanna Spyri's *Heidi* stories.

Helen(a)
From the Greek, meaning "the bright one." The popularity of this name in Britain was due originally to the fourth-century St. Helena. She was the mother of Constantine the Great and was supposed to have been the daughter of the ruler of Colchester, the Old King Cole of nursery rhyme. When she was over 80 she made a pilgrimage to the Holy Land, where she was believed to have found the true cross of Christ. The name is first found as **Elena** and then **Elaine** and **Ellen**. The "H" was not used until the Renaissance, when the study of classical literature brought Homer's story of the Trojan war and the beautiful Greek queen Helen to public notice. **Lena** is a contraction and **Nell** is a short form. **Ilona** is a Hungarian form.

Helga
From the Norse, meaning "holy" (see also **Olga**).

Heloise, Heloïse *see* **Eloise**

Hema
An Indian name that derives from the Sanskrit for "golden."

Henrietta
From the Greek, meaning "ruler of the house," Henrietta is the feminine form of **Henry**. It was introduced into England in the 17th century by **Henriette** Marie, Charles I's French wife. The full form gave way to the

abbreviated **Harriet**, but was revived in the 19th century. Abbreviations are **Etta, Ettie**, and **Hetty**.

Hermione

Hermione (pronounced with four syllables) has recently come to public attention as the name of a major character in J. K. Rowling's *Harry Potter* books. It comes from the Greek meaning "daughter of Hermes." In Greek mythology Hermione was the daughter of Menelaus and **Helen**. Shakespeare's use of the name in *A Winter's Tale* gave rise to its use in modern times. He used another form, **Hermia**, in *A Midsummer Night's Dream*, and this has also been found occasionally.

Hilary, Hillary

From the Latin, meaning "cheerful." The original Latin forms **Hilaria** and **Hilarius** are very occasionally found, and the writer **Hilaire** Belloc used the French form. It was once quite usual as a boy's name, but is now rarely used except for girls.

Hilda

From the Old English word for "battle." There was an Anglo-Saxon St. Hilda, a woman of outstanding ability who founded an abbey at Whitby in the 7th century. When the names of Anglo-Saxon saints were revived in the 19th century, Hilda became popular.

Hina

A Hindu name meaning "henna," the dye used to colour the hair and fingernails. It is also found as **Heena** and **Henna**.

Holly

A plant name used as a first name, currently popular on both sides of the Atlantic.

Honoria

From the Latin, meaning "reputation" or "honour." The Latin forms **Honor(i)a** and **An(n)ora** were predominant until the Reformation, when the Puritans adopted the abstract virtue names and used **Hono(u)r**. They were then used both as masculine and feminine names. In the 19th century the Latin forms were revived (see also **Nora**).

Hope

This Christian virtue was adopted as a first name in the 17th century, in the same way as **Faith** and **Charity**. It was especially popular among Puritans at this time, who used it for both sexes. It is now only used for girls.

Horatia

A rare feminine form of **Horatio**, from the Roman clan named Horatius borne by the Latin poet Horace.

Humayra

This name was given by the Prophet Muhammad to his wife **Aisha**. Its meaning is unclear.

Hunter

A surname that is often used as a first name for boys, but it is increasingly popular as a girl's name, maybe inspired by the actress Hunter Tylo, who appears in the soap opera *The Bold and the Beautiful*.

I

Ianthe
This is an ancient Greek name meaning "violet flower." It has a strong literary flavour, having been used by a number of poets including Byron and Shelley. It is still quietly but steadily used.

Ida
From the Old German, meaning "hard work." The name was introduced by the Normans and lasted until about the middle of the 14th century. In the late 19th century it was revived by Tennyson for the name of the heroine of his poem "The Princess," which Gilbert and Sullivan subsequently took as a basis for the operetta *Princess Ida*. These uses led to a revival of the name at the end of the 19th century.

Imelda
Imelda is probably the Italian form of the Germanic name **Irmhilde** "universal battle." It is the name of a rather obscure saint and had a certain popularity in Ireland in the middle of the 20th century.

Imogen
First appearing in Shakespeare's *Cymbeline*, this name is thought to be a misprint of the name **Innogen**, which appears in Shakespeare's source for the story. It may be derived from the Greek meaning "beloved child." It is a popular choice at the moment.

Ina
This name can come from three different sources. It is an Irish form of **Agnes**, a form of the name **Ena**, and can also be a short form of first names ending "-ina," such as **Christina** and **Georgina**.

India
This was the name of a character in *Gone with the Wind*, but its popularity is more likely to be due to the interest, particularly since the 1970s, in Indian culture and religion and the model India Hicks, given the name as the granddaughter of Lord Mountbatten, last viceroy of India.

Indigo
This name for the plant and the dark blue colour it produced when used as a dye has been coming into use as a fashionable name in the last few years, perhaps helped by its similarity to **India** (the plant's name means "Indian plant," for it came to Europe from India). Indeed, **Blue** itself has recently become immensely high-profile, being chosen by a number of celebrity parents, particularly as a middle name, sometimes in foreign forms such as **Bleu** or **Blu**. Thus we find Cher's Elijah Blue, John Travolta's Ella Blue and Dave Evans, of U2, using Blue Angel.

Indira
An Indian name associated with the goddess Lakshmi, wife of Vishnu. It is usually derived from a Sanskrit word meaning "beauty" but is possibly connected with **Indra**, the name of the god of the sky and rain in Hindu tradition. The meaning of the name is uncertain but may be connected with the Sanskrit for "raindrop."

Inés, Inez *see* **Agnes**

Ingrid
From the Old Norse, meaning "Ing's ride." In Norse mythology Ing was the god of fertility and crops who rode a golden-bristled boar. It is a common name in Scandinavia and was made famous in Britain by the Swedish film star Ingrid Bergman (1915–82). **Ingeborg** ("Ing's fortress") and **Inga**, the short form of these two names, are also found occasionally.

Iola
The Latin form of a Greek name meaning "dawn cloud." In Greek mythology Hercules fell in love with a princess **Iole**.

Iolanthe *see* **Yolanda**

Iona
This is the name of the Scottish island used as a first name. The island seems originally to have been called Ioua, "yew-tree island," but at some point the "u" was misread as "n" and so the island got its present name. The name's popularity has been increasing in recent years. **Ione** ("eye-oh-nee") is not the same name, but a Greek name connected with the word "violet."

Irene
The goddess of peace and also of one of the seasons in ancient Greece. The abbreviation **Renie** is sometimes used and it can also be found in the form **Irena**. Irene is pronounced in two different ways: in the Greek way with three syllables and the final "e" pronounced, and the usual modern way with only two syllables.

Iris
Although this name is usually associated with the flower, it comes from the Greek word for "rainbow," after which the flower was named because of its bright colours. In Greek mythology Iris carried messages from the gods to men, across the rainbow which was her bridge.

Irma
This was originally a German name meaning "universal."

Isabel(le), Isobel
These are forms of **Elizabeth** that developed in medieval France. Elizabeth became **Ilsabeth** and then **Isabeau**, and finally Isabelle. Up to at least the end of the 17th century, the derivatives Isabel(le) in England, Isobel in Scotland, and the Gaelic **Iseabail**, sometimes spelled phonetically as **Ishbel**, were interchangeable with Elizabeth. **Isa** and **Bel(le)** were the common short forms. The Latin **Isabella** and **Bella** were used from the 18th century on.

Isidora
From the Greek, possibly meaning "gift of Isis." There were two Spanish saints of this name. The scandal caused by the private life and dancing style of Isadora Duncan (1878–1927) made the feminine form of the name **Isidore** well known.

Isla
A Scottish island name, used as a girl's name in Scotland since the 1950s. It has now spread to other parts of Britain. The "s" is silent, as in "island."

Isleen *see* **Aisling**

Isolda
From the Old Welsh **Essylt** meaning "fair one." It was a common name in medieval times because of its place in the tragic legend of **Tristan** and Isolda. **Iseult** was the Norman form, which became Isolda in Latin, **Isot(t)** in Middle English. Isolda or **Isolde** had a brief revival in the 19th century owing to the popularity of Wagner's opera *Tristan and Isolde*. It is also spelled **Yseult(e)** and **Ysolde**.

Israel
From Hebrew, although its meaning is disputed; the most likely translation is "may God prevail." In the Old Testament Jacob was named Israel after his struggle with the angel of God. The name was first adopted by Christians after the Reformation.

Ivy
This is a plant name that came into use in the 19th century. Because ivy clings so firmly, the name may have been used to indicate faithfulness.

J

Jacqueline
Jacqueline and **Jacquetta** are French feminines of **Jacques**, the French equivalent of **James** and **Jacob**. Both were introduced into Britain in the 13th century and have been in use there ever since. Jacqueline, with its short forms **Jacky, Jacki(e)**, or **Jacqui**, is found in a very wide range of spellings, which include **Jackalyn, Jacaline, Jacquelyn**, and **Jaqueline**.

Jade
The name of the precious stone used as a first name. Although the names of precious stones have been in use as girls' names since the 19th century, this one seems only to have come into use in the 1970s and has been popular again recently. **Ja(y)da** and **Jaden** can be seen as developments of either Jade or **Jay**. Another variant is **Jaida**.

Jaelin, Jai *see* **Jay**

Jaimal *see* **Jamila**

Jalila
The feminine form of **Jalal**, an Arabic name that means "glory" or "greatness." A similar masculine form is Jalil, meaning "honoured" or "revered." Jalila is the feminine form of both. The name is also found as **Galila**.

Jaleesa
Also spelled **Jalisa**, this newly formed name, blended the "Ja-" of names like **Jane, Janet**, and **Jacqueline** with the sound of **Lisa**. It was introduced in 1988 through a character in the TV sitcom *A Different World*.

Jalisa *see* **Jaleesa**

Jamie
This was originally a Scottish short form of **James**, but it has since spread throughout the English-speaking world and become popular in its own right. Since at least the 1950s it has also been used as a girl's name.

Jamila
An Arabic name meaning "beautiful." Alternate spellings include **Jamil, Jaimal**, and **Jamel**. It is also used in France,

where it can be found as
Djamila.

Jan *see* **Janet**

Jane
This is now the most common
feminine form of **John**. It
comes from the Old French
form **Jehane**. It was very rare
before the 16th century, the
medieval feminine forms of
John being **Joan** and **Joanna**.
An early example was Jane
Seymour, third wife of King
Henry VIII of England and
mother of Edward V. Since Tudor
times the name has been in and
out of fashion. At the moment it
is freely used as a second name,
but rarely as a first unless in
some combination like Sarah
Jane. It can also be spelled
Jayne. The most common short
forms are **Jenny** and **Janey** or
Janie (see also **Janet**). **Jancis**
seems to be a combination of
Jane with **Frances** or **Cicely**.
Other forms include **Jana(e)**,
**Janelle, Janice, Janis, Jeanne,
Joanne, Johanna, Juana**.

Janet
This was originally derived

from **Jeanette**, the French
short form of **Jean**. It was
first used in Scotland. **Janette**
and **Janetta** are also found,
and **Net(ta), Nettie**, and **Jan**
are short forms. A Scottish
short form is **Jessie** (see also
Sheena).

Janey, Janice, Janie, Janis
see **Jane**

Janine
Like **Janet**, this name comes
from a short form of **Jeanne**,
the French form of **Jean**. It
is also spelled **Jannine** and
Janene, and the latinized
Janina is also used.

Jaqueline *see* **Jacqueline**

Jasmine
A flower name also found in its
normal botanical form, **Jasmin**.
The word comes from Persian,
and the name is also used in
the Persian form **Yasmin**, with
variants such as **Yasmine** and
Yasmina.

Jawahir
An Arabic name that means
"jewels."

Jay
Comes from a short form of
any name beginning with a "J,"
or from a surname, originally
a nickname for someone who
chattered like the bird. It is
sometimes spelled **Jaye**. There
are a number of elaborations
such as **Jaelyn** or **Jaylin, Jayla,
Ja(y)den, Jac(e)y** and its
variants.

Jayne *see* **Jane**

Jean
This name started as a Scottish
form of **Jane** or **Joan** derived
from the Old French **Jehane**.
The diminutive **Jeanette** is
also found (see **Janet**). The
most common short forms are
Jeanie and **Jenny**.

Jemima
From the Hebrew, meaning
"dove" or "handsome as the day,"
and the name of one of Job's
daughters in the Old Testament.
First used in the 17th century
by Puritans, it was very popular
in the 19th century and is used
steadily today. **Mima** is a short
form.

Jemma *see* **Gemma**

Jena
Arabic for "little bird."

Jenna
A Cornish version of **Jennifer**, Jenna is increasingly popular in Canada.

Jennifer
An old Cornish form of **Guenevere**, from the Welsh meaning "white ghost," and the name of King Arthur's wife. It was practically obsolete until its 20th-century revival. It spread rapidly and was very popular in the 1950s and 60s. **Jenny** or **Jenni** is the short form, shared with **Jane** and **Jean**. **Gaenor**, **Geunor**, and **Gaynor** are other forms of Guenevere, which is also spelled **Guinevere** and, in Wales, **Gwenhwyfar**.

Jenny *see* **Jane, Jean, Jennifer**

Jessica
The source of this name is much debated, but it was probably invented by Shakespeare for his play *The Merchant of Venice* in which Shylock's daughter is called Jessica. It is shortened to **Jess** or **Jessie** (also a Scottish short form of **Janet**), which is sometimes spelled **Jessye**. It is very popular at the moment.

Joan, Joanna
This is the oldest feminine form of **John** and is a contraction of **Johanna**, the Latin feminine form of **Johannes**. The name came over from France as **Jhone** and **Johan** in the second half of the 12th century, but by the 14th century Joan was the established form. By the mid-16th century it was so common that it became unfashionable, and **Jane** superseded it. It was revived at the beginning of the 20th century. **Joni** is the short form. **Joanne** was a later development of the name. **Juanita** is the Spanish short form, which can be shortened to **Nita**.

Jocelyn, Jo(s)celin
These names seem to be derived from several different names which have come together over a period of time to form one name. The most important source is probably from the Latin, meaning "cheerful, sportive." There is also a possibility that it is derived from an Old German name meaning "little Goth." A further derivation has been traced from the name **Josse**, "champion," a form of **Jodoc**, the name of an early Breton saint, which also gave us **Joyce**. Jocelyn is the usual form for boys, although the name is now rarely masculine.

Jodi(e), Jody *see* **Judith**

Jordan
Jordan was quite a popular name in the Middle Ages when it was given to children baptized with water from the River Jordan brought back by pilgrims from the Holy Land. It has recently been revived as a first name and is currently a popular choice for Canadian girls and boys. The name of the river means "to descend, flow." Other forms include **Jordana, Jorden, Jordin**, and **Jordyn**.

Joscelin *see* **Jocelyn**

Josephine

Josephine is the French feminine form of **Joseph**. It was Napoleon's first wife, the Empress Josephine, who started the fashion for the name in Britain and France. Variants include **Josepha, Joséphine, Josefa, Josefina, Josephina**. Short forms are **Jo(e)** and **Josie**, and in France Josephine has the short form **Fifi**.

Joy

This is the vocabulary word used as a first name. It occurs as early as the 12th century but then disappears, to be revived in the 19th century.

Joyce

In the Middle Ages when this name was most common it usually had the form **Josse**. A 7th-century saint from Brittany, who also gave us the name **Jocelyn**, was the cause of the name's popularity. One of its French variants was **Joisse**, and it was from this that the name's final form was derived. Joyce was little used after the Middle Ages until the general revival of medieval names in the 19th century.

Juanita *see* **Joan**

Judith

From the Hebrew, meaning "a Jewess," and in the Apocryphal Book of Judith the name of the resourceful woman who saves the Israelites by letting the enemy general think he was seducing her, and then cutting off his head with his own sword. The short form **Judy** is often given independently, while the short forms **Jody** and **Jodi(e)** are now the most common form of the name.

Julia, Juliet

Julia is the feminine form of **Julius**, which came to England from Italy as **Giulia** in the 16th century. It did not become common in Britain until the 18th and 19th centuries. **Julie** is the French form. Julia was popular in the middle of the 20th century, then fell out of favour, but is now coming back into use. Shakespeare's heroine in *Romeo and Juliet* gets her name from the Italian short form **Giulietta**, which is **Juliette** in French.

Juliana

This is the feminine form of **Julian**. It was a popular name in the Middle Ages, when the name normally took the form Julian, still occasionally used for girls. The variant forms **Gillian** and **Jill** were among the most common girls' names from the 12th to the 15th centuries. The name subsequently dropped out of use but was revived in the 18th century. The short form **Julie** is shared with **Julia** (see also **Lianne**) and **Julianne** is a common variant.

June

This is simply the name of the month which, like **April**, has been used as a girl's name in the 20th century.

Justine

The old feminine form of **Justin**, from the Latin, meaning "just." These were uncommon names until the later 20th century when they came back into fashion. **Justice** has recently started appearing as a given name for both sexes.

K

Kacey *see* **Casey**

Kadie, Kady *see* **Kay**

Kaitlyn
This, like **Kathleen**, is an Irish form of **Katharine**. The Irish pronounce it with the sound of "cat," but the American pronunciation is reflected in the spelling **Katelynn**. Forms such as **Caitlyn, Caitlynn**, and **Katlin** are also found.

Kalli(e), Kally *see* **Callie**

Kamala
In India this name derives from the Sanskrit, where it means "pale red," but it is specifically associated with the lotus flower. Kamala is one of the goddess Lakshmi's names in classical Hindu texts, where it is also a name of **Shiva**'s wife. The masculine **Kamal** is from

an Arabic word that means "perfection."

Kamila(h)
From the Arabic, meaning "complete" or "perfect."

Kanisha
A modern variation of **Tanisha**, "Monday's child." It is sometimes spelled **Quanisha**.

Kanta
An Indian name, from the Sanskrit for "beautiful, desired."

Kara, Karena, Karissa *see* **Cara**

Karel *see* **Carol**

Karen
A Scandinavian form of **Katharine**. Variants include **Karan** and **Karin, Karyn(a), Caryn**, and **Caron**, although some of these could be analyzed as belonging to **Cara** (see also **Keren**).

Karenza *see* **Kerensa**

Karina *see* **Cara**

Katharine, Katherine, Catharine, Catherine
A name of unknown meaning, but from an early date associated with the Greek *katharos* meaning "pure." The name came to the U.K. in the early 12th century when crusaders brought back the legend of St. Katharine of Alexandria. She was an Egyptian princess who was tortured and put to death in the early 4th century for her learned defence of Christianity. There are a number of further spellings for the name, of which **Kathryn** is one of the most frequent. The most common short forms are **Kate, Kitty, Katie, Cathy**, and **Kay**, all of which are used as independent names. The Irish forms, **Kathleen** and **Cathleen**, are widely used, while **Caitlin** is an older Irish form that has recently become popular. **Kathlyn** is a variant of Kathleen. Russian **Katarina, Katia**, or **Katya** and **Katinka** are occasionally found (see also **Catriona, Karen**).

Katrina, Katrine *see* **Catriona**

Kay

A short form of names beginning with a "K," such as **Katharine**. It has been used as a first name for over a century and can also be spelled **Kai** (also a Hawaiian name meaning "sea") and **Kaye**. Blends such as **Kaylyn (Kaylin, Kaylan**, but see **Keely), Kaya (Kia)** and **Kady** (perhaps a form of **Katie**) are also found.

Kayla

This name may have started as a short form of **Michaela**, particularly as this often takes the form **Makayla** in the United States, or be a variant of **Kayleigh**, especially in the relaxed pronunciation of rural western states such as Montana, where use of Kayla seems to have begun in the 1970s.

Kaylee

Possibly a variant of **Kayla** or a combination of **Kay** and **Lee**. Alternate spellings such as **Caleigh, Cayleigh, Kayley**, and **Kayleigh** are common.

Keanna

A feminine form of the Hawaiian name **Keanu**, meaning "cool breeze over the mountains," widely known.

Keely

This increasingly popular name comes from an Irish word meaning "slender, graceful." In the case of one early popularizer of the name, the American singer Keely Smith (b. 1932), it was originally her surname. The name is also spelled **Keeley**. **Keelin** comes from the same root, and may be a source of **Kaylan** (see **Kay**).

Keira, Kira see **Kiera, Kyra**

Keisha

Possibly originated as a short form for **Lakeisha** which may be adaptation of **Aisha** or **Iesha**, in Arabic meaning "woman."

Kelly

It is an Irish surname that means "warlike" used as a first name. At first mainly a boy's name, it is now more common for girls. **Kelley** is also found (see also **Kayleigh, Kylie**).

Kelsey

The surname, which in turn comes from an Old English name meaning "ship-victory," used as a first name. Despite the success of the American actor Kelsey Grammer, it is more common for girls than boys.

Kendall

The surname, which can have various sources, used as a first name for girls and boys. Another surname, the similar-sounding **Kendrick**, is also used for boys, and from it a feminine form, **Kendra**, has evolved.

Kennedy

Use of this Irish surname is spreading from the United States to the rest of the English-speaking world. Its choice no doubt owes much to the respect and glamour surrounding the assassinated president John F. Kennedy (1917–63).

Kenzie see **Mackenzie**

Kera see **Kyra**

Keren

Although some modern uses of this may be as a form of **Karen**, this is an ancient name, a short form of the Old Testament **Kerenhappuch**, one of the beautiful daughters of Job. The name means "horn (container) of kohl." It has also been found in the form **Kerena** and **Ker(r)yn**.

Kerensa, Kerenza

A Cornish name meaning "affection, love." It is also found as **Karenza**.

Keri *see* **Ceri**

Kerry

The Irish county name used as a given name. It is a modern name, apparently first used in Australia usually for boys, but it is now in general use, mainly for girls. It is also found as **Kerri**. Its spread may have been helped by the Welsh name **Ceri**, pronounced in the same way.

Keshia *see* **Kezia**

Ketana

A Hindu name meaning "home."

Kezia(h)

The Hebrew word for the spice cassia, and the name of one of **Job**'s beautiful daughters in the Bible. The form **Keshia** also occurs, with short forms **Kezie, Kizzie,** and **Kissie** or **Kissy. Cassia** and **Kasia** have also been recorded, with the latter also a Polish short form of **Katharine**.

Khadija

A name from the Arabic, meaning "premature child." Khadiya bint-Khuwaylid, the first wife of the Prophet Muhammad, was the mother of all his children. The name is also spelled **Khadeeja(h)** and **Khadijah**.

Kiara

It probably adapts the word **Tiara**, also used as a first name, making use of the fashionable "K" sound. **Tiana** and **Kiana** (also found in forms such as **Kean(n)a, Keyanna,** and even **Quiana**) are similar coinages; while **Kia** and **Kaya** hover somewhere between this group and **Kay**.

Kiera

A feminine form of the Irish name **Ciaran**, meaning "dark-haired." It was the name of 26 Irish saints and in the last two or three decades it has become increasingly popular. Alternate forms include **Ciara, Ciera, Kiara,** and **Kyra**.

Kim

Probably from Old English *cynebeald*, meaning "royally bold," developing through the surname Kimball. Rudyard Kipling's hero in the novel *Kim* (1901) used a shortened form of his true name, Kimball O'Hara, showing the use of the surname as a first name. More recently the name has been used for girls. **Kym** is also found. *See also* **Kimberley**.

Kimberl(e)y

Another possible source of the name **Kim**. Kimberley is a diamond-mining town in South Africa, and the association with jewels seems to have encouraged its use. It spread rapidly after its first use in the 1940s. There was also a brief fashion for Kimberley as a boy's name at about 1900, commemorating events of the Boer War.

Kirsty, Kirsten
Both these are forms of the name **Christine**. Kirsty was originally a Scottish short form, while Kirsten comes from Scandinavia. **Kiersten** or **Kirstin** are also found.

Kumari
From the Sanskrit, meaning "girl" or "daughter."

Kyla
The feminine form of **Kyle**, a Scottish place and surname meaning "a strip of land."

Kylie
Originally an Australian Aboriginal word for a "curled stick" or "boomerang," it was this name's pleasant sound, at a time when similar-sounding names were popular, rather than its meaning that appealed to parents. It first became familiar to white Australians through the novelist Kathleen Tennant (b. 1912), whose nickname and pen name were both Kylie. Its use spread from Australia throughout the English-speaking world, particularly after being given publicity by the actress and singer Kylie Minogue. **Kylee** and **Kyleigh** are also found.

Kyra
While this name can be interpreted as a feminine form of **Kieran** or **Cyrus**, its popularity may come from the attractive character of **Kira** Neris in the *Star Trek* sequel *Deep Space Nine*. It is also found as **Kera**.

L

Lacey
Although this is on the surface a surname that comes from a French place name used as a first name, its recent popularity in the United States probably owes much to its associations with "lace."

Lachina
The occasionally used feminine form of **Lachlan**. Lachlan is from Gaelic **Lachlann** or **Lochlann**. Primarily a Highland name, it was introduced as a term for Viking settlers there.

Laeta, Laetitia *see* **Letitia**

Laila *see* **Leila**

Lakeisha
An adaptation of the name **Keisha**. The prefix "La-" became fashionable in the early 1970s in names such as **Latasha** and **Latoya**, and was popular until the 90s when it began to be replaced by "Sha-" although this, too, has largely gone out of fashion now. Other frequently used names with this prefix include **Laquisha, Lashay, Lashonda, Latisha, Latrice**, and **Latonya**.

Lakshmi
The name of the Hindu goddess of wealth and good fortune. Lakshmi derives from the Sanskrit for "mark," referring to a lucky birthmark.

Lalage
From the Latin for "one who prattles." Short forms are **Lal** and **Lally**.

Lalita
An Indian name and endearment meaning "playful" or "charming."

As a Hindi term of address the masculine form, **Lal**, means "darling boy," though it derives from a Sanskrit word meaning "caress."

Lana *see* **Alana**

Lara
A short form of the Russian name **Larissa**, the meaning of which is uncertain, although it may well be used by some parents as a variation of **Laura**. Lara came into general use in the 1960s after the success of the film of Pasternak's *Dr. Zhivago*, with its tragic heroine of this name.

Laraine *see* **Lorraine**

Larissa *see* **Lara**

Lashay, Lashonda *see* **Lakeisha**

Latasha
There is a strong tradition of name-creating among certain sections of American society, which goes back to at least the 19th century. This name and **Latoya** are among the most common of a large group of names that have grown in popularity over the last 40 years. They are mostly blends, or combinations of syllables taken from different names, which work because they sound right at the time, echoing the sounds from other popular names. Many of them start with "La" and particularly "Lat." Since names such as **Laverne** were popular with an earlier generation, it may be that the French influence found in place and surnames in the southern United States is the source, although it could just as well come from the many girls' names that begin with these letters (see also **Latisha** at **Letitia**).

Latonya, Latrice *see* **Lakeisha**

Latoya
A name introduced by the well-known singer LaToya Jackson. Her mother invented the name, making use of the fashionable prefix "La-." **LaToy** and **Toya(h)** are also used.

Laura, Lauren
Laura comes from the Latin for "laurel," a symbol in the classical world of victory and poetic genius. **Lauretta** is the diminutive form. Together with **Laurencia** and **Lora** these names were common from the 12th century. Lauren or **Loren** and **Lori** and **Lauryn** are popular variants. Other diminutives that are sometimes used are **Laureen, Laurene, Laurissa, Loretta**, and **Lolly**. **Laurel**, the plant name, sometimes spelled **Lorel**, is also found (see also **Lara, Lorraine**).

Lauraine *see* **Lorraine**

Lavinia
The meaning of this name is unknown, but in classical legend it was the name of Aeneas' wife, for whose hand in marriage he fought and defeated a rival suitor. The town of Lavinium, originally called Latium, was renamed after her. The name was very popular for a while during the Renaissance, but then faded out, only returning to fashion in the 18th century. **Lavina** is probably a variant.

Layla *see* **Leila**

Lea *see* **Leah, Lee**

Leah
A Hebrew name, probably meaning "cow." In the Bible, Leah was the sister of Rachel and the first wife of Jacob. **Lea** and **Lia**, the Italian form of the name, are sometimes used, although they can also be a short form of a number of names ending in the sound.

Leanne *see* **Lianne**

Leanora, Leanore *see* **Leonora**

Lee, Leigh, Lea
From the various forms of the surname meaning "meadow." It may have spread from the southern United States, and probably owes its popularity there to the Confederate general Robert E. Lee (1807–70). See also **Kayleigh**.

Leena
An Indian name that means "devoted." In some cases it may be a form of the Arabic name **Lina**.

Leigh Ann *see* **Lianne**

Leila
A Persian name meaning "night," probably indicating "dark-haired." Byron started the fashion for it in the 19th century by using it in a poem with an oriental setting called "The Giaour." The name also appears in the Persian romantic legend of **Leilah** and Mejnoun, the Persian equivalent of the Greek story of Cupid and Psyche. **Laila** is also used, but the most common variant is **Layla**, the form used by Eric Clapton in his song that managed the remarkable feat of being a hit in 1972, 1982, and 1992.

Lena *see* **Helen**

Lenore *see* **Leonora**

Leonie
From the Latin *leo* for "lion." Six emperors of Constantinople and thirteen popes were named **Leo**. **Leon** is the French form, from which the feminine Leonie comes. Other versions include **Lea, Leola, Leona**, and **Leontine**.

Leonora, Lenore, Leonore
These names are European forms of Eleanor, and their introduction was probably due to contemporary literary and musical influences. The spellings **Leanore** and **Leanora** are also found. A short form that all these names share is **Nora**.

Leslie, Lesley
These were respectively the usual masculine and feminine spellings of the name, although they are both now used for girls. It is a Scottish surname, perhaps meaning "garden of hollies."

Letitia
From the Latin, meaning "gladness." **Lettice** was the usual form of this name from the 12th to the 17th centuries, during which time it was very popular. In the 18th century the Latin **Laetitia** superseded it, now more frequently spelled Letitia. The phonetic form **Leticia** has recently become quite popular in the United States, giving a short form **Tiesha**, used independently and, most importantly, developing into **Latisha**, one of the most

popular of the La- names (see further **Latasha**). **Laeta** is also found. The short forms of Lettice, **Lettie**, and **Letty** are sometimes used independently.

Leverne *see* **Latasha**

Levon
Levon is a feminine form of **Levi**, a Hebrew name, meaning "associated."

Lianne, Leanne
A short form of the name **Juliana**, via the French **Julianne**, which has become popular as an independent name. It can also be spelled **Liane** and occurs in such forms as **Leigh Ann**.

Libby, Liese, Liesel *see* **Elizabeth**

Lillian, Lily
Originally these names may have been short forms of **Elizabeth**. Lillian is found in Shakespeare's time, but the name was probably associated with the lily flower even then. In the 19th century Lily was definitely given as the name of the flower, which is a Christian symbol of purity. **Lil** is the usual abbreviation. Other forms of the name include **Lillah** or **Lila**, and, **Lil(l)ian(n)a** and, in Scotland, **Lillias**.

Lilith
From the Hebrew, meaning either "serpent" or "belonging to the night." In mythology Lilith was an evil spirit who haunted the night and who had been Adam's rejected wife before Eve. It has been used very rarely.

Lina
A short form of names ending in "-lina," such as **Angelina** and **Carolina**, used as an independent name. It can also be used as a short form of these names. In the Arab world it derives from a word meaning "tender." Some Arabic experts refer the name to a type of palm tree.

Linda
This was a common ending for girls' names in Old German, and comes from the word for a snake, an animal that was held in great reverence by primitive German tribes. It represented wisdom and suppleness, and the names derived from it were therefore complimentary. In Spanish *linda* means pretty, and this may also have had some effect on the use of Linda as an English first name, which dates only from the 19th century. It is also used as a contraction of **Belinda**. Linda is also spelled **Lynda**, while **Lin(dy)**, **Lindi(e)**, and **Lyn** are short forms.

Lindsey
From the Scottish surname meaning "pool island." Together with its other forms, **Lindsay**, **Linsey**, and **Linsay**, this name is used for both boys and girls. The form Lindsay tends to be the more usual one for boys. At the moment all forms of the name are used much more frequently for girls than for boys and can then take the form **Linzi**.

Linet, Linette, Linnet *see* **Lynette**

Lois
In the New Testament Lois was the grandmother of **Timothy**.

As the rest of the family had Greek names, Lois is probably Greek also, but its meaning is not known. Like many obscure biblical names, it was adopted in the 17th century by Puritans. It fell out of use but was revived at the beginning of the 20th century.

Lola

This was originally a diminutive of the Spanish **Dolores** and of **Carlotta** (see **Charlotte**). The short form, **Lolita**, became well known in the 20th century through Vladimir Nabokov's novel of that name.

Lolly, Lora, Lorel, Loren, Loretta *see* Laura

Lori *see* Laura, Lorraine

Lorna

This name was created by R.D. Blackmore for the heroine of his novel *Lorna Doone*, published in 1869. In the book she was the lost daughter of the Marquis of **Lorne**, an ancient Scottish first name sometimes used for boys.

Lorraine

This is the French district, whose name derives from the Old German place name Lotharingen, meaning "**Lothar**'s place." Lothar was an Old German warrior name meaning "famous army." Lorraine is the form used in France. In Britain and North America it sometimes takes forms such as **Loraine, Laraine**, or **Lauraine** and it is not always possible to distinguish between variants of this name and forms of **Lauren**. **Lori** is a short form.

Lottie, Lotty *see* Charlotte

Lou, Louie *see* Louisa

Louisa, Louise

Louise is the French, and Louisa the Latin feminine form of **Louis**. Though common much earlier in France, Louise did not come to Britain until the 17th century when Louise de Keroual became Charles II's mistress. It was popular for about a century until Louisa replaced it, but nowadays Louise is once more the popular form. Short forms are **Lulu, Lou(ie),** and **Luella**.

Lourdes

In 1850 St. Bernadette of Lourdes, in south-west France, had numerous visions of the Virgin Mary at a grotto near her home town. It has since become one of the major pilgrimage sites in Europe. When the singer **Madonna** had a daughter, she chose a name linked with her own, which has since come into more general use.

Lowena

Lowena is an old Cornish name meaning "joy," which can also be spelled **Lowenna**. Its popularity has been growing rapidly in Cornwall, and it is beginning to spread to other areas. The name **Lowenek**, "joyful," can also be used. Both names are stressed on the second syllable.

Lucasta, Lucette, Lucia *see* Lucy

Lucille

From the Latin word *lux*, meaning "light" (see **Lucy**). **Lucilla** retains the Latin form, and Lucille is French. The masculine form **Lucius** and its variants **Lucien** and **Lucian** are much less common than the feminine names.

Lucina *see* **Lucy**

Lucinda
Originally a poetic form of **Lucy**, this name is now given independently, and has recently become quite popular. The short forms **Cindy** or **Cind(ie)** are used as names in their own right.

Lucy
Lucy is the usual English form of the Latin **Lucia** from *lux*, "light." In Roman times the name was often used for a child born at dawn; the goddess **Lucina** was the patroness of childbirth, bringing children into the light of day. St. Lucy was a Sicilian martyr who was much beloved in the Middle Ages, and the name became well established after the Norman Conquest. Other forms are **Lucette**, **Lucinda**, **Lucasta**, and **Lulu**.

Lydia
From the Greek, meaning "a Lydian girl." Lydia was a district of Asia Minor where the people were famous merchants and were said to have invented coinage. In the Acts of the Apostles, Lydia was a widow of Philippi who was converted by St. Paul when he stayed at her house.

Lyn
A short form of such names as **Linda, Lynette**, and **Carolyn** (see **Caroline**). It can also take the form **Lin(ne), Linn**, and **Lynn(e)**.

Lynda *see* **Linda**

Lynette
From the Welsh name **Eluned**, which probably comes from a word for "idol," via its short form, **Luned**. The form Lynette was introduced by the poet Tennyson in the story of "Gareth and Lynette" in his *Idylls of the King*. It is also spelled **Lin(n)et** (although this can also be from a bird's name), **Linette** and **Lynnette**, and **Lyn** is used as a short form.

Lynn, Lynne *see* **Lyn**

Lyric *see* **Melody**

M

Mabel
Mabel is a shortening of **Amabel**, with **Mabella** as the Latin form. Both were current from the 12th to the 15th century, but were rare thereafter until Mabel was revived in the 19th century and became very common. It then suffered another fall from favour. The short form often used is **May**. **Maybelle** and **Maybelline** are developments of the name.

Macauley
Made famous by the actor Macauley Culkin, this Scottish surname is now used for children of both sexes, although more frequently for boys. It can be spelled starting with a Mc-, and the final syllable is sometimes -lee or -leigh. The similar-sounding **Mackinley**, originally meaning "son of Finlay," is also found.

Mackenzie
As a Scottish surname, this refers to a "son of Coinneach," a Gaelic name that usually takes

the anglicized form **Kenneth**. It was popularized as a girl's name by the actress Mackenzie Phillips and is in the Top 25 girls' names in Canada. The similar **Mckenna**, originally from a Scottish surname meaning "ardent love," is also found, but more rarely.

Macy

This name, famous in the United States from Macy's department stores, has been popular with American parents for some years. The surname was originally French, from a place name meaning "Marcius' estate." It is also found as **Macey** and **Maci**.

Madel(e)ine

Magdalene, the original form of the name, is Hebrew and means "woman of Magdala," a town on the Sea of Galilee, which was the birthplace of St. Mary Magdalene. From about the 12th century the name was used in England in the French form Madeline, often abbreviated to **Ma(u)dlin**. **Magdalen**, the biblical form, was adopted after the Reformation. It was usually pronounced Maudlin, but because the meaning of this word developed the sense of "weak and sentimental," this form was replaced by the current pronunciation. It shares the short form **Madge** with **Margaret**. **Maddie** or **Maddy** is also used. A short form is **Magda** (shortened from **Ma(g)dalena**) which has also been given as an independent name. It now sometimes takes the form **Mad(e)lyn** or **Madilyn**.

Madge see Madeleine, Margaret

Madison

Madison has made a splash in North America. It was nearly non-existent before 1985. Then it soared in popularity, and is ranked among the five most popular names for baby girls. In provincial rankings, it appears as high as the second most popular name and no lower than sixth place. One theory traces the popularity of the name to the movie *Splash,* in which Daryl Hannah as a mermaid chose the name "Madison" when she saw a Madison Avenue Street sign. Some years later there was a Canadian TV series with the name *Madison,* but the *Splash* theory is much more likely. Variants include **Madisen, Madisyn, Maddison, Madyson**.

Maeve

The more usual phonetic form of the Irish name **Meadhbh**, meaning "she who makes drunk." It was the name of a famous queen in Irish legend. A diminutive is **Meaveen**, and the name is occasionally spelled **Meave** or **Mave**.

Maggie see Margaret

Makenna

A name that is becoming increasingly popular in Canada, Makenna is a variant of **McKenna** from the Gaelic surname Mac Cionnaith.

Mallory

This name has a pleasant sound, but a less pleasant meaning: as a surname it derives from the French and means "ill-omened" or "unfortunate." It was nevertheless well used by parents in the 1990s, having been launched in its first-name role by a character in the TV series *Family Ties*.

Malvina

A name invented by the Scottish poet, James Macpherson (1736–96). He may have taken it from the Gaelic meaning "smooth brow." The form **Melvina** is also found.

Mamie *see* **Mary**

Mandy *see* **Amanda**

Manisha

An Indian name that refers to the Sanskrit for "intellect" or "intelligence."

Manju

An Indian name derived from the Sanskrit for "beautiful." Similar names are **Manjubala** and **Manjulika**, both meaning "beautiful girl."

Manon *see* **Mary**

Marcia

The feminine form of the Latin Marcius, a Roman clan name that probably was derived from Mars, the god of war. St. Marcia was an early Christian martyr. The name can be pronounced with either three syllables or with two, reflected in the alternative spelling **Marsha**. **Marcy** is used as a short form. **Marcella, Marcelle, Marcelline**, and **Marcine** are all developments of the name.

Marcy *see* **Marcia**

Margaret

From the Latin *margarita*, derived from the Greek word meaning "a pearl." However, the ultimate origin is said to be Persian for "child of light," the ancients believing that pearls were formed when oysters rose from their beds at night to look at the moon, and trapped a drop of dew in their shells that was then transformed into a pearl by the moonbeams. The name first appears in Scotland in the 11th century, thanks to St. Margaret, wife of Malcolm III. She was born in Hungary where the name had spread through respect for St. Margaret of Antioch, a 3rd-century martyr. The most common short forms are **Maggie, Madge, Meg**, and **Peg(gy)**. **Maisie** was a particularly Scottish variant, and **Megan**, Welsh. The Irish form is **Mairead** ("mar-ed"). Other diminutives sometimes used are the Swedish **Greta**, French **Margot** (now also spelled **Margaux**) and **Marguerite**, and **Rita**, from **Margarita**, which is also the source of the Scandinavian short form **Meta**. Other forms include **Marghanita, Margaretta**, and **Margoletta** (see also **Daisy, Margery, May, Pearl**).

Margery, Marjorie

Margerie was originally a short form of the French **Marguerite** (see **Margaret**), but it became established in England as early as the 12th century. Marjorie is the spelling in Scotland, where the name was popular from the late 13th century after Robert the Bruce gave it to his daughter, founder of the Stewart or Stuart dynasty through her marriage to Walter the Steward. **Marge** and **Margie** are short forms.

Margot, Marguerite *see* **Margaret**

Mari, Maria(h) *see* **Mary**

Marian
Marian or **Marion** was originally a short form of the French **Marie** (see **Mary**), which was early established as an independent name and was common on both sides of the Channel in medieval times. Marian was later extended to **Marianne**, giving rise to the double name **Mary Anne** in the 18th century. **Marianna** is the Spanish equivalent. Marion is occasionally found as a boy's name, as in the case of Marion Morrison, the real name of actor John Wayne (1907–79). In such cases it uses the surname Marion as a first name, possibly influenced by Francis Marion who played an important part in the American War of Independence.

Marie, Mariel(la), Marielle, Marietta, Mariette *see* **Mary**

Marigold
This name, borrowed from the flower, was adopted with others in the late 19th century but has never been common.

Marilyn
This diminutive of **Mary** is now used independently. Its popularity was heightened by the film actress, Marilyn Monroe (1926–62).

Marina
From the Latin *marinus*, meaning "of the sea." The name has been used occasionally from at least the 14th century, probably on account of St. Marina of Alexandria, a martyr of the Greek church.

Marisa, Marise, Marisol, Marissa *see* **Mary**

Marlene
This is a German shortening of Mary Magdalene (see **Madeleine**). It was introduced to English speakers by the song "Lili Marlene" and by the actress Marlene Dietrich (1901–92). **Marlena** is a form that reflects the German pronunciation of the name, but a two-syllable pronunciation, the second half of the name sounded as in the word "lean" as opposed to the German "lane," is common in Britain (see also **Arlene**). A shortening, **Marlee** (**Marley**) is also used.

Martha
From the Aramaic, meaning "lady." In the New Testament Martha was the sister of Mary and Lazarus. The name was common in France in the Middle Ages, where there was a legend that Martha had come to France after the Crucifixion. It was not adopted in Britain until after the Reformation. Variants include **Marta** and **Martella**. **Martie** is the most common short form.

Martina
The feminine form of **Martin** from the Latin Martinus, a diminutive of Martius meaning "of Mars," the Roman god of war. According to popular legend, St. Martin was a fourth-century soldier who cut his cloak in half to share it with a beggar one winter's night; he later became Bishop of Tours in France. **Martita** is another feminine

form of the name. **Martinella** and the French **Martine** are also found.

Mary

A biblical name, traditionally meaning "dew of the sea," but possibly going back to an ancient Egyptian name. The earliest form of the name was **Miriam**, which later translations of the Bible changed to **Mariam** and **Maria** (now also spelled **Mariah** and pronounced with a long "i" sound), and finally Mary. Out of respect for the Virgin Mary, the name was held to be too sacred for general use until about the 12th century when the French form, **Marie**, and the diminutive, **Marian**, were common. The Scottish kept the French Marie and used the Gaelic **Mairi** and **Mha(i)ri**. **Maire** is the Irish form, and **Mair** or **Mari** the Welsh. The latinized **Maria** was adopted in the 18th century, giving a short form of **Ria**. **Marise** and **Maris(s)a** are other forms of the name. Other elaborations are **Mariel(le)**, **Marietta**, **Mariette**, and **Mariella**. Short

forms of Mary are **Molly**, currently a popular choice, **Polly, Mimi, Mamie**, and **May**, with **Manon** a French short form (see also **Marian, Marilyn, Maureen, Maya, Mia, Miriam, Moira**). A recent trend has been to link Marie with another name, to produce names such as **Marie-Rose** and **Marie-Louise**. One such combination **Marisol**, combining Mary with the Spanish name **Sol**, "sun," is particularly popular with Spanish speakers.

Maryann, Maryanne, Mary Anne *see* Marian

Matilda

From the Old German, meaning "mighty in battle." This name was particularly popular in medieval court circles, introduced by William the Conqueror's wife who bore the name. Later, their granddaughter, sometimes known as **Maud**, fought her cousin Stephen for the throne. The name fell into disuse but returned to favour in the 18th century. **Matty, Tilda**, and

Tilly are short forms. Although by no means common, its use has recently increased.

Maud

The Old French form of the name **Matilda**. This name was popular in Britain after the Norman Conquest, but fell out of use about the 15th century. It was revived in the 19th century by Tennyson's well-known poem "Maud" (1855). It is also spelled **Maude**, and **Maudie** is sometimes used as a short form.

Maura *see* Moira

Maureen

A phonetic form of the Irish **Mairin**, meaning "little Mary." The variant forms in Britain are **Moreen** and **Moira**. The Irish also have a name **Mor** meaning "tall," with a short form **Moirin**, which can be anglicized as **Moreen**.

Mavis

From the old word for song thrush. It was first used by Marie Corelli in her novel *The Sorrows of Satan* (1895).

May

This was originally a short form of **Mabel, Margaret**, or **Mary** but it has more recently been associated with the month, and it is now a separate name. Variants are **Mae**, as in the actress Mae West (1892–1980), and **Mai** (see also **Avril/June**). Forms such as **Mayra** fall somewhere between May and **Maria** (see **Mary**).

Maya

In India this name derives from a Sanskrit word meaning "illusion," an important word in Hindu philosophy. In America the author Maya Angelou has made the name famous. In her case it is a nickname, derived from her brother's way of pronouncing "my sister." The name can also be interpreted as a short form of **Maria** (see **Mary**). It is also found as **Maia** and **Maja**.

Maybelle, Maybelline *see* **Mabel**

Mckenzie, Mckenna *see* **Mackenzie**

Meena

From the Sanskrit for "fish, Pisces," this is the name of a Hindu goddess.

Meera

A Hindi name that means "saintly woman."

Megan

Megan started life as a Welsh short form of **Meg**, itself a short form of **Margaret**. It is popular throughout the English-speaking world, where it is often spelled as **Meghan**, as if it were an Irish name. Other spellings include **Maegan, Maygen, Megane**, and **Mégane**.

Mehul

This Hindi name refers to "rain-clouds." It is also found as **Mehal**.

Melanie

From the Greek for "black" or "dark-skinned." **Melania** is an ancient name used by both the Greeks and the Romans. It came to England from France in the mid-17th century in its French form, Melanie, which

also became **Melony** or **Mel(l)oney** and **Melany** in Britain. It is shortened to **Mel**.

Melissa

From the Greek, meaning "a bee" and the name of a nymph in Greek mythology. It was used occasionally in the 18th century, and has been quite popular in recent years. Other names with the sense of "bee" or "honey" that are used are **Melinda**, sometimes shortened to **Mindy**, and **Melita**.

Melody

From the Greek word for "song." Other names with musical associations that are sometimes used are **Harmony** and **Lyric**.

Mercy

This is the virtue used as a first name, in the same way as **Hope**. The short form is **Merry**, which is also used as an independent name.

Meredith

From the surname from the ancient Welsh **Maredudd** or **Meredydd**, "great chief." It can be spelled **Meridith** and shares **Merry** as a short form with **Mercy**. Use of the name for girls was a 20th-century innovation.

Meriel *see* **Muriel**

Merle
This is the French for "blackbird" originally derived from Latin. It was adopted as a first name in the 19th century. It became well known as the name of the film actress Merle Oberon (1911–79). It is also used as a boy's name.

Merrill *see* **Muriel**

Merry *see* **Mercy, Meredith**

Mia
A Scandinavian short form of **Mary**, although some associate it with the Italian and Spanish word for "my." The actress Mia Farrow brought the name into more general use. **Mya(h)** is also found.

Micah
A variant of **Michael** and the name of a minor prophet in the

Old Testament, was used in the 17th century among Puritans and can now be found used for both sexes, sometimes as **Mica** or **Myka**.

Michelle
Feminine form of **Michael**, from the Hebrew, meaning "who is like the Lord?" In the Bible Michael was one of the seven archangels and their leader in battle, and he therefore became the patron saint of soldiers. The French form of Michelle is **Michele**, which can be shortened to Shelley. **Michaela** is another feminine form with exotic spellings such as **Makayla** or **Mykala** (see also **Kayla**). **Misha** or **Mischa** is in Russia a short form of Michael, but because of the "a" ending is sometimes thought of as a girl's name. The Spanish form is **Miguela**.

Mildred
The 7th-century King Merowald of the Old English kingdom of Mercia had three daughters: Milburga ("gentle defence"), Mildgyth ("gentle gift"), and Mildthryth ("gentle strength").

It was from the last of these that Mildred developed, and the popularity of the three sisters, all of whom became saints, led to the name becoming common in the Middle Ages. It was revived in the 19th century.

Millicent
From the Old German, meaning "strong worker." This name was common in France about a thousand years ago, when it had the form **Melisenda**, now also **Melisande**. The French brought it to England in the late 12th century in the form **Melisent**, and it survived with minor changes of spelling such as **Melicent** well into the 17th century. In the 19th it was revived. **Millie** or **Milly** is a common abbreviation.

Millie, Milly *see* **Amelia, Camilla, Emily, Millicent**

Miranda
From the Latin, meaning "deserving admiration." This name was coined by Shakespeare for the heroine of *The Tempest*, a young woman blessed with many admirable qualities. Like

other Shakespearian names it came into use in the 20th century. **Mirabel (Mirabelle, Mirabella)** from the Latin "admirable, wonderful" is related.

Miriam

This is the old form of **Mary**, and in the book of Exodus in the Old Testament it was the name of the sister of **Moses** and **Aaron**. It is traditionally interpreted as meaning "dew of the sea," but possibly, like Miriam's brothers' names, goes back to ancient Egyptian sources. It first became common in Britain in the 17th century. **Mariam** and **Mariamne** are variant forms that have recently gained popularity. **Mitzi** can be a short form of Miriam or **Maria**.

Mischa, Misha *see* **Michelle**

Mitzi *see* **Miriam**

Mohana

In early times a name of Krishna's, from the Sanskrit for "attractive," bewitching.

Moira, Moyra

Moira or **Maura** is an English phonetic spelling of **Maire**, the Irish form of **Mary**. **Maureen** has the same origin, but has developed as a separate name, though Moira is occasionally used as its short form.

Moirin *see* **Maureen**

Molly *see* **Mary**

Mona

This name is derived from a diminutive of the Irish **Muadhnait** ("mooa-nid"), meaning "noble, good." It can also be a short form of **Monica**.

Monica

The etymology of this name is uncertain, but it could be connected with Greek *monos* meaning "alone" or Latin *monere* meaning "to advise." St. Monica was the mother of St. Augustine and was a paragon of motherly virtues. **Mona** is sometimes used as a short form, and there are French and Scandinavian forms, **Monique** and **Monika**.

Montana

The name of the mountainous American state has been popular as a first name, sometimes spelled **Montanna**.

Morag

A Scottish name from the Gaelic and Irish name **Mor** meaning "great" or "tall" (see also **Maureen**).

Moreen *see* Maureen

Morgan

In its earliest form, **Morcant**, this name meant "sea-bright" (see **Muriel**), but it later absorbed another name, **Morien**, meaning "sea-born." Its earliest celebrated male bearer was the first recorded British heretic, who was known as Pelagius, a Greek translation of the name. It was almost always a male name until the 20th century, but now is more common for girls. The most famous female precedent for the name was **Morgan(a)** le Fay, King Arthur's wicked half-sister.

Morna, Myrna

Both these names come from the Gaelic name **Muirne**, which means either "gentle," the traditional interpretation, or possibly "high-spirited."

Morwenna

Morwenna comes from Welsh and probably means "maiden." There was a fifth-century saint of this name about whom little is known, and the name used to be confined to Wales and Cornwall but now seems to be spreading. It is also found as **Morwen**.

Muhsina

A popular name derived from an Arabic word meaning "charitable" or "benevolent."

Munira

From the Arabic, for "brilliant" or "illuminating."

Murali

From the Sanskrit word for "flute." The reference is to the young Krishna, who played the flute to attract female cowherds to his side.

Muriel, Meriel

A Celtic name meaning "sea-bright." It came to England at the time of the Norman Conquest, via the many Celts who had settled in Brittany and Normandy in earlier centuries. Both forms were in common use until the mid-14th century. Muriel was revived in the 19th century and Meriel came back into use at the beginning of the 20th century. Other forms such as **Meryl** and **Merrill** have appeared more recently.

Myfanwy

A well-known Welsh name meaning "my fine one." The most common short forms in Wales are **Fanny** and **Myfi**.

Myra

This name appears to have been invented in the 16th century by Fulke Greville, Lord Brooke, for the heroine of his love poems, and until the 19th century it was used exclusively by poets and novelists. He may have wanted to echo the sound of "admired." The variant form **Mira** is found, but this can also be a short form of **Mirabel**, "admirable," or **Miranda**.

Myrtle

One of the flower names that has been used as a name since the 19th century. The name is Greek, and in Ancient Greece the myrtle was a symbol of victory, while more recently, myrtle was a traditional element in a bride's bouquet. The variant form **Myrtill(a)** is also found occasionally.

N

Nadine

A French name, derived from the Russian for "hope." Variants are **Nada** and **Nadia**.

Nafisa(h)

The feminine form of **Nafis** From the Arabic, for "precious, delicate." Used for both boys and girls, but more common for girls. It can also be spelled **Nafeesa**.

Naima

From the Arabic, word meaning "comfortable," "contented," or "tranquil." Some families prefer to spell the names **Naeem** and **Naeema**.

Nan *see* **Anne**

Nancy

This was originally a short form of **Anne**, but has long been established as a name in its own right. **Nancie** is occasionally found, and **Nanette** and **Nana** are French forms.

Nanette, Nanny *see* **Anne**, **Nancy**

Naomi

From the Hebrew, meaning "pleasant." In the Old Testament Naomi was the mother-in-law of Ruth, and loved her daughter-in-law so much that when their menfolk died, she left her home to travel back to Israel with Ruth. The name was adopted by the Puritans in the 17th century and has recently increased in popularity. The French forms **Noemie** and **Noémie** are popular in Quebec. Other forms include **Naëmi, Noemi, Noomi**, and **Noémia**.

Natalie, Natasha

These names come from the Latin *natale domini*, meaning "the birthday of the Lord," and were originally restricted to children born around Christmas. Natalie comes from Russia, where it is spelled **Natalya**, and has the short form Natasha, both popular choices in recent years. Natasha is sometimes spelled **Natacha** or **Natasja**, and can have the short form **Tasha**. **Natalia** or **Natalie** can be shortened to **Talia, Talya**, or **Tally**.

Nayana

An Indian name derived from the Sanskrit for "eye." The feminine form refers to a girl with lovely eyes.

Neha

This Indian name comes from the Sanskrit for "rain."

Nell, Nelly

These are short forms of **Helen** and **Eleanor**. They were already in use in Britain in the Middle Ages. A famous holder of the name was Nell (Eleanor) Gwyn, the mistress of Charles II.

Nerissa

This is one of the less common names taken from Shakespeare, in this case **Portia**'s witty maid from *The Merchant of Venice*. It is not clear what Shakespeare meant by the name, but he may have taken it from *nereis*, the Greek word for a sea-nymph.

Nerys

An unusual Welsh name, meaning "lady."

Nevaeh

"Heaven" spelled backwards. Its use as a girl's name is growing in Canada, while its popularity seems to have peaked in the United States.

Nia

A Swahili word meaning "intention, purpose."

Niamh

This name, pronounced "nee-av" or "neev," is currently very popular in Ireland. It means "radiance, brightness" and was originally the name of a pagan goddess. In Irish legend Niamh was a fairy woman who fell in love with **Ossian** and carried him off to the magical Land of Promise.

Nicola, Nicole
Nicola is one of the Italian forms of **Nicholas** ("victory of the people"), others being Nocolo and Niccolo. The feminine Italian form is **Nicoletta**. Nicola is preferred in England, but in other parts of the world, Nicole is more common, the French feminine form of Nicholas. The names are also spelled **Nichola** and **Nichole**, and **Nicolette** is also used. **Nickie, Nikki**, and **Nicci** are short forms shared with Nicholas (see also **Colette**).

Nikita
Nikita was originally a Russian, masculine name, from the Greek meaning "unconquered" and adopted by Russians in honour of a second-century pope. However, in many languages it looks like a feminine name, and after its use for a woman in the successful 1990 French film *La Femme Nikita* and the subsequent American television series based on it, it has come to be used as a girl's name. Nikita or **Nikhita** is also an Indian name used for both sexes, from the Sanskrit for "the earth."

Niloufer
An Indian name that means "celestial being." It occurs in various spellings, such as **Neelofar**.

Nina
A short form of various Russian names ending "-nina," which is now established as a name in its own right.

Nisha
A Sanskrit name meaning "night." **Nishant** means "dawn," the end of the night.

Nita *see* **Joan**

Noelle
Noelle is the feminine form of **Noel**, an old French name derived from the Latin *dies natalis*, meaning "birthday."

Noemie
The French form of **Naomi** (from the Hebrew, meaning "pleasant.")

Nora(h)
An Irish abbreviation of **Honoria**, now used as a separate name. It is also found as a short form for **Eleanor** and **Leonora**. In Ireland the short forms **Noreen** and **Nonie** are used.

Norma
Possibly from the Latin, meaning "rule" or "precept." The great success of Bellini's opera *Norma* (1831) brought the name into popular favour. It has been used as a feminine counterpart of **Norman**.

O

Octavia
A Roman family name derived from the Latin, meaning "eighth." It was also used as a given name for an eighth child in the 19th century, but now that such large families are rare it is used without regard to its original sense. The short forms **Tavia, Tavian**, and **Tavius** are sometimes used independently.

Olga
From the Norse word *helga*, meaning "holy." The founder of the Russian monarchy is

supposed to have been a Scandinavian traveller, and it was in Russia that Olga evolved from the Scandinavian form, **Helga**. St. Olga was the wife of the Duke of Kiev in the 10th century, and she helped spread Christianity in Russia.

Olivia

The feminine form of **Oliver**, but even more strongly associated with the Latin *oliva*, meaning "olive." St. Oliva was venerated as the protectress of the olive crops in Italy. Olivia was first found in England in the early 13th century, was used by Shakespeare in *Twelfth Night*, and is currently very popular. **Olive** is a rarer form, although well known as the name of the cartoon character Olive Oyl, Popeye's girlfriend.

Olwen, Olwyn

From the Welsh, meaning "white foot-print." The name first occurs in an old Welsh legend in which Olwen, a giant's daughter, is wooed by a prince, who has to get help from King Arthur to do the tasks that are set him. She was named Olwen because

white clover sprang up wherever she trod. The name became very popular in Wales and spread to England in 1849 when a new translation of the story was published.

Ophelia

From the Greek, meaning "help." Its use is due to Shakespeare's *Hamlet* (1601). In the play, Ophelia is Hamlet's lover but goes mad after he murders her father and abandons her, and is finally drowned.

Oprah

This name is well known through the talk show host Oprah Winfrey, but perhaps because of this close association with one person, it has not yet come into general use. Oprah Winfrey has explained that her parents intended to call her **Orpah**, a biblical place name which possibly means "gazelle." The registrar misspelled the name as Oprah, which her parents then preferred.

Oriel, Oriole *see* Aurelia

Orla

An Irish name meaning "golden

princess." It also occurs as **Orlagh** and in the Old Irish spelling **Orlaith**, and is currently popular in Ireland.

Ottilie

This is a modern form of **Ottilia**, which comes from the Old German meaning "prosperity." St. Ottilie is the patron saint of Alsace. **Ottoline** is another form of the name, and the French **Odette** and **Odile** have also been used in Britain. The masculine form, **Otto**, is less common there.

P

Padma

This Indian name, usually identified with the goddess Sri or Lakshmi, derives from a Sanskrit word meaning "lotus." Other forms are **Padmal, Padmini**, and **Padmavati**. In some parts of India **Padma** and **Padman** are used as boys' names.

Paige

A surname originally given to someone who acted as a page.

Paige is now a popular girls' name in North America, where it is twice as popular in Canada than the United States.

Paloma
The Spanish word for "dove," the symbol of peace. Its use by the artist Pablo Picasso for his daughter made the name more widely known.

Pamela
From the Greek, meaning "all honey." This name dates from the late 16th century when it was coined by Sir Philip Sydney for his romance *Arcadia*. It did not come into general use until the publication of Samuel Richardson's novel *Pamela* (1740). It has been most used in the 20th and 21st centuries, and **Pam(mie)** is the usual short form.

Pandora
In Greek legend Pandora ("all-giving") is a beautiful but foolish woman created by the gods to plague mankind. She opened the box that contained all the ills that afflict us. After their escape, only hope, which had been sealed up with them, was left to help mankind.

Paris
This has been an increasingly popular choice in the United States. It is difficult to tell if parents choose it for the glamorous associations of the French capital, or for the Trojan prince who had to choose between three goddesses and was given the beautiful Helen of Troy as his reward, although the former seems the more likely.

Parvati
An Indian name, from the Sanskrit, meaning "of the mountain," a reference to the wife of **Shiva**.

Pascale
A French name meaning "Easter," which has come into general use since the 1960s.

Patience
This name was fashionable in the 17th century when girls were named after abstract virtues and Sir Thomas Carew could call his four daughters **Patience, Temperance, Silence**, and **Prudence**.

Patricia
The feminine of Latin *patricius*, meaning "nobleman." It was originally only used in Latin records to distinguish a female bearer of the name **Patrick** then used for both sexes, but it was used independently from the 18th century. It has become common only in the last hundred years, possibly encouraged by the popularity of Queen Victoria's granddaughter Princess Patricia of Connaught. Current abbreviations are **Pat, Patsy, Patti(e), Patty**, and **Tricia**.

Paula, Paulina, Pauline
The feminine forms of **Paul**. The fourth-century St. Paula founded several convents in Bethlehem, and thus established the name in the Middle Ages. Paulina and Pauline or **Paulette** are respectively the Latin and French forms. **Polly** is sometimes used as a short form.

Payal

An Indian name meaning "anklet." It is also spelled **Paayal**.

Pearl

This name first became common in the 19th century, with other gem names such as **Beryl** and **Ruby**. It has also been used as a pet name for **Margaret**, which is derived from the Greek for "pearl."

Penelope

In Greek legend Penelope was the name of Odysseus's faithful and astute wife, who waited 10 years for her husband to return from the Trojan Wars. The name has been used regularly since the 16th century. It is often abbreviated to **Pen** or **Penny**.

Perdita

This is from the Latin, meaning "lost." It was coined by Shakespeare for the heroine of *A Winter's Tale*, who was lost at birth.

Petronella, Petronilla

These are derived from Petronius, a Roman family name. Petronilla, a first-century martyr, came to be connected with St. **Peter**, and was even thought by some to be his daughter; because of this the name was popular in the Middle Ages and used as Peter's female equivalent.

Phebe *see* **Phoebe**

Philippa

This is the feminine form of **Philip**, but originally was only used to distinguish women (who shared the name Philip with males in the Middle Ages) in Latin records. Its use as a separate name dates from about the 19th century. Often abbreviated to **Pippa**, an Italian form, it can be found as **Phillip(p)a**. **Philippine** is a much rarer feminine form of Philip.

Philomena

This name comes from the Greek for "beloved." It used to be a popular name in Ireland, but is now rather out of fashion. It was thought that there were two saints of this name, but when it was realized that the word Philomena on the inscription on their graves was an address to the reader and not their names the cult was suppressed; hence the name's fall from favour.

Phoebe

From the Greek, meaning "the shining one." It is one of the titles given to the Roman moon goddess, **Diana**. It occurs as a personal name in St. Paul's Epistle to the Romans and, perhaps for this reason, was adopted after the Reformation, reaching its peak of popularity in the 17th century. It is currently enjoying another rise in popularity and is sometimes spelled phonetically **Phebe**. It can be used as a short form of **Euphemia**.

Phyllis, Phillis

From the Greek, meaning "leafy." In legend it was the name of a girl who died for love and was transformed into an almond tree. **Phyllida** is an alternative form which is sometimes found in use.

Pia
From the Latin, meaning "pious."

Pippa see **Philippa**

Polly see **Mary, Paula**

Pooja, Poojan
This Hindi name, which can also be spelled **Puja** and **Pujan**, means "worship." **Poojita**, also found as **Pujita**, means "worshipped."

Poonam
A Hindi name that refers to the "full moon." The spelling **Punam** is also used.

Poppy
The flower used as a name. It was particularly popular at the end of the 19th century and the beginning of the 20th, and is now back in fashion.

Portia
Portia is an old Roman family name with the unfortunate meaning of "pig." However, Portia, wife of Brutus, became famous for her stoicism and bravery, which probably inspired Shakespeare to choose this name for the heroine of *The Merchant of Venice*. This Portia is beautiful, rich, wise, witty, and charming, and it is thanks to her that the name has come into use as a modern girls' name.

Priscilla
The Latin diminutive of *prisca*, meaning "ancient." It was the name of a woman mentioned in the Acts of the Apostles and as with other New Testament names it was a favourite with the 17th-century Puritans. It also appears as **Prisca**, but this form is very rare. **Pris** and **Prissy** are sometimes found as short forms, but **Cilla** is the most used form.

Priyal
An Indian name from the Sanskrit for "beloved." Other forms include **Priyam, Priyanka**, and **Priyasha**.

Prudence
Prudence first appears as a name in Chaucer's books, and it was one of the first abstract virtues to be adopted by the Puritans. It is usually abbreviated to **Prue** or **Pru** (see also **Patience**).

Prunella
Probably from the Latin *prunus*, meaning "little plum." It is also the name of a kind of silk and the Latin name for a wild flower, the self-heal, and a bird, the hedge sparrow or dunnock. The actress Prunella Scales has made the name more widely known. It shares short forms with **Prudence**.

Punita
A Hindi name that means "pure."

Q

Queenie
This name is sometimes given independently, but it is really a pet name for **Regina**, which is Latin for "queen." This name also appears as **Reina** in Spanish, **Regine**, or **Reine** in French and **Raina (Raena, Rayna)** in Polish, all forms that are showing signs of increasing popularity in the United States. Regina was used from the Middle Ages, possibly with reference to the Virgin Mary, Queen of Heaven. Queenie was

also used as a nickname for girls christened **Victoria** during Queen Victoria's long reign.

Quinn

Quinn is an old Irish family name, literally meaning "descendant of Connm," but used to indicate "chief, leader." It has recently come into use for both sexes.

R

Rabiah

An Arabic name that means "garden."

Rachel

From the Hebrew for "ewe," a symbol of gentleness and innocence. In the Book of Genesis, Rachel was "beautiful and well-favoured," and **Jacob** laboured seven years to win her (Gen. XXIX, 20). In Britain the name was adopted after the Reformation and was very popular in the 17th and 19th centuries and is popular today. The usual short forms today are **Rach, Rachie, Rae, Rai**,

and **Ray**, and it can be spelled **Rachael** or **Raechel(l)**. The actress **Raquel** Welch has the Spanish form of the name. From Rachel have developed the forms **Rachelle** (sometimes pronounced with a "sh" sound) and **Rochelle**, the French for "little rock," a place name taken from Brittany. **Shelley** is a short form.

Radha

Radha is the name of the cowherd loved by Krishna. It derives from the Sanskrit for "success." Another form of this Indian name is **Radhika**.

Rae, Rai *see* **Rachel**

Raelene *see* **Darlene**

Rahil

An Arabic form of **Rachel**. It is also found as **Raheel** and **Raheela**.

Rahima(h)

The feminine form of **Rahim**, from the Arabic, meaning "merciful" and "compassionate." The spellings **Raheema** and **Raheemah** are also found.

Raina *see* **Queenie**

Rajani

From the Sanskrit, meaning "the dark one" or "night." This is one of the names of the Hindu goddess **Durga**.

Rajni

An Indian name from the Sanskrit for "queen," this name can also be a contracted form of **Rajani**.

Raven

The name of this large, sleek, black bird increased in popularity when an actress of that name appeared in TV's *The Cosby Show*. Other bird names such as **Finch, Lark**, and **Swan** have occasionally been used in the past.

Raymonde, Ramona

The feminine form of **Raymond** from the Old German meaning "counsel protection." The Normans brought the name Raymond to Britain and it was particularly popular in crusading times. Two 13th-century saints bore the name. The short form, **Ray**, is sometimes given independently. Other short forms are **Rai** and **Rae**. The Spanish form is **Ramona**.

Razina
A Muslim name from the Arabic, for "contented."

Rebecca
In the Old Testament **Rebekah** (the name's Hebrew form) was the wife of **Isaac** and was famous for her beauty. It was a favourite name among Puritans, who took it to North America. It is occasionally spelled **Rebeca, Rebe(k)ka**, and **Rebekah**.

Reese
The feminine form of **Rhys**, an old Welsh name meaning "rashness, ardour." It has had many famous bearers, including a Prince Rhys who checked the Norman advance into Wales. Reese is twice as popular as a name for girls in Canada than in the United States.

Renée
A girls' name derived from the Latin *renatus*, meaning "reborn."

The Latin form was sometimes used by Puritans in the 17th century. The Latin feminine form, **Renata**, is also used occasionally.

Reshma
An Indian name that means "silken."

Rhiannon
The name of an important figure in medieval Welsh literature. There is evidence that she was originally a Celtic goddess connected with horses. The name means "great queen, goddess" and is spreading outside Wales. The old form was **Riannon**, and a new form **Rhianna** (also **Reanna**) is also found. **Reanne, Rhian(n)e**, and **Riann** are also used, although some forms shade into feminines of **Ryan**.

Rhoda
Derived from the Greek for "rose," this is a New Testament name that was taken into use in the 17th century. It was popular in the early years of the 20th century.

Rhona *see* **Rowena**

Rhonda
This is a simplified spelling of the Welsh place name Rhondda, which has been used as a first name since the early part of this century.

Ria *see* **Mary**

Ricarda
Feminine form of the name **Richard**. Richard first appears in Anglo-Saxon as Ricehard meaning "strong ruler," which was later developed into **Ricard**. Variants include **Richelle** and **Richenda**.

Riley
Riley **(Rilley, Reilly)** is an Irish surname of unknown meaning, used for both boys and girls. It is also found as **Rylee** or even **Ryleigh**.

Rio
This is a recent addition to the store of names, its spread probably helped by a 1982 Duran Duran hit song. It comes from the Spanish word for "river," and is also the short form of the glamorous Brazilian city of Rio de Janeiro.

Riona *see* **Catriona**

Rita

This is an abbreviation of **Margarita** (see **Margaret**). However, it is used much more often as a separate name, and some of its popularity in the 20th century may have been due to its use by the film star Rita Hayworth (1918–87).

Roberta, Robina, Robin, Robyn

Feminine forms of the name **Robert**. Robert is derived from the Old German meaning "famous and bright." Although there was an equivalent Anglo-Saxon name, it was the French form that took hold in Britain after the Norman Conquest. Robin or Robyn, a French short form of Robert, is now popular in its own right for both boys and girls. Roberta and Robina are feminine forms particularly used in Scotland. **Bobbie** is also found.

Rohan

This name comes from a Sanskrit word that can mean either "ascending" or "medicine," although some like to interpret the meaning as "sandalwood." In Sri Lanka it is the name of a sacred mountain, also known as Adam's Peak, which has on its summit a mark like a footprint which features, with different interpretations, in the legends of all three of the island's great religions—Muslim, Hindu and Buddhist.

Roisin *see* **Rose**

Ronat

The feminine form of **Ronan**, an Irish and Scottish name meaning "little seal," borne by a number of early saints. **R(h)ona** (see **Rowena**) is also used.

Rosalie

From Latin *rosalia*, the name of a Roman festival when garlands of roses were draped on tombs. Its use as a first name is due to St. **Rosalia**, a 12th-century hermit, the patron saint of Palermo in Sicily. Rosalie is the French form.

Rosalind

The origin of this name is the Old German **Roslindis**, either made from elements meaning "horse" and "serpent" or "fame" and "shield"—the experts disagree. When the Goths took it to Spain it was interpreted as *rosa* and *linda*, "pretty rose," and it was with this meaning that it came to England in Elizabeth I's reign. It was used by Shakespeare for the heroine of *As You Like It* and in another form, **Rosaline**, in two other plays. Largely due to this literary association it has been popular ever since. It developed a number of different forms such as **Ros(a)lyn, Rosalin, Rosalinda**, and **Rosaleen**, which is used in Ireland as an alternative form of **Roisin** (see **Rose**). A short form is **Roz**.

Rosamund, Rosamond

This comes from the Old German words meaning "horse" and "protection," but it has generally been associated with the Latin *rosa munda*, meaning "pure rose" or *rosa mundi*, "rose of the world." A short form is **Roz**.

Rose

This flower, the symbol of the Virgin Mary, has been the most popular of all flower names that are used as personal names. The Normans brought the name to England and it has been consistently popular, giving rise to many derivatives, like **Rosalba** ("white rose"), **Rosetta** ("little rose"), and **Rosabel(la)** ("beautiful rose"), as well as **Rosina, Rosita,** and the short form **Rosie** or **Rosy**. **Rosa** is a Latin form that has been used occasionally since the 19th century. In Ireland **Roisin**, sometimes spelled **Rosheen** to reflect its pronunciation, is popular. It means "little rose." Rose is used as a short form of all the girls' names that begin with its sound.

Roseanne

This is one of the many developments of **Rose**, here combined with **Anne**. Variants include **Ros(e)anna, Rosanne,** and **Rosannah,** as in Rose + **Hannah**.

Rosemary

This is generally considered to be a plant name, although it is sometimes analyzed as a combination of **Rose** and **Mary**. The plant name is derived from the Latin *ros marinus*, meaning "dew of the sea," which describes the misty blue-green of its leaves. It can be spelled **Rosemarie**, and **Rom(e)y** and **Rosie** are short forms.

Rosetta, Rosheen, Rosina, Rosita *see* Rose

Roshan, Roshni

A name from the Persian for "shining" or "famous," used by both Muslims and Hindus in India.

Roslyn *see* Rosalind

Rowanne

From the Irish **Ruadhan**, meaning "little red-(haired) one." **Rowan** was the name of an Irish saint. Once used exclusively for boys, it is now also found as a girl's name.

Rowena

Probably best thought of as a form of the Welsh **Rhonwen**, meaning "fair (woman), slender as a lance." Rowena was the daughter of the Saxon chief Hengist and her beauty bewitched the British king Vortigern, bringing about his downfall; she may have had a truly Saxon name, but her story is transmitted through Welsh-speaking British writers and seems to have taken on a Welsh form. Its modern use is due to Sir Walter Scott, who gave this name to the heroine of his novel *Ivanhoe* (1819). **Rowina** is another spelling. **R(h)ona** has been claimed as a short form of Rhonwen, although it is also the name of a Scottish island.

Roxana, Roxan(n)e

The English form of the name **Roshan**, usually interpreted by users as meaning "dawn light." It was the name of one of Alexander the Great's wives.

Ruby

This is one of many jewel names introduced during the 19th century. Other precious substances used as first names include **Diamond, Amber, Beryl,** and **Pearl**.

Rupli

An Indian name from a Sanskrit word meaning "beautiful." Other names that have a basic meaning of "beauty" include **Rupashi** and **Rupashri**.

Ruth

A biblical name that came into use just after the Reformation, after the Old Testament heroine who gave her name to the Book of Ruth. The name is also associated with the abstract noun *ruth* meaning "sorrow" or "pity." **Ruthie** is a short form.

S

Saagar *see* Sagar

Sabah

An Arabic name that means "morning" or "dawn." The Lebanese singer of this name has made it well known. In India it is often **Saba**.

Sabina

A Latin name, meaning "a Sabine woman." It has been used in Ireland for the Irish **Sadhbh**; **Sive** in its phonetic spelling, meaning "sweet." There is also a French form, **Sabine**.

Sabrina

This is a very ancient name, used for the River Severn before the Romans came and probably the name of the goddess of the river. The poet John Milton (1608–74) used it as the name of the nymph of the Severn in his masque *Comus*, and subsequent uses of it as a first name probably stem from this, although nowadays it is probably better known from the television series *Sabrina The Teenage Witch*.

Sacha

A Russian short form of **Alexander**. Although originally a man's name, the "a" ending has led to its use for girls. **Sasha** is an alternative form.

Sade

Made famous by the British-Nigerian singer, Sade is a short form of the Yoruba name **Falasade**, meaning "honour bestows a crown." Phonetic spellings such as **Shardai** or **Sharday** are also found.

Sadie *see* **Sarah**

Saffron

The name of the golden-yellow crocus pollen used as a spice, which has come to be given as a first name in modern times.

Sagarika

The feminine form of the Indian name **Sagar** from the Sanskrit meaning "ocean." Sagarika means "wave."

Sage

This is one of the most recent plant names to come into fashion as a first name, its use boosted by several American entertainers choosing it for their children. The aromatic plant sage gets its name from the ancient reputation tea made from its leaves had for boosting memory and wisdom. The spelling **Saige** is occasionally used.

Sahila

An Indian name from the Sanskrit for "guide."

Saliha(h)

A name from the Arabic, for "goodness, righteousness."

Salima
An Arabic name that means "safe" or "unharmed."

Sally
Originally a pet name for **Sarah**, but one that is nowadays used independently. It is shortened to **Sal**.

Salma
From an Arabic word meaning "peaceful." The word for "peace" is much used as a greeting in the Middle East, as in the Arabic *salaam* or the Hebrew *shalom*. The latter forms the basis of names like **Salome** and **Solomon**, both of which mean "peaceful."

Salome
The Greek form of an Aramaic name meaning "peace." In the New Testament Salome was one of the women at Jesus' tomb on Easter Sunday. However, it is better known from the story of the Salome who danced the dance of the seven veils and, at her mother's insistence, asked Herod for John the Baptist's head as a reward.

Samantha
Probably an 18th-century coinage, meant to be a feminine version of **Samuel**. It first became popular in the 1950s, when it appeared in the film *High Society* and in the title song, *I Love You, Samantha*, and is well used once again. It shares short forms **Sam** and **Sammy** with Samuel.

Samimah
From the Arabic, for "true" or "sincere." The name is also spelled **Sameema(h)**.

Samira(h)
An Arabic name that means "one whose conversation in the evening or at night is lively," thus an entertaining companion. The spellings **Samara** and **Sameera(h)** are also used.

Sana
This Arabic name means "resplendence" or "brilliance." **Saniyya** has the same meaning.

Sanchia
A Provençal and Spanish name derived from the Latin *sanctus*, meaning "holy." The name came

to England in the 13th century when the Earl of Cornwall married Sanchia, daughter of the Count of Provence.

Sandip
This Indian name means "beautiful."

Sandra
This is a short form of Italian **Alessandra**, now used as a name in its own right (see **Alexandra**). **Sandie** or **Sandy** (also used for **Cassandra**) are short forms. It also appears as **Sondra**, and the designer **Zandra** Rhodes uses an unusual alternative form.

Sandy *see* **Alexander, Sandra**

Saniyya *see* **Sana**

Sara(h)
Sarah comes from the Hebrew, meaning "princess" and was the name of Abraham's wife in the Old Testament. Sara is the Greek form found in the New Testament. **Sal(ly)** and **Sadie** started life as short forms. In Ireland Sarah has been used to

render the Irish **Sorcha** ("sorr-ha," the "h" as in Scottish "loch") meaning "bright," and **Saraid** ("sahr-it") meaning "excellent."

Sarika

An Indian name that refers to the "koel" or "black cuckoo."

Saskia

This was the name of the wife of the Dutch artist Rembrandt (1606–69), whose paintings of her introduced the name to Britain. It may be connected with the word for Saxon.

Savannah

The name of a river and city in the state of Georgia. The name comes from Spanish "sabana," a treeless plain. It can appear with spellings such as **Savan(n)a**.

Scarlett

The use of Scarlett as a first name is due entirely to the success of Margaret Mitchell's *Gone with the Wind*. In the novel, Scarlett O'Hara is given her grandmother's maiden name as a middle name, but is always called by it. **Scarlet** is also used.

Sean

The Irish form of **John**, developed from the French **Jean**. It is also spelled as it is pronounced, **Shaun** or **Shawn**. **Shane** is a variant form. Shawn and Sean are used now for girls, along with **Shawna** and **Shawndelle**.

Sejal

This Indian name means "river" or "water."

Selina

The etymology of this name is disputed. One possible derivation is from **Selene**, the Greek moon goddess; another is from the Latin name **Coelina**, from *caelum*, meaning "heaven," through the French form **Céline**. **Celina** and **Selena** are also found.

Selma

Selma is the name of a castle in James Macpherson's 18th-century poems about Scottish heroes. When the poems were translated into Swedish, the translator failed to make the meaning clear, and it was taken

by many Swedish readers to be a personal name; some then used it for their children. Immigrants took the name to the U.S., where it is still more common than in Britain.

Serena

This is a Latin word meaning "calm, serene (woman)." **Serenity** is also used for girls.

Shahida(h)

An Arabic name that means "witness" or "martyr."

Shaina

From a Yiddish word meaning "beautiful," Shaina is also found as **Shayna, Sheyna**, or **Cheyna**.

Shakila

An Arabic name meaning "beautiful, handsome." Can also take forms such as **Shakeela, Shaquil(le),** and **Shaquilla(h)**.

Shakira

This is an Arabic name meaning "grateful." Shakira was publicised first by the actress Shakira

Caine, and more recently by the Spanish-language singer Shakira. **Zshakira** is an alternative form.

Shamina(h)
An Arabic name from a word meaning "scent" or "flavour."

Shanel(le), Shannel see **Chanel**

Shani see **Sian**

Shania
A name of Ojibwa origin, meaning "on the way." It was made popular by the singer Shania Twain, whose birth name was **Eileen** and whose adoptive father is a member of the Ojibwa First Nation.

Shanice
A blend of the fashionable "Sha-" prefix and **Janice**. The name has been given publicity by singer Shanice Wilson, who uses only her first name as her stage name. Spellings such as **Chaniece** or **Chanise** are also found. **Shaniqua (Shanika)** is a similar blend of Sha- and **Monica**.

Shannon
This is the Irish river and place name, meaning "the old one," which has become a popular first name in recent years. **Shanna** can be seen as either a variant of this or of **Sean** or **Shanae**.

Shante, Shanti see **Ashanti**

Shantal see **Chantal**

Sharada
From an Indian word for "autumn." An alternative form is **Sharadini**.

Sharifa(h)
This Arabic name means "eminent" or "honourable." It is also used as a title for descendants of the Prophet Muhammad.

Sharlene see **Charlene**

Sharmaine see **Charmaine**

Sharon
In the Bible Sharon, which means "the plain," is an area of rich natural beauty and to compare a woman to it came to be a great compliment. It has been used as a first name only since the 20th century. It is occasionally spelled **Sharron**. **Shari** is a short form.

Shaun(a), Shawndelle, Shawn see **Sean**

Shayla, Shaylee, Sheela see **Sheila**

Shayna see **Shaina**

Shea
An Irish surname meaning "descendant of the fortunate one" now used as a first name. **Shay** is also used.

Sheena
This is a phonetic form of **Sine**, the Gaelic for **Jane**. An alternative form of Jane is **Siubhan**, which in Irish becomes **Siobhan**, with phonetic spellings **Shevaun** and **Chevonne**. **Shona**, the Scottish form of **Janet**, comes from the same root and is a phonetic form of **Seonaid**, in Irish **Sinead** (shin-aid).

Sheila
A phonetic spelling of **Sile**, the Irish form of **Cecilia**. It can also be spelled **Shelagh, Shiela**, and **Sheela**. In the United States it has developed the forms **Shayla** and **Shaylee**.

Shelby
An English place name and surname. The original meaning was probably "settlement with willow trees." Its use as a first name started in the United States and was sparked by a character in the 1989 film *Steel Magnolias*.

Shelley
This is a short form of **Michelle** and **Rachel** as well as being a variant of the name **Shirley**. From the 1940s the name was brought to public attention by the actress Shelley Winters.

Sheree, Sherrie, Sherry *see* **Cherie**

Sheril, Sheryl *see* **Cheryl**

Shirley
This was originally a place name meaning "shire meadow." From this it became a surname in Yorkshire and elsewhere. It was primarily a boy's name until Charlotte Brontë started the fashion for it as a girl's name in 1849, when her novel *Shirley* appeared (see also **Shelley**).

Shyama
From the Sanskrit for "dark," but identified with **Krishna**. Shyama is a name of the goddess **Durga**. Similar names, with a basic meaning of "dusky," include **Shyamal(a), Shyamalendu, Shyamali(ka), Shyamalima, Shyamari**, and **Shyamasri**.

Sian
This is the Welsh form of **Jane**, properly spelled **Siân**. **Siani** is a short form, which may appear as **Shani**.

Sibyl, Sibylla *see* **Sybil**

Sidney, Sydney
This is a surname used as a first name from at least the beginning of the 18th century. The spelling Sydney did not appear until the 19th century, and the city in Australia was named after Viscount Sydney, who was then Secretary of State. The short form is **Sid**. In the 18th century, girls were given surnames as first names more often than was usual until very recently, and Sydney as a girl's name may date from this. Alternatively, it may be a form of the Latin name **Sidonia** ("woman of Sidon"), which became **Sidonie** in French and **Sidony** in English. Sydney is more common as a female name, and can appear as **Sydnee** or **Sidni(e)**.

Sienna
Like **Florence**, this is the name of an Italian city that has come to be used as a first name in recent years. The Italian spelling, **Siena**, is also used.

Sierra
The Spanish word for a mountain range. Spellings such as **Cierra** are also found.

Sigourney
The actress Sigourney Weaver chose to call herself Sigourney

while still a child, inspired by the character Sigourney Howard in F. Scott Fitzgerald's 1925 novel *The Great Gatsby*. Fitzgerald in turn is thought to have been inspired by the name of Lydia Huntley Sigourney (1791–1865), one of the earliest American women to earn her living by writing, although the name was already in use when Fitzgerald was writing, and it may be no coincidence that there was a prominent New York socialite at the time called Sigourney Thayer.

Silvia, Sylvia
This is the Latin word meaning "(woman) of the wood." Rhea Silvia was the mother of Romulus and Remus, the founders of Rome. This may have been the reason why the name was adopted during the Renaissance in Italy. Like other classical names, it came to England in Elizabethan times. Shakespeare used it in *Two Gentlemen of Verona*, and this probably gave rise to its use in Britain. The diminutive form is **Silvie** or **Sylvie**.

Simone
This is the better-known feminine English form of the New Testament **Simeon**, the name of the man who blessed the baby Jesus in the Temple. The short form is **Sim**. Simone is the feminine form taken from the French.

Sine, Sinead, Siobhan *see* **Sheena**

Sis, Sisley, Sissy *see* **Cecilia**

Sita
From the Sanskrit for "furrow," the reference being to the goddess who personifies agriculture and is wife to Rama. **Seeta** and **Seetha** are other spellings of the name.

Siubhan *see* **Sheena**

Sive *see* **Sabina**

Sneha(l)
From a Sanskrit word that originally meant "oil" but later came to mean "friendly affection."

Sol *see* **Mary**

Sonal
An Indian name meaning "golden." **Sonali** and **Sonika** are variants.

Sondra *see* **Sandra**

Sonia
This is a Russian short form of **Sophia**. **Sonya** and **Sonja** are other spellings of the name.

Sonika *see* **Sonal**

Sophia, Sophie
From the Greek, meaning "wisdom." Hagia Sophia ("Holy Wisdom") is a common dedication for Orthodox churches as in the case of the great cathedral at Constantinople. This led to Sophia's use as a name in Greece. The name spread through Hungary to Germany and then to England when George I became king. Both his mother and his wife had the name. Sophie is the anglicized form. The forms **Sophy** and **Sofia** are also used (see **Sonia**).

Sri

This Indian name is from the Sanskrit meaning "light" or "beauty," later developing into "majesty" and used as a title as well as a name. Sri is one of the names of Lakshmi, goddess of prosperity and beauty. **Shree, Shr**i, and **Sree** are variants.

Stacey, Stacy

This is a short form for boys or girls which has become popular as an independent name. As a woman's name it was originally short for **Anastasia**. Currently, it is mostly given to girls, sometimes in the form of **Stacie**.

Stella

This is the Latin word for "star." Its use stems from its literary associations. An early use was in Sir Philip Sidney's *Astrophel and Stella* (1591). Then, in the early 18th century, Jonathan Swift used it as a pet name in letters to **Esther** Johnson. The French form **Estella** was popularized by Charles Dickens, when he used it for the main female character in his *Great Expectations* (1861). **Estelle** is another

French form. These share the short forms of Esther.

Stephanie

Feminine form of **Stephen**, from the Greek *stephanos* meaning "crown" or "wreath." The laurel wreath was the highest honour a man could attain in the classical world. Variants include **Stefanie, Steffany**, and the Italian form **Stefania**.

Sumayyah

A Muslim name of uncertain meaning, borne by the first martyr in the cause of Islam. It also occurs as **Sumay(y)a** and **Sumayah**.

Sunila

Sunila comes from an obscure, ancient Sanskrit word meaning "very dark blue." Its use as a first name is modern. It has become a popular choice for parents in India and is sometimes interpreted as "sapphire."

Sunita

This name comes from the Sanskrit for "of good conduct"

or "righteous" and was the name of a princess in epic poetry who was the daughter of the King of Bengal. **Suniti** is another form of the name.

Surinder

This is a development of the name **Indra** and can be interpreted as meaning "mightiest of the gods." It is also found in the form **Surendra**. It is less often used for girls than for boys.

Susan, Susana(h)

Shushannah is Hebrew for "lily" and Susanna(h) was the earliest form of this name in England, occurring in the Middle Ages and becoming quite common after the Reformation. Susan was adopted in the 18th century. In the 20th century the French forms, **Suzanne** and **Suzette**, and spellings such as Susana and **Suzanna** have been found. **Sue, Sukey, Susie**, and **Suzy** are short forms.

Sybil

In classical times the Sibyls were prophetesses, and some

of them were supposed to have foretold the coming of Christ. Sybil or **Sibyl** had a revival in the second half of the 19th century after Disraeli had published his political novel of that name (1845). The actress **Cybill** Shepherd has introduced another form of the name.

Sydney *see* Sidney

Sylvestra, Sylvana
Rare feminine forms of **Silvester** and **Sylvester**, Latin for "wood-dweller."

T

Tabitha
This name derives from the Aramaic word for "gazelle." In the New Testament it is the name of a Christian woman of Joppa who showed great charity towards the poor and was raised from the dead by St. Peter. The Greek translation of her name is **Dorcas**. **Tabatha** is a modern spelling of the name.

Tallulah
This name is well known from the American actress Tallulah Bankhead (1903–68). She was named after her grandmother, who was in turn named after a place, Tallulah Falls in Georgia. The place name is said to come from a Native American word meaning "terrible." The name was given further publicity by a character in the 1976 film and musical *Bugsy Malone*.

Tally, Talya *see* **Natalie**

Tamara
Tamara is the Russian form of the biblical name **Tamar**, which means "date palm." Tamara was the name of a famous Russian queen and remains a popular name in Russia. A short form is **Tammy**.

Tammy
A short form of **Tamara** and **Tamsin**, now used as an independent name. In 1957 a film called *Tammy* and a song of that name, which was the bestselling record in the United States, started a vogue for the name's use. It is also a Scottish form of **Tommy**. **Tamia** (**Tamya**) is probably a blend of **Tammy** and **Tanya**.

Tamsin
A feminine form of **Thomas**. It can also be found as **Tamsine**, **Tamzin**, and **Tamzen**. It also comes from **Thomasin** or **Thomasine**, which have been used since the Middle Ages. **Thomasina** is an old latinized version which was revived in the 19th century. **Tammy** is a short form of these names.

Tanisha
A Hausa name from West Africa, meaning "girl born on Monday." It comes in a variety of forms, including **Tane(i)sha**, **Taniesha, Tenecia, Tenesha**, and **Tenisha**.

Tanith
The name of a Phoenician goddess of love that has recently come into occasional use as a first name. It can also take the form **Tanit**.

Tanya *see* **Tiana**

Tara

Tara is the name of the hill where the ancient High Kings of Ireland held court and which plays an important part in Irish legend. It has been used as a first name only since the end of the 19th century. It is occasionally used for boys. As an Indian name it means "star."

Taryn

Part of a group of names with varied origins. Taryn was coined by the actors Tyrone Power and Linda Christianson for their daughter, also an actor, Taryn Power in 1953, and use spread after she started appearing in films in the 1970s. In addition, the American author Lloyd Alexander coined the name **Taran** (probably based on **Tara**) for the hero of his Celtic fantasy novels *The Chronicle of Prydain*. Many other variants of these names have appeared in recent years.

Tasha *see* **Natalie**

Tasia, Tassia *see* **Anastasia**

Tasnim

An Arabic name meaning "fountain of paradise." It is also found as **Tasneem**.

Tatiana *see* **Tanya**

Tatum

This name, which seems to have been coined for the actress Tatum O'Neal (b. 1963), comes from a surname which in turn comes from an Old English place name meaning "homestead of a man named Tata."

Taylor

This English surname, indicating an ancestor who was a tailor, has been made familiar as a first name by the American author (Janet Miriam) Taylor Caldwell, who chose to use it as her pen name in order to obscure her gender.

Tea *see* **Tia**

Tegan

This is an old Cornish name meaning "lovely little thing" or "ornament." The name first got more general exposure in the 1980s in the television series *Dr. Who*, when it was used for an Australian air hostess who became involved in the doctor's adventures. The name seems to have reappeared in the form **Tiegan** in the Australian soap opera *Home and Away*. Tegan is pronounced with a short "e" sound, but Tiegan with the sound of "tea," hence the common American spelling **Teagan**. The word "teg," meaning "pretty, fair," is found in Welsh as well as Cornish, for they are closely related, and there are a number of Welsh names that use it, of which **Tegwen**, "pretty and fair," is the most common.

Tejal

A Sanskrit name meaning "lustrous."

Teresa, Theresa

The meaning of this name is obscure. The first recorded Theresa was the wife of the 5th-century St. Paulinus and was responsible for his conversion. The name was for a long time confined to Spain until the fame of St. Teresa of Avila (1515–82) spread the name to all Roman Catholic countries, but it did not become common in the U.K. until the 18th century. It is often abbreviated to **Tess(a)** or **Tessie**. The form **Teri** or **Terry**, shared with some boys' names, is also found. A variant is **Tracy**. The French form, **Thérèse**, is also found occasionally.

Tessa

From the Greek, meaning "reaper" and a short form of **Theresa**. Other forms include: **Tesa, Tess, Tesha, Tes(s)ia, Tezla**.

Thelma

Like **Mavis**, this name was introduced in the 19th century as a character in a novel by the writer Marie Corelli and spread quickly throughout the country. There is a Greek word *thelema* meaning "will," which may have had some influence on its development.

Theodora

The feminine form of **Theodore** from the Greek meaning "gift of God." There are 28 saints called Theodore in the Church Calendar. In England the name did not become general until the 19th century, but in Wales it has long been used as a form of Tudur or Tudor, which in fact probably comes from a Celtic name. The feminine form has been used since the 17th century. It is usually abbreviated to **Theo** (sometimes used as an independent name), **Thea**, and **Dora**. The rare **Theodosia** has a similar meaning.

Theresa, Thérèse *see* Teresa

Thora

From the Norse, meaning "Thor-battle." Its earlier form was **Thyra**. Thor was the god of thunder in Norse mythology, and he also gave his name to "Thursday."

Thyra *see* Thora

Tia

Tia is a Spanish word for "Auntie"; but although its use in such contexts and the liqueur named Tia Maria may have helped its spread, it is probably best regarded as a pet or short form of such fashionable names as **Tiana** and **Tiara** (see **Kiara**) or **Tierra**; or of names ending in -tia. It appears in numerous spellings, including **Téa** (which can also be a short form of **Teodora**, in Italian form of **Theodora**) and **Tya**.

Tiana

Tiana, **Tanya**, or **Tania** is a short form of **Tatiana**, which has been popular in Russia for many years, inspired by St. Tatiana, a martyr revered by the Orthodox Church. **Tonya** is also found although, properly, this is the Russian pet form of **Antonia**. Other spellings include **Tean(n)a** and **Tiahna**.

Tiesha *see* Letitia

Tiffany

Originally a short form of the name **Theophania**, from the Greek meaning "the manifestation of God." Tifainé was the Old French form, and this name was given to girls born at the time of the Epiphany, the words having the same meaning. The names were fairly rare until recently when Tiffany became popular.

Timothea

A rare feminine form from *Timotheos*, an old Greek name meaning "honouring God." Its use as a first name is due to **Timothy**, the companion of St. Paul. It was not used widely until the 16th century when many classical and biblical names were introduced.

Tina

Originally a short form for girls' names ending in "-tina," most common of which is **Christina** (see **Christine**). It is now used in its own right.

Tracy

This popular girl's name seems to have started life as a short form of **Teresa**. It is also found as **Tracey** and **Tracie**. Its beginnings as an independent name were probably helped by the use of the surname Tracy (from a French place name) as a boy's name, particularly as at the time when it first became popular Spencer Tracy (1900–67) was a well-known film star. **Trace** is used as a boys' name, and as a short form of the girls'.

Trinity

From the three forms of God in the Christian faith, it's becoming popular as a girl's name in the United States and Canada.

Triss *see* **Beatrice**

Tulasi

This Indian name is from the Sanskrit word meaning "sacred basil." Tulasi is also the name of a goddess based on the same word.

Tya *see* **Tia**

Tyla

The feminine form of **Tyler**, a surname, from the job, used as a first name. It has been popular in the United States for some years and can be shortened to **Ty**.

Tyra

The feminine form of **Tyrone**, the name of the Irish county, which means "Eoghan's land" (see also Taryn).

U

Uma

A Sanskrit name of a goddess, meaning "flax, turmeric," which has been made internationally famous by the actress Uma Thurman.

Una

The etymology of this ancient Irish name is obscure. It is also found in the forms **Oonagh** or **Oona** (pronounced "oo-na"), both of which are also found in Scotland. **Juno**, influenced by the name of the Roman queen of the gods, is another Irish form, best known from Sean O'Casey's play *Juno and the Paycock* (1924). The Elizabethan poet Edmund Spenser took the Irish name Una and gave it its Latin sense, "one, unity," in his epic poem *The Faerie Queene*.

Unice *see* **Eunice**

Unity

This is one of the abstract virtue names that became quite common among Puritans after the Reformation. It is rarely found today.

Ursula

From the Latin, meaning "little she-bear." The name was fairly common in the Middle Ages on account of St. Ursula, a 5th-century Cornish princess who, along with her companions, was murdered near Cologne while on a pilgrimage. The name had a revival after Mrs. Craik chose it for her heroine in her popular novel, *John Halifax, Gentleman* (1856).

V

Valentine

From the Latin *valens*, "strong" or "healthy." St. Valentine was a third-century Roman priest martyred on 14 February, the eve of the celebrations of the pagan goddess Juno, when lots were drawn to choose lovers. The feast was absorbed into the Christian calendar. **Valentina** is an alternative form. **Val** is a common diminutive, shared with **Valerie**.

Valerie

This is the French form of the Roman family name **Valeria**, and was taken into use in Britain in the late 19th century. It comes from a word meaning "to be in good health." It has the short form **Val**.

Vanda see Wanda

Vanessa

A name invented in the early 18th century by the writer Jonathan Swift as a pet name for **Esther** Vanhomrigh. He took the first syllable of her surname and added **Essa**, which was probably a short form of Esther.

Vanna see Gianna

Velma

A name of unknown origin, first used in the 1880s in the United States.

Venetia

The Latin name for the Italian city of Venice, used as a first name. It was previously thought to have a connection with Venus, the Roman goddess of love, which is very occasionally used as a first name.

Vera

This name has two possible derivations. One source is the Russian for "faith," another is the Latin meaning "true." It was used in English literature in the 19th century and became popular in Britain at the beginning of the 20th. It is sometimes used as an abbreviation of **Veronica** (see also **Verena**).

Verena

The name of a rather obscure 3rd-century saint. Its meaning is not known, but may well come from the same source as **Vera**. St. Verena lived in Switzerland and her name is popular there, but use among English speakers probably owes something to the name's prominence in Henry James's novel *The Bostonians*.

Verity

From the Old English word for "truth." It was first used by the Puritans in the 17th century and has been quite common ever since. The variant **Verily** ("truly") is also found occasionally.

Veronica

Traditionally, this name is thought to derive from the Latin *vera icon*, meaning "a true image." St. Veronica wiped the sweat from Christ's face on his way to Calvary, and a "true image" of his face was said to have been left on the cloth. It is more likely, however, that the name is a form of **Berenice**. **Véronique** has long been popular in France, and from there the name reached Scotland in the late 17th century. It does not appear much in England before the late 19th century (see also **Vera**).

Veva *see* **Genevieve**

Victoria

From the Latin for "victory." This name was hardly used in Britain until the reign of Queen Victoria, who was named after her German mother. In the recent past the name has been very popular and is often found in one of its short forms, **Vicky, Vickie, Vikki**, and **Tori(e)** or **Toria**. **Vita** and **Viti** and the nickname **Queenie** are also found.

Vida *see* **Davida**

Vijaya

The feminine form of **Vijay**, an Indian name from a Sanskrit word meaning "victory." Vijaya, is also applied to the goddess **Durga**, wife of Shiva.

Vinaya

An Indian name that means "educating to act in a proper way." For Buddhists it suggests the modest behaviour appropriate to a monk.

Viola, Violet

Viola is Latin for "violet." Although it does occur in the Middle Ages, the modern use of this name comes from Shakespeare, who gave it to the heroine of *Twelfth Night*. **Violette** and **Violetta** have also been used.

Virginia

Although there was a Roman family called Virginus, the modern use of this name dates only from 1587. Sir Walter Raleigh had called his newly founded colony in North America Virginia, after Elizabeth

I, the "Virgin Queen," and the name Virginia was given to the first child born to the settlers there. **Ginny, Gini**, or **Jinny** is a common short form.

Vishala

An Indian name that means "immense, spacious." **Vishalakshi** is also used, with the meaning "wide-eyed."

Vita, Viti *see* **Victoria**

Vivian, Vivien

From the Latin *vivianus*, which means "lively." Vivian is now used for both sexes, but was originally the masculine form, with Vivien, **Vivyan**, or **Vyvyan** mostly used for girls. The French **Vivienne** is always female as is **Viviana**. **Viv** is used for short.

Vonda *see* **Wanda**

W

Wanda

This is a Polish girl's name that is probably connected with the word "vandal." Its wider use may have started when a novel of the same name by Ouida was published in 1883. **Vanda** and **Vonda** are both variants.

Wasimah

From the masculine Arabic name **Wasim**, which means "handsome" or "graceful." The feminine form, Wasimah, also means "pretty."

Wendy

This name was first used by James Barrie in *Peter Pan* (1904). The name started as "Friendy-Wendy," a pet name for Barrie used by a child friend of his, Margaret Henley. **Wenda** has been described as a variant of Wendy, but is more probably a form of **Gwenda** (see **Gwen**).

Wenonah *see* **Winona**

Whitney

This name, made famous by the singer Whitney Houston, was originally a surname meaning "(living) at the white island." Its use as a first name in the United States may be due to its being

the surname of both a wealthy family prominent in national politics and arts, and of Josiah Dwight Whitney (1819–96), geologist and surveyor, after whom the United States's highest mountain outside Alaska, Mount Whitney in south California, is named.

Willow

A recent plant name, usually used for girls, but occasionally for boys.

Wilma

The feminine form of **William**, from the Old German, meaning "desiring protection." It also appears as **Wilhelmina** with short forms **Willa** or **Vilma**, **Minnie** and **Minna**, and **Elma**.

Winifred

From the Welsh feminine name Gwenfrewi, anglicized as Winifred and later confused with the Old English male name **Winfrith**, meaning "friend of peace." St. Winifred, a 7th-century saint, is said to have been decapitated by a Welsh prince when she rejected his

advances, but then was restored miraculously to life. Although she was a popular saint in the Middle Ages, her name was not used much until the 16th century, but was very popular at the turn of the 19th–20th centuries. **Win(nie)** and, less often, **Freda** are short forms. **Winifrid** is also used.

Winona

This is a Sioux word meaning "eldest daughter." It is also the name of a city in Minnesota. The name occurs as **Wenonah** in Longfellow's poem "Hiawatha" (1855) and can also be found as **Wynon(n)a**.

X

Xanthe

From the Greek, meaning "yellow."

Xara *see* **Zahra**

Xenia

The Greek word for "hospitality." **Xena** is also used (see also **Zena**).

Y

Yael
From the Hebrew, meaning "strength of God."

Yessenia
Still mainly restricted to the Americas, this name of unknown meaning became popular with Spanish speakers as that of the titular gypsy heroine of a Mexican film (1971), later made into a television series.

Yoko
Japanese for "good girl."

Yolanda
From the Greek, meaning "violet flower." The name of the Gilbert and Sullivan opera *Iolanthe* has the same root. **Yolande** is the French form.

Yseult(e), Ysolde *see* **Isolda**

Yvonne, Yvette
These are French names meaning "yew." They are feminine short forms of the Breton boy's name **Yves**.

Z

Zahara
From the Swahili for "flower."

Zahra, Zara
A Muslim name that means "to flower" or "to achieve splendour." It was the family name of the Prophet's mother and is traditionally used in her honour. The English form came to the attention of the British public in 1981 when Princess Anne, the Princess Royal, used it as her daughter's name. It is occasionally found as **Xara** or **Zaria**.

Zainab *see* **Zaynab**

Zakiyah
An Arabic name meaning "pure, chaste." It can also be spelled **Zakiy(y)a**.

Zaynab
A popular Muslim name of uncertain meaning. Some scholars link it with a fragrant plant, and it was borne by several members of the Prophet Muhammad's family. It is frequently found as **Zainab**.

Zena
One theory is that this name comes from a Persian word meaning "woman." Another makes it a short form of various other names such as **Zinaida**, which comes from Zeus, the Greek king of the gods, and is the name of two Russian saints; and another a variation of **Xenia**. It is also found as **Zina**.

Zenobia
This was the name of a great Queen of Palmyra (modern Syria) in the 3rd century A.D. She was seen as a threat to the Eastern Roman Empire, and her aggressive foreign policy forced the Emperor Aurelian to invade. This he did successfully and put an end to her power, though he spared her life. The name appears in Cornwall from the 16th century, but the reason for this is unknown.

Zillah
From the Hebrew for "shade." The name occurs in the Old

Testament (Genesis IV, 19–23) and was used occasionally after the Reformation.

Zina, Zinaida *see* **Zena**

Zita
The name of the last Empress of Austria who, although deposed just after the end of the First World War, died only in 1989. It comes from an Italian word for "little girl" and was the name of a humble but good maid who became the patron saint of domestic servants.

Zoe, Zoë
This is the Greek word for "life." The Alexandrian Jews used it to translate the Hebrew equivalent for **Eve** into Greek. The name spread throughout the Eastern Church but has been used in Britain only in the last hundred years. It also appears as **Zoey** and **Zoie**. Zoe is still one of the most popular girls names in Canada.

Zorah
An Arabic name meaning "light of dawn," also found as **Zora**. It can also be understood as a Hebrew name, taken from a place name of unknown meaning found in the Bible.

Zshakira *see* **Shakira**

Zubaida
An Arabic name, popular in India, meaning "marigold."

Zuleika
From the Persian meaning "brilliant beauty." The name is known from Max Beerbohm's satirical novel *Zuleika Dobson* (1911), whose heroine is so beautiful that all the young men at Oxford University kill themselves for love of her. The Arabic spelling is **Zulekha**.

Zsa Zsa
Hungarian form of **Susan**. Also spelled as **Zsuzanna**.

Boys' Names A–Z

A

Aaron

In the Old Testament, Aaron was the brother of **Moses** and the first High Priest of Israel. The traditional interpretation links this name to the Hebrew for "high mountain," but like Moses, Aaron is probably an Egyptian name of unknown meaning. It is connected with the Arabic names **Harun** and **Haroun** and has been in use since the Reformation. In the past it was pronounced with a first sound as in "air," but now it is also found with a short "a," a pronunciation reflected in the spelling **Ar(r)on**.

Abdullah

A Muslim name from the Arabic, for "servant of Allah." The short form **Abdul** also occurs.

Abe, Abie *see* **Abel**, **Abraham**

Abel

In the Old Testament, Abel was the second son of Adam and Eve and murdered by his brother Cain. The name may come from a Hebrew word for "breath," but like so many of the earliest names, its meaning is doubtful. The name has been used in England since before the Norman Conquest. The short forms include **Abe** and **Abie**.

Abner

From the Hebrew words for "father of light." In the Bible it is the name of King Saul's cousin, who was commander of the army. In England it came into common use, together with other biblical names, after the Reformation in the early 16th century. It is still found occasionally in North America.

Abraham

This is the name of the Old Testament patriarch who, for the first 90 years of his life, was called **Abram**, "high father," but then was told by God that he should be called Abraham, "father of many nations." It was used in England regularly after the Reformation and became popular in North America, where the abbreviation **Abe**, as in President Abe Lincoln (1809–65), was widely used. Other short forms are **Abie, Bram**, and **Ham**. (See **Ibrahim**.)

Adam

From the Hebrew, meaning "red," possibly referring either to skin colour or to the clay from which God formed the first man. The name was adopted by the Irish as early as the 7th century, when St. Adamnan, "Little Adam," was Abbot of Iona. It was very common in the 13th century and has been in use ever since. Other forms include **Adamo, Adán, Adão, Addam**, and **Addison**.

Adil
An Arabic name meaning "just, honest." It is also spelled **Adeel**.

Adnan
An Arabic name of uncertain meaning. According to tradition, Adnan was the ancestor of the North Arabians.

Adrian
From the Latin, meaning "man from Adria," and a form of the name of the Roman Emperor **Hadrian**, who built the wall across northern England. It has been used since Roman times; a St. Adrian was the first British martyr in the fourth century. **Adrien** is also found.

Aeneus, Aengus *see* **Angus**

Ahmad
This Arabic name is often spelled **Ahmed**. It is one of the names applied to the Prophet Muhammad and means "more praiseworthy."

Aidan, Aiden
An ancient Irish name that means "little fire." It was the name of a 7th-century Irish missionary who founded the monastery of Lindisfarne in Northumbria. The name was revived during the 19th century, and both Aidan and Aiden are in the Top 50 list for boys' names in Canada. Aidan is sometimes anglicized as **Edan** and is also found as **Ayden**.

Ailbhe *see* **Elvis**

Ajay, Ajit
Popular Indian names from the Sanskrit for "invincible."

Akash
This Indian name is sometimes found as **Aakash**. It is from the Sanskrit and means "the sky."

Akhil
An Indian name from the Sanskrit meaning "whole, complete."

Akshar
An Indian name that comes from the Sanskrit meaning "imperishable."

Alan
An old Celtic name of unknown meaning. It has appeared in various forms from early times. In England it first became popular after the Norman Conquest as **Alain** or **Alein**, the French forms. These developed into **Alleyne**, which is preserved as a surname. Alan, **Allan, Allen**, and **Alun** (strictly speaking, a Welsh river name used as a first name) are in use today.

Alastair
Also spelled **Alasdair, Alistair** and **Alister**, this is the Gaelic form of **Alexander**, "defender of men." It is shortened to **Al(i), Alli**, or **Ally, Alec**, and **Alick**.

Alban
From the Latin *Albanus*, meaning "man from Alba" (a Roman town whose name means "white"), and the name of the earliest British saint. The town of St. Albans, where he was martyred, is called after him. **Albin** and **Albinus** are variants that appear occasionally.

Alberic *see* **Aubrey**

Albert
An Old German name meaning "noble and bright." The Old English form was **Ethelbert**, the name of the Kentish king who welcomed Augustine to Canterbury when he came to convert the Anglo-Saxons to Christianity. This was replaced after the Norman Conquest by the French form, **Aubert**. Albert became so popular after the marriage of Queen Victoria to Prince Albert of Saxe-Coburg that it became over-used and so went out of fashion. **Bert** and **Bertie** are short forms.

Alby *see* **Elvis**

Aldous
From the Old German *Aldo*, meaning "old." It has been used in the eastern counties of England since the 13th century and has given rise to various surnames like **Aldhouse** and **Aldiss**. **Aldo** is still used in North America. The writer Aldous Huxley (1894–1963) is the best-known British example.

Aldwyn
This Anglo-Saxon personal name, meaning "old friend," has been revived in modern times. Some parents prefer the spelling **Aldwin**.

Alec *see* **Alastair, Alexander**

Aled
The name of a Welsh river used as a first name.

Alexander
Currently one of the most popular boys' names, this comes from the Greek, meaning "defender of men." It was made famous in the 4th century B.C. by Alexander the Great, and was very popular in England in the Middle Ages. **Sandy** is a short form, particularly in Scotland. **Alex** is the most common of the many short forms, others being **Al(i)**, **Alec**, **Lex**, **Sacha**, **Xan**, and **Xander** or **Zander**. Variants include **Alexandre**, **Alessandro**, **Alejandro**, and **Aleksander**.

Alexis
From the Greek word meaning "helper" or "defender," Alexis is the name of one of the great saints of the Orthodox church.

Originally a man's name, it is now more frequently used for women. Alternative forms are **Alexie, Alexus** and short forms such as **Lexi(e)** and even **Lexus**.

Alfred
From two Old English words, meaning "elf" (hence "good") and "counsel." It is also a possible development of the Anglo-Saxon name **Ealdfrith**, meaning "old peace." It is sometimes written **Alfrid**. When Alfred was written down in old Latin, the name was spelled **Alured** and developed into **Avery** (now used for both sexes). **Alf(ie)** and **Fred** are diminutives.

Algernon
From a Norman French nickname meaning "with whiskers." It was popular in the 19th century but is not much used today. The usual diminutive is **Algie** or **Algy**.

Ali
Ali is a popular Arabic name meaning "exalted, noble," and as one of the terms used of Allah, invokes God's protection for the

child. As a western name **Ali** is also a short form of **Alastair**.

Aloysius

This is the Latin form of **Aloys**, an old Provençal form of **Louis** (see **Lewis**). There was a popular Spanish saint of this name in the 16th century and Roman Catholics continue to use the name in Britain.

Alvin

From two Old English names, Alwine, "friend of all" and Athelwine, "noble friend." **Aylwin, Alvan**, and **Alvy(n)** are alternative forms. The similar-sounding **Alvar** means "elf army."

Ambrose

From the Greek for "divine." There was a fourth-century St. Ambrose who was Bishop of Milan. The name is found in the Domesday Book and has been used occasionally ever since. The Welsh name **Emrys** is derived from the Latin form of the name.

Amin

From the Arabic for "honest," "trustworthy," or "reliable."

Iman, "faith, belief" comes from the same root.

Amit

An Indian name from the Sanskrit for "without limit." It is also a simplified short form of names like **Amitbikram** ("limitless prowess") and **Amitjyoti** ("limitless brightness").

Amitabh

A name of the Buddha, from the Sanskrit meaning "limitless splendour." The spelling **Amitav** is also used.

Amos

A Hebrew name, possibly meaning "he who carries a burden." It was the name of an Old Testament prophet and was adopted by English Puritans after the Reformation, when saints' names fell out of favour. Popular until the 19th century, it is at present uncommon.

Amrit

In the Vedic epics of the Hindus, this Sanskrit name refers to immortality or that which confers it, such as the "water of life, soma juice, nectar, [or] ambrosia." Amrit can be used for both sexes.

Anand

From the Sanskrit for "happiness," "joy," or "bliss." It is the name of a god in the *Veda*, sacred book of the Hindus.

Andrew

From the Greek for "manly." Andrew is the name of the Apostle who is patron saint of Scotland, Russia, and Greece, and first appears in England in the Domesday Book. It has been used in Britain continuously and has enjoyed particular favour in Scotland. The short forms include **Andy**, **Dandy** (Scottish), and **Drew**, which is also used as an independent name. The Italian form, **Andrea**, is actually a boys' name in Italy, but is often used as a girls' name. The French boys' form, **André**, is likewise sometimes used for girls. **Andra** is both a traditional Scottish form of the boys' name and used for girls.

Aneurin

This name is traditionally interpreted as the Welsh form of Latin *Honorius*, meaning "honourable." It also appears in the form **Aneirin**. Short forms are **Nye** and **Neirin**.

Angus

From the Gaelic **Aonghas**, meaning "one choice." It appears in Irish legend in the form **Aengus** or **Oengus**, but is more common in Scotland. The name became associated with the classical myth of **Aeneas** (which is close to the Irish pronunciation) in the 15th century, and this form was also used.

Anil

The name of the wind-god in the Hindu Vedic epics. It is derived from the Sanskrit meaning "air" or "wind." Anil is the driver of Indra's golden chariot, which is pulled by a thousand horses.

Anish

A Sanskrit name, one of the thousand borne by the Hindu god Vishnu. Its meaning is possibly "without a master."

Anthony, Antony

A Roman family name. Its most famous member was Marcus Antonius, the Mark Antony of Shakespeare's *Julius Caesar* and *Antony and Cleopatra*. The name was very popular in the Middle Ages as a result of the influence of St. Antony the Great and St. Antony of Padua. The alternative and commoner spelling Anthony was introduced after the Renaissance, when it was incorrectly thought that the name was derived from the Greek *anthos* meaning "flower," as in Anthea. The usual short form is **Tony**. **Anton, Antonio** (shortened to **Tonio**), and **Antoine** (often in phonetic spellings such as **Antwan** or **Antuan**) are often used.

Anup

An Indian name from the Sanskrit meaning "without comparison." The spelling **Anoop** is also used.

Archibald

From Old German words meaning "truly bold." The Old English form was used in East Anglia before the Norman Conquest. Thereafter, it was primarily Scottish and was associated particularly with the Douglas and Campbell families. The most usual diminutive is **Archie**, now sometimes given to a child rather than the full name.

Ardal

This is an Irish name of disputed meaning, either "high valour" or coming from the word for "bear."

Ariel

A Hebrew name, traditionally said to mean "lion of God."

Arjun

A Hindu name from the Sanskrit for "white" or "bright." It was the name of a famous Pandava prince, son of the god Indra.

Armaan

Persian word meaning "desire" or "goal." Armaan and **Arman** are popular in Canada, but don't appear as frequently in the United States.

Arnold

From the Old German, **Arnwalt**, meaning "eagle's

power." It appeared in various forms, both Germanic and French, in the Middle Ages, but dropped out of use from the 17th century until the late 19th when it had a revival.

Arthur
The origin of this name is disputed. Possible sources are the Celtic word for "bear" and the Roman name Artorius. Whatever its source, its use comes entirely from the fame of its first known bearer, King Arthur. Victorian interest in things medieval made it popular in the 19th century when Queen Victoria gave the name to one of her sons. Over-use in the late 19th and first quarter of the 20th centuries led to a decline, but there are now distinct signs of a revival in popularity. **Art(ie), Arty, Artur(o)** are some of the variants.

Arun
An Indian name from the Sanskrit for "reddish brown," a colour associated with the dawn. It became the name of the mythical personification of the dawn, charioteer of the sun. **Aroon** is an alternative spelling.

Asa
From the Hebrew word meaning "physician." In the Bible it is the name of a king of Judah, noted for his piety.

Asher
The name of one of the tribes of Israel. It means "happy." Although it is an unusual name, there are signs that its use is on the increase, along with other names from the Bible. It is, of course, also a common surname meaning "ash tree," and some uses may be from this.

Ashish
A relatively modern Indian name, probably derived from the Sanskrit for "prayer" or "benediction."

Ashraf
A popular Muslim name from the Arabic for "more noble" or "more honourable."

Ashton
An Old English surname

meaning "ash farm," which is now commonly used as a first name for both boys and girls.

Aslam
A Muslim name from the Arabic, meaning "safer" or "sounder."

Athol
Athol or **Atholl** is the Scottish place name, used as a first name. The place name means "New Ireland."

Aubrey
From the Old German, meaning "elf ruler." In medieval romance the diminutive **Auberon** was used and Shakespeare adopted it as Oberon in *A Midsummer Night's Dream*. The German form, **Alberic**, developed first into **Albery** and later into Aubrey.

Augustus
From the Latin for "venerable." Augustus was a title given to the first Roman Emperor. **Augustine**, the name of two important saints, one of whom converted the English to Christianity, is another form of the name. It was so popular in

the Middle Ages it developed the shorter forms **Austin, Austyn**, and **Austen**, a name that has been popular for some years.

Aurelius
From the Latin *aurelius*, meaning "golden." It has been used since the 17th century, and recently a short form, **Auriol, Auriel, Oriel**, or **Oriole**, has shown some popularity.

Austin *see* **Augustus**

Avery
Old English, meaning "elf ruler" and a variant of **Alfred** and **Aubrey**.

Ayden *see* **Aidan**

Azim
This Arabic name means "determined."

Aziz
This Arabic name means "friend." **Azeez** is a common alternative spelling.

B

Bailey
Once a surname, this name comes from the job of steward or bailiff of an estate. Popular as a girls's name too.

Bairre *see* **Barry**

Bala
An Indian name from the Sanskrit for "young child." Variants include **Balu** and **Balan**.

Barnabas
From the Hebrew, meaning "son of exhortation or consolation," it is best known as the name of the New Testament companion of St. Paul. The diminutive, **Barnaby**, is rather fashionable at the moment, more so than the full form. **Barney** is a short form that is also shared with **Bernard**.

Barney *see* **Barnabas, Bernard**

Barry
The English form of a variety of Celtic names, most prominently **Bairre**, a short form of the Irish **Finbarr (Finnbar, Fionnbharr)** meaning "fair-haired." Barry can also be spelled **Barrie**.

Bartholomew
From the Hebrew, meaning "son of Talmai," Talmai meaning "full of furrows." It was the surname of the Apostle **Nathaniel** and was very popular in the Middle Ages when the cult of St. Bartholomew was at its height. The name is still in use and has the short form **Bart**, made famous by the cartoon character Bart Simpson.

Basil
From the Greek *basileios*, meaning "kingly." It was probably brought to England by the Crusaders, and it has remained in use ever since. Diminutives include **Bas** or **Baz, Basie,** and **Bazza**. These were common in the Middle Ages, but are hardly ever found today.

Bastian, Bastien *see*
Sebastian

Benedict
From the Latin *benedictus*,
meaning "blessed," and most
familiar as the name of St.
Benedict, founder of the
Benedictine Order. It was
common in medieval England
in the forms **Bennet** and
Benedick. The latter is
the name of a character in
Shakespeare's *Much Ado About
Nothing*.

Benjamin
From the Hebrew, meaning "son
of the south" or "right hand,"
which might imply strength
and good fortune. The Old
Testament story of Benjamin,
son of Jacob, gave the name
the added implications of a
favoured youngest son. The
most common short forms are
Ben(nie), Benny, Benjie,
and **Benjy**. Variants include
**Beniamino, Bejamím,
Benjamim**.

Bernard
A Germanic name meaning
"brave as a bear." It was very

popular in the Middle Ages.
Two important saints bearing
the name were St. Bernard
of Menthon after whom St.
Bernard dogs are named, and
St. Bernard of Clairvaux who
inspired the Second Crusade. It
has remained in use ever since.
The most usual short forms are
Bernie and **Barney**, which
is shared with **Barnabas**. The
German form is **Bernhard**.

Bert, Bertie
A short form of a large number
of names including **Albert,
Bertram, Bertrand, Gilbert,
Herbert, Hubert, Robert**.
In all these cases, the "-bert"
part of the name is a Germanic
element meaning "bright." The
name is sometimes used as a
given name, when it may take
the form **Burt**.

Bertram
From the Old German,
meaning "bright raven," the bird
associated with the god Odin.
The name has been used in
England since the early Middle
Ages and has the short forms
Bert and **Bertie**, and the less
common **Berry**. **Bertrand**,

meaning "bright shield," is often
treated as the French form of
Bertram.

Beverl(e)y
From an Old English surname
meaning "of the beaver-meadow."
It is shortened to **Bev** and is
now only rarely used for boys.

Bevis
This is a French name, possibly
meaning "bow," introduced
into England at the Norman
Conquest. It was popular in the
Middle Ages and revived again
after Richard Jeffries' *Bevis, The
Story of a Boy* was published in
1882.

Bharat
This was the name of several
famous heroes in the Hindu
epics, and derives from the
Sanskrit for "being maintained."
India officially became Bharat
when it achieved independence.

Bhaskar
A Hindu name from the Sanskrit
for "the sun." Bhaskara, the
famous 12th-century Indian
astronomer and teacher, shows
an earlier form of the name.

Billie, Billy
This short form of the boys' name **William**.

Björn
A Scandinavian name that means "bear." The name has become widely known in modern times through the Swedish tennis champion Björn Borg.

Blaise
From the French, meaning either someone from the Blois region, or derived from the Latin for "stammerer." It is also spelled **Blase** or **Blaze**.

Blake
A surname, from the Old English meaning "black, dark-complexioned," used as a first name.

Bobbi(e), Bobby
These short forms of **Robert** are used as names in their own right and in combinations such as **Bobby Joe**.

Boris
From the Russian word for "fight." It was used in Britain and North America in the 20th century, possibly due to cultural influences such as Moussorgsky's opera *Boris Godunov*, the film actor Boris Karloff, and the author of *Dr. Zhivago*, Boris Pasternak, as well as the large number of Slavic immigrants who have come to the West.

Boyd
From a Gaelic word meaning "yellow," referring to the colour of the hair. It is the name of a Scottish clan, though the surname can also derive from "isle of Bute." Boyd became more widespread outside Scotland after its use in Margaret Mitchell's *Gone With the Wind*.

Braden, Brayden, Braydon
A now-fashionable first name that derives from the surname. It is from the Old English, meaning "descendant of Bradan," an Irish hero who acquired the gift of prophecy from the Salmon of Knowledge.

Bradley
A surname from the Old English, meaning "wide meadow," now popular as a first name.

Brad(d) is a short form.

Brady
An Irish surname, possibly meaning "broad-chested," now increasingly popular as a first name for boys.

Brendan, Brandon
An Irish name meaning either "with stinking hair" or, according to one authority, from the Welsh word meaning "prince." It is most famously found in the sixth-century Irish St. Brendan the Navigator, credited in legend with the discovery of America. The form **Brandan** or Brandon has a long history as an alternative form of Brendan, but can also come from an Old English place and surname meaning "a hill where broom grows." The name is also spelled **Brandin, Brandyn, Brenden,** and **Brendon**.

Brennan
Brennan is a short form of the Irish name **Bren**, which probably means "tear, sorrow." Since the earliest records this name and **Bran**, "raven," and its short form **Brannan** have

regularly been confused, and it is not always possible to tell which form of the name has come from which source.

Bret(t)
From an Old French word meaning "a Briton" or "a Breton."

Brian
A Celtic name, the origin of which is obscure, though it may be derived from words meaning "hill" or "strength." It was known mainly in Celtic areas until the Norman Conquest, when it was introduced to England. Brian Boru was a famous Irish King of the 11th century, who defeated the invading Vikings. The name continued to be popular in England until Tudor times, but after that it disappeared until it was reintroduced from Ireland in the 18th century. Today the spellings **Bryan, Brien**, and **Brion** are found, and **Bryant** or **Briant**, originally a surname developed from the name Brian, is also found.

Brice
Brice, possibly meaning "speckled," is an old Gaulish name, the name of a 5th-century French saint and bishop. The surname that developed from the first name, **Bryson**, is also found used as **Bryce**.

Bruce
A French surname that came to Britain at the time of the Norman Conquest. Members of the family moved to Scotland, where a descendant of one, Robert Bruce, became King of Scots, and was the ancestor of the Stewart or Stuart Kings. Bruce has only been used as a first name since the 19th century, but it proved so popular in Australia in the mid-20th century that it is almost a nickname for an Australian man.

Bruno
This is a German name meaning "brown," probably imported to the U.K. via the United States, where it has been established for longer.

Bryan *see* **Brian**

Bryce *see* **Brice**

Bryn
A Welsh name, originally describing where someone lived, meaning "hill." It can be found as **Brin**, and **Brynmor** ("large hill") is also used.

Buddy
This word for a friend is occasionally used as a first name but is usually a nickname. The singer Buddy Holly, for example, was christened Charles.

Burhan
An Arabic name meaning "evidence" or "proof." **Burhanuddin** means "proof of faith."

Byron
A name more frequently used in America than Britain, though it honours the English poet Lord Byron (1784–1824). Byron comes from the word "byre," which means a cow-shed or barn. The name may have originally indicated someone who lived near a barn.

C

Caius *see* **Kai**

Caleb
From the Hebrew *kalebh*, meaning "dog" or "intrepid." It first appeared in England in the 16th century and is now popular in Canada. It can be shortened to **Cale** and spelled **Kaleb**.

Callum
Callum comes from the Latin *columba*, "a dove." When the Irish St. Columba went as a missionary to Scotland in the sixth century, he introduced the name there and it became a typically Scottish name, along with **Malcolm**, which comes from it. It is found spelled **Calum** and **Colum**, while the form **Colm** is particularly popular in Ireland.

Calvin
From the surname of the 16th-century French religious reformer Jean Cauvin or Chauvin, which was latinized to Calvinus and adopted as a first name by Protestants. The surname may mean "bald." It is most commonly found in North America and Scotland and can be shortened to **Cal**. Other spellings include **Kelvan, Kelvin**, and **Kelvyn**.

Cameron
From the Gaelic, meaning "crooked nose," this is the name of a Scottish clan. Its popularity has spread from Scotland and is one of the Top 50 boys' names in Canada. **Camryn** is a popular variant.

Caradoc
From the Welsh for "beloved." In the form Caratacus, the name of a Briton who fought against the Romans in the first century, it is one of the earliest recorded British names.

Carl, Karl
German forms of **Charles**.

Carlo *see* **Charles**

Carlton, Charlton
These names are both forms of an Old English place name and, later, a surname meaning "countryman's farm."

Carson
Old English for "son of marsh dwellers."

Carter
This is another surname that has recently accelerated in popularity as a first name. Of Old English origin, it means literally "one who transports goods by cart."

Cary
A surname that was only rarely used as a first name until it became famous through the film star Cary Grant. Ultimately, it probably goes back to one of a number of Irish surnames, including ones meaning "battle-king" or "dark brown."

Casey
This comes from an Irish surname meaning "vigilant in war." It can also be a form of the Polish name **Casimir**, "proclamation of peace." The name takes various forms, often spelled with a "K."

Caspar *see* **Jasper**

Caspian

Although at first this looks like the name of the great Asian inland sea, use of Caspian as a first name comes from the character of Prince Caspian in C. S. Lewis's *Chronicles of Narnia* books, particularly the 1951 volume named after him.

Cecil

From the Latin, meaning "blind." It was the name of a famous Roman clan and was first adopted into English as a girls' name. The popularity of the name in its masculine form only became marked in the 19th century, probably as one of several aristocratic surnames which it was then fashionable to use as first names.

Cedric

This name seems to have been a creation of Sir Walter Scott's for a character in the novel *Ivanhoe*. Scott is said to have used it by mistake for Cerdic, who was the first king of the West Saxons. However, as there is a Welsh name **Cedrych** ("pattern

of generosity"), it may well be from this. Cedric became popular with parents as a result of the book *Little Lord Fauntleroy* (1886) by F. H. Burnett whose hero bore that name, and it may well also owe its fall in popularity to its association with the book and its hero's smugly virtuous image. It does, however, show signs of coming back into fashion, particularly in the United States.

Chad

The name (of uncertain meaning) of a 7th-century saint who was Bishop of Lichfield. The name became quite popular in America in the 20th century. A famous holder of the name was the Rev. Chad Varah, founder of The Samaritans.

Chae *see* **Charles**

Champak

The Hindu name of a god and of a tree bearing yellow flowers.

Chandan

An Indian name from the Sanskrit for "sandalwood." The paste derived from sandalwood

is important in Hindu religious ceremonies, when it is used to anoint statues of the gods and to make a mark on the forehead of worshippers. Chandan occurs as a divine personal name in traditional Hindu texts.

Chander

An Indian name from the Sanskrit meaning "the moon." In the Hindu religion, the moon is a god rather than a goddess, but the name **Chandra** is nevertheless a popular one for girls. The variant **Chander** is often used for boys.

Chandler

The success of the television series *Friends* has led to an increased use of the name, originally a French surname meaning "candle maker."

Chandrakant

From the Sanskrit for "loved by the moon," referring to a mythical jewel mentioned in classical Hindu texts, supposedly formed by the moon's rays. It is also the name of a white water-lily that blossoms at night.

Charles

Originally from an Old German word *carl*, meaning "man," which was latinized as **Carolus** and then changed by the French to Charles. The Normans brought the name to England, but it did not become popular until its use by the Stuart kings of Britain caused it to be taken up by Royalists in the 17th century and Jacobites in the 18th century. Its popularity has continued ever since. The short form **Charlie** is now common as the given form of the name. **Chas**, originally a written abbreviation, has come to be used as a short form. **Chuck** is also used, and in Scotland **Chae** or **Chay**. **Carlo**, the Spanish and Italian form, is much used in North America.

Chase

The rise in popularity of this surname, meaning "hunter," as a first name in the United States probably owes much to its use for a character in the 1980s television series *Falcon Crest*.

Chay *see* **Charles**

Chester

A surname taken from the English city, used as a first name. The word comes from the Latin for "fort."

Chetan

A Hindu name meaning "consciousness" or "awareness."

Christian

This name has been used in Britain since the 13th century. It became more popular after its use by Bunyan for the hero of *Pilgrim's Progress*, but has never been as common as the feminine form, **Christine**, although it is currently enjoying some popularity.

Christopher

From the Greek, meaning "bearing Christ." As a first name it is used in honour of the saint who was believed to have carried the infant Christ to safety across a river. Thus St. Christopher became the patron saint of travellers. The Scottish equivalent of the name was **Chrystal** or **Crystal**. Abbreviated forms are **Kester, Kit, Chip**, and

Chris. **Christie** or **Christy** is a short form particularly used in Ireland.

Clarence

In the 14th century **Lionel**, son of King Edward III of England, married the heiress of the town of Clare in Suffolk. He was later created Duke of Clarence, the name Clarence meaning "of Clare." This title seems to have been first used as a name in the early 19th century in Maria Edgeworth's novel *Helen*.

Clark

The surname meaning "a clerk," used as a first name. Famous users were the actor Clark Gable and in fiction Clark Kent, the everyday name for Superman. **Clarke** is also found.

Claud

From the Roman name Claudius, itself derived from the Latin, meaning "lame." In homage to the Emperor Claudius, who was ruler when Britain was conquered by the Romans, the name was used in Britain in the 1st and 2nd centuries. Its use soon lapsed in that country though not in France, where it is spelled **Claude** and used for either sex. It was from the French that it was revived in Britain in the 16th century by the Scottish family of Hamilton. A derivative is **Claudian**, and the short form **Claudie** can be found.

Claus *see* **Nicholas**

Clayton
Clayton, from a place name, later a surname, meaning "settlement on clay," is enjoying some popularity in the United States as a boy's name, as is the shorter **Clay**. Both are also found spelled with a "K."

Clement
From the Latin, meaning "mild, merciful." Clement was the name of an early saint and of several popes. Its abbreviated forms are **Clem** and **Clemmie**, which are shared with the feminine forms **Clementina** and **Clementine**.

Clifford
There are several places named Clifford ("ford by the cliff")

in Britain, any of which could become a surname. Towards the end of the 19th century, the surname came into use as a first name. It is now most often used in its short form **Cliff**. **Clifton**, "settlement by the cliff," is also found.

Clint
A short form of **Clinton**, an aristocratic surname meaning "farm by the river Glyme," used as a first name. The short form has been given fame by the actor Clint Eastwood.

Clive
A surname meaning "dweller by the cliff," which has come to be used as a first name, probably in honour of Robert Clive (1725–1774), known as Clive of India, who was prominent in the British conquest of India.

Clyde
Clyde is an ancient Scottish river name meaning "the washer," possibly from the name of a local goddess and used since before the Roman occupation. It became a surname, then a first name.

Cody
This is said to be an Irish surname meaning "descendant of a helpful person." It has been popular in the United States, where it is also a place name and well known as the surname of the Wild West hero, Buffalo Bill Cody. **Codey** and spellings with "K" have also been recorded.

Coinneach *see* **Kenneth**

Colby
An English place name and surname, now used as a first name in the United States, where it grew steadily in popularity in the early 1990s. The name originally indicated a farmstead owned by a Norseman called Koli. **Colton**, however, comes from a place name meaning "farm by the River Cole."

Cole
An English place name, now gaining popularity as a first name. It means "swarthy," as in "coal." The best-known person with this first name was the composer/lyricist Cole Porter (whose first name was his mother's maiden name).

Colin

This has a similar origin to **Colette**, for it was a French short form of **Nicholas**. In Scotland, it was also interpreted as coming from the Gaelic word *cailean*, meaning "puppy" or "youth."

Conan

From the Irish, meaning "hound, wolf." A famous holder of the name was Arthur Conan Doyle, creator of Sherlock Holmes, but the name is probably best known today from the fictional stories and films.

Conn, Connor, Conny *see* Conor

Conor

From the ancient Irish name **Conchobar** or **Conchobhar** meaning "lover of hounds." It was the name of one of the great kings in Irish heroic stories and has long been a popular name in Ireland. Its popularity has spread around the world, often spelled **Connor**. It can be shortened to **Con** or **Conny** and sometimes **Conn**, which is also a separate name, perhaps meaning "wisdom."

Constantine

The masculine form of Constance comes from the Latin, Constantia for "firm, constant." Three Scottish kings were named Constantine after a Cornish saint who was believed to have converted their ancestors to Christianity in the 6th century. It became popular in England from the 12th to the 17th centuries, and was the origin of the surnames Constantine, Considine, Costain, and Costin. The composer Constant Lambert (1905–51) shows an English form of the name.

Conrad

From the Old German words for "bold counsel." The name is found mostly in Germany, where in the 13th century Duke Conrad was a greatly beloved figure. Objection to his public execution by the conquering Charles of Anjou led to a widespread use of this name in German-speaking states. **Curt** or **Kurt** is a short form used as an independent name, now used rather more frequently than the full form.

Cooper

Becoming more popular in Canada, Cooper is derived from the Old English name for a barrel maker. The short form is **Coop**.

Corbin

Corbin comes from a surname based on the Old French word for "raven." Its spread owes much to the success of the actor Corbin Bernsen.

Corey

This is an Irish surname of unknown meaning, which has come to be used as a first name. It has been popular in the United States for some years. It is also spelled **Cory**.

Cormac

This Irish name is of doubtful meaning, although it is sometimes said to mean "a charioteer." It appears frequently in Irish legend, but through its prevalence in early Irish history and the Irish Church the name was accepted as having a

Christian character in Ireland and so remained in steady use. A variant is **Cormick**.

Cornelius
From the Latin *cornu*, meaning "a horn," also the name of a famous Roman clan. The masculine form was used in Ireland as a substitute for the native **Conchobar** (see **Conor**). Its abbreviated forms are **Corn(e)y** and **Cornie**.

Cosmo
From the Greek *kosmos*, meaning "order." It is the name of one of the two patron saints of Milan and was used by the famous Italian family of Medici in the form **Cosimo** from the 14th century onwards. It was the name of the 3rd Duke of Gordon, who was a friend of Cosimo III, Grand Duke of Tuscany, and the name was introduced into several other Scottish families.

Courtney
An aristocratic surname used as a first name. It comes from **Courtnay**, a French place name, although the name is often interpreted as coming from *court nez*, the French for "short nose." It is currently more used for girls than for boys.

Craig
The place and surname meaning "crag," used as a first name.

Crispin, Crispian
From the Latin *crispus*, meaning "curled." The third-century martyrs Crispinus and Crispinianus were the patron saints of shoemakers. Crispin was popular in Britain in the Middle Ages and has recently enjoyed a revival.

Cruz
The Spanish word for "cross" has always been used for both sexes, and is increasingly popular as a boy's name in the United States.

Curtis
A surname from the French meaning "courteous," used as a first name.

Cuthbert
From the Old English words *cuth* and *beorht*, meaning "famous" and "bright." It was in common use both before and after the Norman Conquest, and was the name of a 7th-century saint who was Bishop of Lindisfarne in Northumbria. It sometimes appeared as **Cudbert** and had the short form **Cuddy**. The name fell out of use just after the Reformation until the 19th century, when it was brought back by the Oxford Movement. It was a slang term for someone who avoided military service during the First World War, and it may be partly due to this usage that the name is not popular today.

Cynan
This is a Welsh name based on the word *cyn*, meaning "chief" or "outstanding." It can also be found spelled **Cynin** or **Cynon**. There are a number of other Welsh names formed from this word, including **Cynyr**, which means "chief hero."

Cyprian
From the Latin *Cyprianus*, meaning "from Cyprus." It was the name of a Christian martyr of the third century.

Cyril

From the Greek *kyrios*, meaning "lord." There were two saints of this name in the 4th and 5th centuries, and it was a 9th-century Saint Cyril who took Christianity to the Slavs, and devised the Russian Cyrillic alphabet. The name was first used in England in the 17th century but did not become common until the 19th century. The name shares the abbreviation **Cy** with **Cyrus**, and has been recorded spelled **Syril**.

Cyrus

A Greek form of the Persian word meaning "sun" or "throne." This is the name of the founder of the Persian Empire in the 6th century B.C., as well as a number of other Persian kings. It was first used in Britain in the 17th century among Puritans, probably in honour of the fact that the Emperor Cyrus allowed the Jews to return to Palestine from their Babylonian captivity. They took it to North America, where the short forms are **Cy** and **Cyro**.

D

Dakota

The American place name is more commonly used for girls, but does appear as a name for boys too.

Dale

The Old English for "valley." At first more common as a girls' name, it is now more frequently used for boys. There are a number of other surnames from place names starting with the same sound, such as **Dalton, Dallas**, and **Dallin**, which may owe their use as boys' names to the popularity of Dale.

Damian, Damien

From the Greek, meaning "tamer." There have been four saints called by this name.

Damon

From the Greek, meaning "to rule" or "guide." In Greek legend, Damon and Pythias were inseparable friends, famous for their willingness to die for each other.

Dan *see* Daniel

Dana

As a boys' name this comes from the surname, the Old English word for a Dane. **Dane** is another form.

Daniel

Daniel, meaning "God has judged," is the Hebrew name of an Old Testament prophet. It was found in England before the Norman Conquest, but only among priests and monks. It became more widespread in the 13th and 14th centuries. It can be found as a version of the Irish **Domhnall** (see **Donald**) and Welsh **Deiniol**, meaning "attractive, charming." Its shortened forms are **Dan** and **Danny**.

Dara

This is an Irish name, a shortened form of Mac Dara "son of the oak," the name of a popular Connemara saint. It is also spelled **Darragh**. Although traditionally a masculine name, it is now also used for girls.

Darcy

Darcy can be either from a

French surname meaning someone from a place called Arcy, hence the form d'Arcy, or an Irish surname meaning "descendant of the dark one."

Darian, Darien *see* **Dorian**

Darius
Darius was the name of the sixth-century B.C. king of the Persians who was defeated by the Athenians at Marathon. The name means "protector."

Darrel(l)
Also spelled **Dar(r)yl**, this is another surname used as a first name. In this case the surname comes from a French village, the village name meaning "courtyard, open space."

Darren
A surname of unknown meaning used as a first name. It seems to have been introduced in the 1950s and become popular in the 1960s. **Darran** is also found.

Darshan
An Indian name from the Sanskrit meaning "to see." Darshan refers to being in the presence of, or being near enough to touch and see with one's own eyes, a holy or revered person. It is thought to bestow spiritual enrichment on the observer.

Dashiell
The American detective novelist Dashiell Hammet (1894–1960), best known for *The Maltese Falcon*, first brought the name to public attention. He was named from his mother's surname. As well as being a noted writer he was something of a hero of the left, having gone to prison rather than testify during McCarthy's anti-Communist witch-hunts. The name has been used quietly ever since and has been used by a number of celebrities, including Cate Blanchett and Alice Cooper.

David
The Hebrew name of the second king of Israel in the Old Testament, meaning "beloved." This name absorbed the Celtic **Daithi**, meaning "nimbleness" (the "th" is pronounced "h"), and became very popular in Wales and Scotland. The patron saint of Wales is a 6th-century David. There were Scottish kings of this name in the 10th and 14th centuries. The name did not appear in England before the Norman Conquest, but it was a common medieval surname in the variant forms **Davy**, **Davit**, and **Deakin**. Short forms are **Dave**, Davy, **Davie**, and in Wales **Dafydd** becomes **Dai** or **Taffy**, the latter being an English nickname for a Welshman. Other forms include **Davide** and **Davi**.

Dean
A surname, meaning "valley," adopted as a first name. It seems to have become popular in the United States first, but has been widely used in the U.K. since the 1960s.

Declan
The name of an early Irish saint associated with Ardmore. It is rising in popularity as a boys' name in Canada.

Dee
This is usually a nickname, given to anyone with a name beginning with the letter "D,"

but is occasionally found as a given name. Compounds such as **Deedee** also occur.

Deepak

An Indian name from the Sanskrit meaning "little lamp." It is one of the descriptive names applied to Kama, god of love. The spelling **Dipak** is also used.

Deiniol *see* **Daniel**

Delbert

This name has been in use since at least the beginning of the 20th century. It is probably formed on the pattern of several surnames such as **Delroy** ("of the king") and **Delmar** ("of the sea"), which are also used as first names, keeping the "Del-" part and adding "-bert" from the many Germanic names that end in this suffix. The short forms **Del** or **Dell** are also used as first names and can be short forms of **Derek** too.

Demetrius

This is an ancient Greek name that means "follower" or "devotee of **Demeter**," the Greek pagan goddess of corn and agriculture,

whose name in turn means "earth mother." It was the name of a highly successful general who died in 286 B.C. In the form **Demetrios**, it is the name of a Greek saint and as **Demitrus** it is found in the Bible. **D(i)mitri** is the form the name takes in Russia, where it has been long established.

Denholm

A place name, meaning "island valley," used as a first name. The similar **Denham**, "home in a valley," is also used.

Denzel, Denzil

In the form **Denzell**, this is an old Cornish surname derived from a place name.

Derek, Derrick

This is from the Old German **Theodoric**, meaning "people's ruler." Variants are **Deryk, Deric**, and the Dutch form **Dirk**, popularized by the actor Dirk Bogarde. Short forms are **Derry, Rick(ie)**, and **Del(l)**.

Dermot

This is the anglicized spelling of **Diarm(a)it** or **Diarm(a)id**,

the Irish name possibly meaning "free from envy," or "free man." The legendary character who bore this name eloped with **Grainne** who was betrothed to **Finn**. Finn pursued the lovers for a long time and finally brought about Dermot's death.

Desmond

From the Irish *Deas-Mumhain*, meaning "(man) of Desmond," an old name for Munster. It was originally used as a surname in Ireland. Later it became a first name and came to England in the late 19th century. **Des** and **Desi, Desy**, or **Dezi** are short forms.

Dev

An Indian name from the Sanskrit meaning "god." Deva is also the term used to address royalty, Brahmins, and priests. Dev becomes **Deb** or **Deo** in different parts of India. **Devdan** means "gift of the gods." The forms **Debdan** and **Deodan** are also used.

Devon

This name appears to be the name of the English county, but

American parents usually stress it on the second syllable. The alternative spelling **Devin** is frequent and forms such as **DaVon** are also found.

Dexter
This is a surname, originally given to a dyer, now used as a first name.

Dezi *see* **Desmond**

Diego
This popular Spanish name is much used in the United States. It is a form of **James**, through the intermediary forms **Tiego** and **Tiago**, from Sant Iago, "Saint James."

Digby
A place and surname, meaning "the settlement by the dike," used as a first name.

Dilip
The name of several kings in the Hindu epics. It probably comes from the Sanskrit words meaning "protecting Delhi." An alternative form of the name is **Duleep**.

Dinsdale
A place and surname used as a first name. It means "settlement surrounded by a moat."

Dirk *see* **Derek**

Dominic
From the Latin *dominicus*, meaning "of the Lord." It probably became more widespread on account of St. Dominic, founder of the Order of Preachers known as the Black Friars early in the 13th century. Until this century it was almost exclusively a Roman Catholic name, but is now widely used. **Dominick** is also found, and the name can be shortened to **Dom** and **Nic**.

Donald
From the Irish **Domhnall** or **Donal(l)** (the second reflecting the pronunciation, with a long "o" as in "doe") meaning "world mighty." It was the name of a number of medieval Irish kings. The name became Donald in Gaelic. Common short forms are **Don** and **Donny**.

Donovan
An Irish surname, meaning "dark brown," used as a first name. It gained popularity as the name of a well-known singer from the 1960s.

Donte
The Italian name **Durrante**, meaning "steadfast," developed the shortened form Donte, and **Dante**, famous as the name of the medieval poet. Donte (pronounced with two syllables) has been much used in the United States in recent years.

Dorian
The ancient Greek people known as Dorians came from Doris in the north but later dominated southern Greece. The best-known group was the Spartans. The word was introduced as a first name in Oscar Wilde's *The Picture of Dorian Gray* (1891). Like so many boys' names, it is now used as a girls' name as well. It is now also spelled **Dor(r)ien**. Forms such as **Darian** and **Darien** can be seen as either a form of this name or a blend of such names as **Darius** and **Darren**.

Dougal, Dugal(d)
From the Irish *dubh ghall*, meaning "dark stranger," a name given to the Danish Vikings. It was a common first name in the Scottish Highlands, and while it still has strong Scottish associations, it now has a more general use.

Douglas
From the Gaelic *dubh glas*, meaning "black stream." It was first a Celtic river name, then the surname of a powerful Scottish family famous for its strength and bravery in fighting, and, from about the late 16th century, a first name for both girls and boys. It is now restricted to boys. **Duggie** and **Doug(ie)** are short forms.

Drew
From the Old German **Drogo**, meaning "to carry" or "to bear," a name that was brought to Britain by the Normans and later became a surname. This surname, which like any other can also be used as a first name, may also come from two other sources: as a short form of

Andrew, probably the most common form of Drew as a first name, and from an old French word for "lover." Parents wishing to use this name may take their choice. It has recently been used occasionally for girls.

Duane, Dwayne
An Irish surname, probably meaning "black," used as a first name. Variants include **DeWayne** or **Du'aine**.

Dudley
Originally a surname from the place name in Worcestershire. Robert Dudley, Earl of Leicester, was the favourite of Queen Elizabeth for many years. Like other aristocratic names it came into general use as a first name in the 19th century. **Dud** is a short form.

Duncan
The Scottish form of the Irish **Donnchadh** (pronounced don-ne-ha, the "h" ideally the sound in Scottish "loch"), meaning "brown." It was the name of two Scottish kings and at one time was almost entirely confined

to Scotland, although this is no longer the case.

Dunstan
From the Old English words *dun*, meaning "hill" and *stan*, meaning "stone." It was the name of a famous 10th-century Archbishop of Canterbury. It appears from time to time before the Reformation, and was revived by the Oxford Movement in the 19th century.

Dustin
Best known from the actor Dustin Hoffman, this name may be from a place name meaning "dusty," or could be a form of **Thurstan**, a Norse name meaning "Thor's stone," i.e., an altar dedicated to the thunder god Thor.

Dwayne *see* **Duane**

Dwight
Originally an English surname, which may go back to the same source as **Denis**. The use of this name as a first name in the United States probably arose from respect for Timothy Dwight,

President of Yale University (1795–1817). U.S. President Dwight D. Eisenhower gave a wider circulation to the name.

Dylan

This is the name of a legendary Welsh hero, son of the sea god, possibly meaning "son of the wave." It was rare outside Wales, but the Welsh poet Dylan Thomas made it more familiar to the general public. The singer Bob Dylan, often referred to by his second name, took his stage name from the poet.

E

Eachan *see* **Hector**

Eamon(n) *see* **Edmund**

Earl

From the title, in Old English meaning "nobleman" or "chief." It has been used as a first name for about a century, mainly in North America. **Erle** is a variant spelling.

Earnest *see* **Ernest**

Ebenezer

From the Hebrew, meaning "stone of help." In the Old Testament it is the name of a stone monument set up by Samuel, in memory of the triumph of the Jews over the Philistine army and in thanks for God's help. It was first used as a first name in the 17th century among the Puritans. It is now used mainly in North America, with the shortened form **Eben**.

Edgar

From the Old English, meaning "fortunate spear." Owing to the popularity of King Edgar, King Alfred's grandson, the name continued in use after the Norman Conquest, but it faded out at the end of the 13th century. It was then used by Shakespeare in *King Lear* and revived with other Old English names by 18th-century writers of fiction. Its popularity in the 19th century probably stems from its use for the hero of Scott's novel *The Bride of Lammermoor*. It is shortened to **Ed(die)**.

Edmund

From the Old English Eadmund,

meaning "happy protection." It was the name of two kings of England and of two saints. **Edmond** is a French form, which was used from the late Middle Ages. **Eamon(n)** is the Irish form. Shortened forms are **Ed(die)** and **Ted(dy)**.

Edward

From the Old English, meaning "fortunate guardian." Edward the Confessor established its popularity in England and ensured its survival after the Norman Conquest. It was further strengthened by the accession of Edward I in 1272, after which there was an Edward on the English throne for over a hundred years. It has remained in use ever since. The short forms **Ned** and **Ted**, together with **Neddy** or **Teddy**, have been used since the 14th century, but **Ed** and **Eddie** are the more common abbreviated forms found today. Other forms include **Édouard, Edoardo**, and **Eduard(o)**.

Edwin

From the Old English meaning "fortunate friend." Edwin was

the first Christian king of Northumbria, in the 7th century. The name survived the Norman Conquest and became popular in the 18th century.

Egbert

From the Old English meaning "bright sword." This was the name of the first king of a united England and of a 7th-century Northumbrian saint. It enjoyed some degree of popularity in the 19th century, but is now rarely found.

Eli

From the Hebrew, meaning "elevated." It was the name of the high priest in the Old Testament who looked after the prophet Samuel when he was given to the Temple as a baby. It was used as a first name in the 17th century. Eli is also a shortened form of **Elias**, and **Elihu**, which means "God is the Lord."

Elias, Elijah

From the Hebrew, meaning "Jehovah is God." Both forms were very common in the Middle Ages, along with the short forms **Elia, Ellis**, and

Eliot(t), or **Elliot** which became surnames, and are now used as first names. **Elisha**, "god is," is often thought of as a variant of this name.

Eliot(t) *see* Elias

Elmer

This is a surname that comes from both the Old English Ethelmer, "noble and famous" and Ethelward, "noble guard." It became a first name in the United States in honour of two brothers with the surname Elmer who were prominent in the American War of Independence. **Aylmer** is another form of the name.

Elton

A surname, probably meaning "Ella's settlement," used as a first name. The singer Elton John, effectively began its first-name use.

Elvis

A name that was almost unknown until given world fame by Elvis Presley. It is probably a version of the name of the Irish saint **Alby** or

Ailbhe (a name that in Irish can be used for either sex and that is pronounced "alva"), which is found in Wales in the form St. Elvis. Although Presley was not the first member of his family to bear the name, modern uses come from him.

Emanuel

From the Hebrew, meaning "God with us." It was the name given to the promised Messiah by the prophet Isaiah in the Old Testament. It was introduced as a first name by the Greeks in the form **Manuel**. This is also the Spanish form. **Manny** is used as a short form.

Emlyn

A common Welsh name, possibly derived from the Latin *Aemilius*, but which is more likely to be from a Welsh place-name.

Enoch

From the Hebrew, meaning "trained, skilled" or "dedicated." It was the name of an Old Testament patriarch and was adopted in the 17th century by the Puritans. It is now rare, although a well-known modern example is the politician Enoch Powell (1912–98).

Eoan, Eoghan *see* **Eugene, Evan**

Eoin *see* **Eugene, John**

Ephraim
From the Hebrew, meaning "fruitful," an Old Testament name that was revived in the 17th century by the Puritans. **Eph** is a short form.

Eric
From Scandinavia; the second syllable means "ruler," the first is doubtful but may mean "ever." The name was brought to Britain by the Danes about the 9th century. Possibly Dean Farrar's book *Eric or Little by Little* was responsible for its popularity with 19th-century parents. Eric is sometimes spelled with a "k" instead of "c." Short forms are **Rick(y)** or **Rickie**.

Ernest
From the Old German, meaning "vigour" or "earnestness." It is sometimes spelled **Earnest**. It was introduced by the Hanoverians in the late 18th century and was common in the 19th century. Oscar Wilde's play *The Importance of Being Earnest* (1899) increased its popularity. Shortened forms are **Ern** and **Ernie**.

Errol
Probably a surname used as a first name, although it is not certain whether the surname is a development of **Eral**, a medieval form of **Harold**, or whether it is a variant of **Earl**.

Esmond
From the Old English *east* and *mund*, meaning "grace" and "protection." This name was never common and fell out of use in the 14th century. Its modern use probably dates from Thackeray's novel *The History of Henry Esmond* (1852). It is nowadays rather rare.

Ethan
This is a Hebrew name meaning "firmness," which occurs several times in the Old Testament. Ethan is the most popular name for Canadian boys.

Eugene
From the Greek, meaning "well-born." The Celtic names **Eoghan** (pronounced "eoh-un") or **Eoan** ("ohn"), and their Scottish form **Ewan, Ewen**, or **Euan** have traditionally been interpreted as forms of Eugene, although sometimes confused with **Eoin**, a form of John. However, some would claim that they are a native Celtic name meaning "born of the yew."

Eustace
From the Greek, meaning "rich in corn" and hence "fruitful" generally. Because of the two saints Eustachius, this name was in use in Britain before the Norman Conquest and was popular from the 12th to the 16th centuries.

Evan
This is a Welsh form of **John**, the anglicized form of the Welsh spelled variously **I(e)fan** or **Ieuan**. In Scotland it is also an anglicized form of the Irish **Eoghan** (see **Eugene**).

Everard
From the Old German

for "brave boar." The name was brought to Britain by the Normans and was fairly common in England in the 12th and 13th centuries and has been used occasionally ever since. In Scotland, it became **Ewart**. The surname **Everett** comes from Everard and is also used as a first name.

Ewan, Ewen *see* **Eugene**

Ezekiel

From the Hebrew, meaning "may God strengthen." It is the name of an Old Testament prophet and was used from the 17th century in Britain. It is still current in North America and is beginning to re-appear in Britain. **Zeke** is the usual short form.

Ezra

From the Hebrew, meaning "help," Ezra is the name of the author of one of the books of the Old Testament. It was adopted as a first name by the Puritans in the 17th century. The name is no longer common, but a well-known example from the 20th century is the American poet Ezra Pound.

F

Fabian

From the Latin family name Fabianus, possibly meaning "bean-grower." There was a pope of this name and a St. Fabian in the 3rd century, and there is a record of the name's use by a 13th-century sub-prior of St. Albans. There is little other evidence of it until the 16th century, but its use as a surname shows that it was known previously. The Roman general **Fabius**, known as the "delayer" for his tactics of awaiting the right moment to achieve his ends, was the inspiration for the socialist Fabian Society, founded in 1884. The Spanish form is **Fabio**.

Faysal

This Arabic name indicates one who decides between right and wrong, a decision-maker or a judge. This has been a royal name in modern times, borne by kings of Iraq and Saudi Arabia. The name is also found as **Faisal** and **Feisal**.

Feargus *see* **Fergus**

Feisal *see* **Faysal**

Ferdinand

From the Old German for "brave journey." Never a popular name in Germany, it was common in Spain, especially in the forms **Fernando** and **Hernando**. Short forms are **Ferd(ie)** and occasionally **Nandy**.

Fergal

This is an Irish name meaning "valorous." The surnames **Farrell** and **Farall**, which come from it, reflect the Irish pronunciation.

Fergus

Fergus or **Feargus** comes from the Irish words for "man" and "strength." **Fergie** is a short form.

Fingal

This is the name given to the Scottish legendary hero (the equivalent of the Irish **Finn**), who figures in the 18th-century Ossianic poetry. He was a mighty warrior, a defender of the underdog, and righter of wrongs. Fingal's Cave is named after him. The name means "blond stranger" and was a term used of the Vikings.

Finlay

This is a Scottish name meaning "fair hero." It is also found as **Finley** and **Findlay**.

Finn

Finn, **Fynn**, or **Fionn** is an Irish name meaning "white, fair" or can also be used as a short form of **Finbar** (see **Barry**). Finn Mac Coul (Finn mac Cumaill) is a great hero of Irish mythology and folklore. He was chosen to lead the Fenians (an elite armed troop) because of his truthfulness, wisdom, and generosity, but he was also of great physical strength. However, all these qualities were not enough to prevent Finn's fiancée **Grainne** from running away with his companion, **Dermot**. **Finnian** or **Finian** comes from the same root, and was the name of a sixth-century British saint.

Fintan

From the same root as **Finn**, Fintan means either "white ancient one" or "white fire."

Flann

This is an Irish name meaning "red" that would have started life as a nickname. **Flannan** started as a short form of this.

Forbes

Forbes is a Scottish surname now used as a first name. It comes from a place near Aberdeen, meaning "field, district."

Forrest

This is the word "forest" in its surname form. It was originally used as a first name in the southern U.S. in the late 19th century, when it was fashionable to name boys after Confederate generals—in this case, General Nathan Bedford Forrest. It is sometimes found as **Forest**.

Francis

From the Latin, meaning "little Frenchman." The name became popular in Europe in the 13th century because of St. Francis of Assisi. The Italian word *Francesco* was the saint's nickname, his Christian name being Giovanni, the Italian form of **John**. It was given to him in his worldly youth because of his love of fashionable French things. It was first used in Britain in the 15th century. **Fran** is a short form along with **Frank(ie)**. Frank can be used as an independent name. The German form is **Franz**. Other forms include **François, Franco**, and **Frans**.

Frank, Frankie *see* **Francis**

Franklin

From a medieval English word meaning "free." A franklin was a man who owned land in his own right but was not a noble. The name came into use in America in honour of Benjamin Franklin (1706–90), statesman, writer, and inventor. A famous holder of the name was Franklin D. Roosevelt (1882–1945), 32nd U.S. President.

Fraser, Frazer

A Scottish surname of unknown meaning, used as a first name. **Frasier** is another form of the name.

Fred, Freddie, Freddy *see* **Alfred, Frederick**

Frederick

From the Old German, meaning "peaceful ruler." It is also found with such spellings as **Frederic** and **Frederik**. Common abbreviations are **Fred(die)** and **Freddy**, also used as independent names.

G

Gabriel

From Hebrew, containing the elements "God," "man," and "strength," and possibly implying the phrase "strong man of God" or "God is my strength." In St. Luke's Gospel, Gabriel is the Archangel who announces to Mary that she is to bear the baby Jesus. Use as a first name used to be restricted to Ireland, where it can be shortened to **Gay**, but it is increasingly popular in Canada.

Ganesh

A title of the Hindu god **Shiva**, and the name of his elder son, derived from the Sanskrit for "lord of the hosts." It is customary to appease Ganesh at the beginning of Hindu ceremonies.

Gareth

From the Welsh, meaning "gentle." This name was used for one of King Arthur's knights by the 15th-century writer Malory in his *Morte d'Arthur*, and later by Alfred Tennyson, the 19th-century poet, in his version of Malory's story, "Gareth and Lynnette." It was due to the latter that the name was revived in the 20th century. **Garth** and **Gar(r)y** can be used as short forms.

Garfield

A surname meaning "spearfield" in Old English, used as a first name, probably after J. A. Garfield (1831–81), 20th president of the United States. The cricketer Sir Garfield (**Gary**) Sobers is a well-known holder of the name and also shows its short form.

Garret, Garrett *see* Gerard

Garth, Garry *see* Gareth

Gary

While this can be used as a short form of both **Gareth** and **Garfield**, its use as an independent name owes much to the film star Gary Cooper (1901–61). He was born Frank James Cooper and chose his stage name from the American town of Gary. **Garry** is also found, reflecting the usual pronunciation, although Gary Cooper pronounced his name to rhyme with "airy."

Gaspar, Gaspard *see* Jasper

Gaston

A French name, originally spelled **Gascon** and meaning a man from the region of Gascony. It is a common French first name which has been used occasionally in Britain.

Gavin

The name of Sir **Gawain**, King Arthur's famous nephew, was **Gauvin** in Old French, and from France was adopted in Scotland as Gavin.

Geoffrey, Jeffrey

From the Old German *Gaufrid*, the second half of which means "peace," but the meaning of the first half is unclear. Geoffrey or Jeffrey was popular between the 12th and 15th centuries in England resulting in many surnames e.g. Jeffries, Jeeves, Jepson. It fell from favour from the 15th until the 19th century, when it was revived. **Geoff** and **Jeff** are common abbreviations.

George

From the Greek for "farmer." The famous St. George is said to have been a Roman soldier who was martyred in Palestine in A.D. 303. In early Christian art many saints were represented as trampling on dragons, as a symbol of good conquering evil. This may be an explanation of how the legend of St. George and the dragon originated. In the Middle Ages, St. George was closely associated with knighthood and chivalry, and after 1349, when Edward III of England founded the Order of the Garter and put it under St. George's protection, he became the patron saint of England. Despite this, the name was not much used until the Hanoverian succession in 1714 brought a line of four Georges to the throne. It is currently popular with parents. **Geordie** is a Scottish and North Country short form, which is used as a nickname for Tynesiders. Other forms include **Georg, Georges, Giorgio, Jorge**, and **Jerzy**.

Geraint

This is a very old Welsh name, a variant form of the Latin Gerontius, which is in turn derived from a Greek word meaning "old." The 19th-century poet Alfred Tennyson used the old Welsh story of Geraint and Enid in his *Idylls of the King*, and it was from this that the name's modern use has stemmed. The real-life hero on which the fictional character is based died in battle about A.D. 530.

Gerald

From the Old German, meaning "spear rule." It was used in England from the 11th to the 12th century and was probably introduced by the Normans. The name flourished in Ireland due to the influence of the Fitzgerald ("Sons of Gerald") family, the powerful rulers of Kildare. It was probably from Ireland that the name returned to England in the late 19th century. Shortened forms are **Ger(ry)** and **Jerry**.

Gerard

From the Old German, meaning "spear-brave." It was brought to Britain by Norman settlers and was very common in the Middle Ages. The surnames Gerrard and Garret(t) are derived from it, and these were the most common medieval pronunciations of the name, although it is not always possible to distinguish between forms of Gerard and **Gerald**. **Ger, Gerry**, and **Jerry** are its short forms.

Gervais, Gervase

From the Old German, meaning "spear vassal" or "armour bearer." The name was first used among English churchmen of the 12th-century in honour of the 1st-century martyr St. Gervase. It spread to the general public, giving rise to the surname **Jarvis**. Gervais is the French spelling.

Gideon

From the Hebrew, now generally thought to mean "having a stump for a hand," although the traditional translation was "a hewer." It is the name of an Old Testament Israelite leader who put the forces of the Midianites to flight. The name was adopted at the Reformation and was a favourite among the Puritans, who took it to North America where it is still in use.

Gilbert

From the Old German, meaning "bright hostage." The Normans brought the name to England and it was common in medieval times, when St. Gilbert of Sempringham (died 1189) was much admired. Shortened forms are **Gib, Gilly**, and **Bert(ie)**.

Giles

According to legend, St. Giles was an Athenian who took his name, Aegidius, from the goatskin that he wore. He left Greece in order to escape the fame that his miracles had brought him and became a hermit in France. There the name became **Gilles**. The name is first recorded in England in the 12th century, but it was not popular. It has been suggested that this may be because of St. Giles's association with beggars and cripples, of whom he is the patron saint. However, recent years have seen an increase in its popularity. It is sometimes spelled **Gyles**.

Glen(n), Glyn(n)

These are both forms of Celtic words for "a valley." In the last 40 years they have become popular names throughout the English-speaking world.

Godfrey

From the Old German, meaning "God's peace." It was brought to Britain by the Normans.

Gopal

This Indian name can be taken to mean "a devotee of Krishna." It derives from the Sanskrit words meaning "cow-protector," indicating a cowherd, but the name was applied to Krishna in medieval devotional texts. In southern India the name is sometimes given as **Gopalkrishna**.

Gordon

Originally a Scottish place name from which the local lords took their name, it later became the name of a large and famous clan. It was rarely used as a first name until 1885, when the dramatic death of General Gordon at Khartoum gave the name immense popularity.

Govind

This Indian name is similar to **Gopal**, deriving from the Sanskrit words that mean "cow-finding," a reference to a cowherd, but the 12th-century Song of Govind associated the name firmly with Krishna. The form **Gobind** is also found.

Graham

Like **Gordon**, this was originally a place name that developed into a family name, particularly on the Scottish/English border. At first restricted to this area, it gradually came into general use as a first name. **Graeme** and **Grahame** are also found.

Grant

A surname from the French for "tall, large" used as a first name. It seems to have come to Britain from the United States, where its use may have been connected with the popularity of General Ulysses Grant (1822–85), the 18th president.

Gregory

From the Greek, meaning "watchman." The name first came to Britain through St. Gregory the Great, the pope who sent St. Augustine to England. It was in common use from the Norman Conquest, when most Latin names were introduced, until the Reformation when, because of its association with the papacy, it fell out of favour. **Gregour** was the usual medieval form, which is still found as **Gregor** in Scotland, and hence the surname MacGregor. The most common shortened form is **Greg**.

Griffin

From the Latin for "hooked nose," Griffin is also the name of a mythical beast usually half-eagle, half-lion. Variants include **Griffen, Gryffen, Gryffin**, and **Gryphon**.

Griffith

From the Welsh name **Gruffud** or **Gruffydd**, meaning "lord" or "strong warrior." It has always been fairly popular in Wales and was the name of several Welsh princes. **Griff** is a short form.

Guy

From the Old German Wido, the meaning of which is uncertain, possibly "wide" or "wood." Wido became **Guido** in Latin records and Guy was the French form introduced to Britain by the Normans. Medieval clergy identified the name with the Latin *Vitus* meaning "lively," hence the disease St. Vitus' Dance is known in France as *la danse de Saint Guy*. St. Vitus was a Sicilian martyr who was invoked for the cure of nervous ailments. Guy fell out of use after Guy Fawkes' gunpowder plot of 1605. It was revived in the 19th century with the help of Walter Scott's novel, *Guy Mannering*.

Gwyn

From the Welsh, meaning "white" or "blessed." This name has been anglicized as **Wyn(ne)**. Its use is mainly confined to the Welsh. **Gwynfor** or **Wynfor** is Gwyn with the word for "great" added to the end.

H

Hadrian *see* **Adrian**

Hal *see* **Henry**

Hamish

The anglicized form of *Seumas* (see **Seamas**), the Gaelic form of **James**. This name became popular in the second half of the 19th century and is still used, mostly in Scotland.

Hamzah

The name of the Prophet Muhammad's uncle, probably From the Arabic, for "lion." It is also spelled **Hamza**.

Hani

The masculine form of **Hana** From the Arabic for "bliss"

or "happiness." Hani meaning "joyful, delighted" comes from the same root.

Hank *see* Henry

Hari

This Indian name occurs frequently in classic Hindu texts and is often applied to Vishnu or Krishna. It derives from a Sanskrit word that indicates a yellowy-brown colour.

Harley

Harley (sometimes **Harleigh, Harli(e)**, or **Harlee**, particularly for girls) is an English aristocratic surname, but its use as a first name probably owes much to the glamour of the Harley Davidson motorbike. Use of the similar-sounding **Harlan**, although found in the 19th century, is increasing.

Harold

From the Old Norse, meaning "army-power"; **Harald** is the original Scandinavian form. It was used in the Middle Ages, but went out of fashion until it became popular again in the

18th century. It is not much used at the moment. It shares the abbreviation **Harry** with the name **Henry**.

Haroun *see* Aaron

Harrison *see* Henry

Harvey

From the French, meaning "battle-worthy." It was common until the 14th century and had a slight revival in the 19th. Its modern use as a first name may be due in part to its widespread use as a surname.

Hasan

One of the most popular Muslim names, derived From the Arabic, for "handsome" or "good." Al-Hasan was the Prophet's grandson. Similar names derived from the same Arabic word are **Hasin, Hassan, Husayn, Husni, Hussain**, and **Hussein**.

Hayden

This appears to be a form of **Haydn**, a name used in honour of the Austrian composer Franz Josef Haydn. As a first name, it

is also spelled **Haydon**. The surname Haydn in its turn derives from the Old German word for "heathen." Once restricted to boys and used mainly in Wales, it has been much used in the United States for some years as a name for both sexes, and its popularity is spreading.

Hector

From the Greek, meaning "hold fast." It was the name of the Trojan hero who was killed by the Greek Achilles and took quite a strong hold in Scotland, where it was used as an equivalent for the quite unconnected Gaelic name **Eachan**, which means "a horseman."

Heena *see* Hina

Henry

From the Old German, meaning "home ruler." The Latin Henricus became **Henri** in France. **Harry**, reflecting the French pronunciation, was the original English form of Henri, used until the 17th century and often abbreviated to **Hal**.

Today, Harry is used as the short form of Henry and increasingly as a name in its own right. **Hank** is a short form more common in the United States. **Harrison**, "son of Harry," has become well known through the actor Harrison Ford. Its use as a first name is influenced by the fact that it was the surname of two U.S. presidents, William (1773–1841) and his grandson, Benjamin Harrison (1833–1901).

Herbert
From the Old German for "bright army." It seldom appeared before the Norman Conquest, after which it became quite common. It was revived at the start of the 19th century and became quite popular again towards the century's end, due in part to the fashion for using aristocratic surnames as first names. **Herb(ie)** and **Bert(ie)** are short forms.

Herman
A Germanic name meaning "soldier." The French form of the name is **Armand**, and the Old English form **Armin** or **Arminel**, which can also be used as a feminine name.

Hilary, Hillary
From the Latin, meaning "cheerful." The original Latin forms **Hilaria** and **Hilarius** are very occasionally found, and the writer **Hilaire** Belloc used the French form. It was once quite usual as a boys' name but is now rarely used except for girls.

Hiram
From the Hebrew,, meaning "brother of the high one," and the name of an Old Testament king of Tyre. It was a favourite 17th-century name and was taken at that time to North America where it still flourishes.

Homer
The name of the famous ancient Greek author, known as "the father of literature" and author of the *Iliad* and *Odyssey*. It means "pledge, hostage." It was once very popular in the United States but then became deeply unfashionable. Despite being so strongly associated with the television show *The Simpsons*, it is now creeping back into fashion, having been recently chosen as a baby name by a number of stars, including Richard Gere and Anne Heche.

Horace, Horatio
From the Roman clan named Horatius borne by the Latin poet Horace. Horatio seems to have come from Italy to England in the 16th century and has been kept alive by the fame of Nelson, although Horace is the form more likely to be found today.

Howard
Like other aristocratic family names, this was adopted as a first name by the general public in the 19th century. The origin of the surname is disputed. It may be from the Old German meaning "heart-protection" or the French for "worker with a hoe," or even from the medieval official the "hogwarden," who superintended the pigs of a district. **Howie** can be used as a short form.

Hubert
From the Old German, meaning "bright mind." This name was popular in the Middle Ages,

probably as a result of the fame of St. Hubert of Liège, the patron saint of huntsmen. It was not much used from the 16th to the 18th centuries, after which it was revived to some extent, but it has since gone out of fashion again. **Bert** is the short form.

Hugh, Hugo

From the Old German, meaning "heart" or "soul." It appears frequently in the Domesday Book. It was further strengthened by the popularity of St. Hugh, Bishop of Lincoln in the 14th century. Hugo is the Latin form. **Hew** and **Huw** are Welsh forms of the name; **Hughie** and **Huey** are used as short forms.

Humphrey

From the Old German, meaning "peace." This name was originally spelled with an "f," the "ph" coming in when it was equated with the name of the obscure Egyptian saint, Onuphrios, in order to Christianize it.

Hunter

The Old English word used as a first name, this is another surname that has come to be used as a girls' name and boys' name and is increasing in popularity in Canada.

Husayn, Husni, Hussain, Hussein see Hasan

Huw see Hugh

Hywel

A Welsh name, meaning "eminent."

I

Ibrahim

The Arabic form of **Abraham**.

Idris

This is a Welsh name meaning "fiery lord." In Welsh legend, Idris the Giant was an astronomer and magician, who had his observatory on Cader Idris.

Iefan, Ieuan, Ifan see Evan

Ifor see Ivor

Ignatius

Ignatius or **Inigo** is a Latin name, derived originally from a Greek name of obscure origin, possibly meaning "fiery." It took root mainly in Russia and Spain and was carried further afield by the Jesuits whose founder was Iñigo López de Recalde, better known as St. Ignatius of Loyola.

Ike see Isaac

Inderjit

An Indian name from the Sanskrit meaning "conqueror of the god Indra." The spelling **Indrajeet** is also used.

Ira

A name from the Old Testament meaning "watchful." The name was used by the Puritans, who took it over to America where it is now much more common than in Britain. The song-writer Ira Gershwin was a famous bearer of the name.

Irving

Irving and **Irvine** are Scottish place names that were used first as surnames and then as first names.

Isaac

From the Hebrew, meaning "laughter." It was the name given by **Sarah**, wife of **Abraham**, to the son born in her old age, traditionally because she laughed when she was told that she would conceive. The name appears in Britain in the Middle Ages and came to be regarded as a specifically Jewish name. It came into general use in the 16th and 17th centuries, when it was spelled with a "z" as in **Izaak** Walton, the author of *The Compleat Angler*. In the mid-17th century the "s" spelling came into fashion, as in Sir Isaac Newton, the great scientist. **Zak** or **Ike** are used as short forms.

Isaiah

From the Hebrew, meaning "Jehovah is salvation," and the name of the great Old Testament prophet. It was first used by the 17th-century Puritans.

Ishmael *see* Ismail

Ismail

This is the Arabic form of **Ishmael**. Arabs are sometimes known as Ismailites, "descendants of Ismail."

Ivan

The Russian form of **John**.

Ivo

From the Old German, meaning "yew." It was common in Brittany in the form **Yves** and was brought to Britain at the time of the Norman Conquest. It has been used occasionally since.

Ivor, Ifor

Ifor is a Welsh name that means "lord," and Ivor is the anglicized spelling. It was originally **Ior** but was probably influenced by **Yves**.

J

Jack

Originally the short form of **John**, this is now a very popular name in its own right. In the Middle Ages **Jan** evolved from John, and then developed the short form **Jankin**, later shortened to Jack. **Jock** is a traditionally Scottish form. Jack shares the short form **Jake**, now a name in its own right, with **Jacob**. **Jackson**, a surname meaning "son of Jack," is also found as a first name.

Jacob

The meaning of this Hebrew name is uncertain. In the Old Testament, it was the name of Isaac's younger son, who tricked his brother Esau out of his inheritance. This explains the popular interpretation of the name as "he supplanted." There were two Latin forms, Jacobus and Jacomus. Jacob came from the former and **James** from the latter. Jacob has survived as a first name because translators of the Bible kept this form for the Old Testament Patriarch, although they called the two New Testament apostles James. **Jake** is an abbreviation shared with **Jack** and now a popular choice as a name in its own right. Jacob has long been a popular choice in Canada, especially in New Brunswick, where it is the number one boys' name.

Jadon *see* **Jay**

Ja(i)mal
An Arabic name meaning "beautiful." The name is popular in the masculine and feminine form in the Arab world and in the United States, where it is also spelled **Jamil** and **Jamel**.

Jalal
An Arabic name that means "glory" or "greatness." A similar name is **Jalil**, meaning "honoured" or "revered." The names are also found as **Galal** and **Galil**.

James
This name has the same root as **Jacob**. It became established in Britain in the 12th century when pilgrims started to visit the shrine of St. James at Compostella in Spain. At that time the name was more common in Scotland. With the accession of James VI as the first king of both Scotland and England in 1603, the name became more popular in England. It was unfashionable in the 19th century but is now probably the most used boys' name. The short forms are **Jim(my)** and **Jamie**. The Irish form is **Seamas** and the Scottish **Hamish**.

Jamie
This was originally a Scottish short form of **James**, but it has since spread throughout the English-speaking world and become popular in its own right. Since at least the 1950s it has also been used as a girls' name, particularly in the United States.

Jared
A biblical name meaning "to descend" and connected with **Jordan**. It was used in the past by the Puritans but had become very rare until the mid-1960s when it became popular in the United States and Australia. It is also found in the forms **Jarred** and **Jar(r)od**, although some of these forms may be influenced by similar surnames. **Jaron** is also used.

Jarvis *see* **Gervais**

Jason
This name was adopted in the 17th century when biblical names became popular, because it is the traditional name for the author of Ecclesiasticus. It has been a popular name in recent years, when parents probably associated it more with the Greek hero Jason, who won the Golden Fleece. A short form, **Jace**, is sometimes used.

Jasper
Gaspar or **Caspar** (**Kaspar**) is the traditional name of one of the three kings or wise men of the Christmas story. It may mean "keeper" or "bringer of treasure." **Gaspard** is the French form which became Jasper in English.

Jay
As an Indian name, Jay comes from a Sanskrit word for "victory" and can also be spelled **Jai**. Otherwise it comes from a short form of any name beginning with a "J," or from a surname, originally a nickname for someone who chattered like the bird. It is sometimes spelled **Jaye**. There are a number of elaborations such as **Jac(e)y**

and its variants **Jaden, Jadon**, or **Jayden**.

Jed
A short form of the biblical name **Jedidiah**, which means "beloved of the Lord."

Jeff, Jeffrey *see* **Geoffrey**

Jem *see* **Jeremy**

Jeremy
From the Hebrew,, meaning "may Jehovah exalt." **Jeremiah** was the Old Testament prophet who wrote the Book of Lamentations. The traditional English form is Jeremy, which appears from the 13th century onwards, although in the 17th century, the two forms **Jeremias** and **Jeremiah** were more common. **Jerry** is a short form, which is shared with **Gerald**, and **Jem** and **Jez** are also used. **Jerrell** is a recent variant.

Jerome
From the Greek Hieronymos, meaning "holy name." This name is pre-Christian in origin but soon became popular with the early Church. St. Jerome translated the Bible into Latin in the 4th century and was an important religious influence in the Middle Ages. The name appears in England in the 12th century as Geronimus, which gradually gave way to the French form Jerome.

Jerry *see* **Gerald, Gerard, Jeremy**

Jesse
From the Hebrew, meaning "God exists," and in the Old Testament, the name of King David's father. It was adopted in the 17th century by the Puritans who took it to America where it has been commoner than in the U.K. Jesse James, the outlaw, and the politician Jesse Jackson are probably the best known examples. **Jess** is a short form. The name is sometimes spelled **Jessie**.

Jethro
From the Hebrew, meaning "abundance" or "excellence." In the Bible it is the name of Moses' father-in-law. It has been used as a first name since the Reformation.

Jim, Jimmy *see* **James**

Jo(e) *see* **Joseph**

Job
From the Hebrew, meaning "hated" or "persecuted." **Jobie** or **Job(e)y** are short forms of the name.

Jocelyn, Jo(s)celin
These names seem to be derived from several different names that have come together over a period of time to form one name. The most important source is probably from the Latin, meaning "cheerful, sportive." There is also a possibility that it is derived from an Old German name meaning "little Goth." A further derivation has been traced from the name **Josse**, "champion," a form of **Jodoc**, the name of an early Breton saint which also gave us **Joyce**. Jocelyn is the usual form for boys, although the name is now rarely masculine.

Jock *see* **Jack**

Joel
From the Hebrew, meaning "Jehovah is God" and the name of one of the minor Old Testament prophets. It was adopted by the Puritans, like many other biblical names, after the Reformation.

John
From the Hebrew, meaning "the Lord is gracious." Its earliest form in Europe was the Latin **Johannes**, which was shortened to **Johan** and **Jon** before becoming John. However, in France the name became **Jean**, and both forms of the name were introduced into the British Isles, which resulted in two groups of names developing. Thus the Johannes-form, where the "J" was pronounced as an "I," gives us the Gaelic **Ian** and **Iain**, **Ieuan** and **Evan** in Welsh, and **Eoin** ("oh-n") in Irish, while the Jean-form gives **Sean** or **Shane** in Irish and **Sion** in Welsh (see also **Ivan**, **Jack**).

Jolyon *see* **Julian**

Jon *see* **John, Jonathan**

Jonah, Jonas
From the Hebrew, meaning "dove." The Old Testament story of Jonah and the whale was very popular in the Middle Ages and because of this the name was common. It continued to be used occasionally until the 19th century, when it became rare probably because of the association of the name with bad luck. Jonas is the Greek form of the name and is now the more common of the two.

Jonathan
A Hebrew name meaning "the Lord has given." In the Old Testament, Jonathan was the son of King Saul and it was his great friendship with David that gave rise to the expression "David and Jonathan" to describe two close friends. The name came into use at the time of the Reformation, and it is popular today. The short form, **Jon**, is often used as a separate name and the name is sometimes spelled **Jonathon**.

Jordan
Jordan was quite a popular name in the Middle Ages when it was given to children baptized with water from the River Jordan brought back by pilgrims from the Holy Land. It has recently been revived as a first name and is currently a popular choice for both girls and boys. The name of the river means "to descend, flow" and comes from the same word that gives us the name **Jared**.

Jos *see* **Joseph, Josiah**

Joseph
From the Hebrew, meaning "the Lord added" (i.e., to the family). In the Old Testament it was the name of Jacob and Rachel's elder son who was sold into slavery in Egypt. In the New Testament, there are Joseph, the husband of Mary, and Joseph of Arimathea, who is believed to have buried Jesus and whom legend connects with Glastonbury and the Holy Grail. The name was not often used until the 17th century, when Old Testament names were adopted by the Puritans

and Joseph became a favourite.
Joe and **Jo** are common
abbreviations and much used as
names in their own right, and
Jos is also found.

Joshua

From the Hebrew, meaning
"the Lord saves." In the Old
Testament Joshua succeeded
Moses and finally led the
Israelites to the Promised Land.
Josh is a short form. **Jesus** is
the Greek form of the name,
popular as a first name with
Spanish speakers. Other forms
include **Josua, Giosué, Josué**,
and **Jozue**.

Josiah

From the Hebrew, meaning
"may the Lord heal." **Josias** is
an alternative form of the name,
and **Jos** a short form.

Joyce

In the Middle Ages when this
name was most common it
usually had the form **Josse**. A
7th-century saint from Brittany,
who also gave us the name
Jocelyn, was the cause of the
name's popularity. One of its
French variants was **Joisse**, and

it was from this that the name's
final form was derived. Joyce
was little used after the Middle
Ages until the general revival
of medieval names in the 19th
century. It is now very rare as a
name for men.

Jude

The Hebrew form of this name
is **Yehudi**, which was rendered
as **Judah** in the Authorized
Version of the Old Testament.
Judas Iscariot bore the Greek
form, and because of him Jude
was not used by Christians until
the Reformation. The name was
brought back to public attention
by Thomas Hardy's novel *Jude
the Obscure* and the Beatles' song
"Hey Jude." It means "praise."

Julian

Julianus was a Roman family
name that meant "connected
with the family of **Julius**." Julius
probably comes from the same
root that gives the Latin word
for "god," but in Roman times
the family believed that it
referred to the soft growth of
hair that forms a boy's first sign
of a beard, as this was the state
of development that a founding

member of the clan had reached
when he first distinguished
himself in battle. The most
famous of numerous saints of
this name was St. Julian the
Hospitaller, who devoted himself
to helping poor travellers. The
name came to Britain in the
Latin form, which was anglicized
as **Julyan**, and in the North of
England as **Jolyon**. **Jules**, the
French form of Julius, is also
used as a short form of Julian.

Junayd

An Arabic name meaning
"warrior." It also occurs as
Junaid.

Justin

From the Latin, meaning "just."
An uncommon name until the
later 20th century when it came
back into fashion.

K

Kacey *see* **Casey**

Kadin

An invented name or possibly
from the Arabic, meaning

"friend." The use of Kadin and its variants **Caiden, Cayden, Ka(e)den, Kaiden, Kayden** has grown dramatically in both Canada and the United States.

Kai

The Welsh names **Cai, Kai**, or **Kay** (well known as the name of Sir Kay, King Arthur's foster-brother) are derived from **Caius**, a Roman first name, meaning "rejoice."

Kamal

In India this name derives from the Sanskrit, where it means "pale red," but it is specifically associated with the lotus flower. Kamala, the feminine form, is one of the goddess Lakshmi's names in classical Hindu texts, where it is also a name of **Shiva**'s wife. In the Arab world Kamal is from an Arabic word that means "perfection."

Kamil

From the Arabic, meaning "complete" or "perfect."

Kashif

An Arabic name that means "discoverer."

Kaspar *see* Jasper

Keanu

The actor Keanu Reeves has made this Hawaiian name, meaning "cool breeze over the mountains," widely known.

Keegan

This name is of Gaelic origin. Its meaning is "small flame" or "little fierce one." **Kagan, Kagen**, and **Kegan** are variant forms.

Keenan

Kean, whose name means "ancient," was a leader of the victorious Irish troops against the Vikings in the great battle of Clontarf in 1014. Kean, also found as **Cian, Kian, Keen**, and **Keane**, developed the short form Keenan (**Keenen, Keenon**), well known as a surname, and now increasingly used once more as a first name.

Keiran *see* Kieran

Keith

This is a first name from Scotland that has spread throughout the world. It was originally a surname that was taken from the Scottish place name, probably from the Gaelic meaning "wood" or "windy place."

Kelly

A modern first name that has rapidly become very popular. It is an Irish surname, which means "warlike," used as a first name. At first mainly a boy's name, it is now more usual for girls. **Kelley** is also found.

Kelsey

The surname, which in turn comes from an Old English name meaning "ship-victory," used as a first name. Despite the success of the American actor Kelsey Grammer, it is more common for girls than boys.

Kelvin

This is the name of the river that flows through Glasgow, used as a first name. The river's name possibly means "narrow water."

Kendall

The surname, which can have various sources, used as a first name. Another surname, the similar-sounding **Kendrick**, is also used.

Kennedy

Use of this Irish surname is spreading from the United States to the rest of the English-speaking world. Its choice no doubt owes much to the respect and glamour surrounding the assassinated president John F. Kennedy (1917–63).

Kenneth

This is the English form of the Gaelic **Coinneach**, meaning "handsome," and equivalent to modern Welsh **Cenydd**. It is basically a Scottish name that became popular when Kenneth MacAlpine became first King of Scotland in the ninth century, uniting the Picts and the Scottish. From there it gradually spread over Britain. It is often shortened to **Ken(ny)**.

Kent

This is the surname taken from the English county used as a first name. It first became popular in the United States. The county name is an ancient one, meaning "border" from its position on the coast. The similar-sounding **Kenton** is from a different surname, a common place name meaning "royal manor," and now used as a first name.

Kentigern *see* **Mungo**

Kerr

An ancient Scottish aristocratic surname, now sometimes used as a first name, and pronounced as in "care." The surname originally referred to someone who lived in wet scrubland, although it is traditionally associated with a Gaelic term for "left-handed."

Kerry

The Irish county name used as a given name. It is a modern name, apparently first used in Australia usually for boys, but is now in general use, mainly for girls. It is also found as **Kerri**.

Kester *see* **Christopher**

Ketan

A Hindu name meaning "home."

Kevin

From the Irish, meaning "handsome birth." The name was very popular in Ireland on account of St. Kevin, a sixth-century hermit and abbot of Glendalough. It is now widely used around the world.

Kiefer

The actor Donald Sutherland named his son Kiefer after the writer-director Warren Kiefer, who had been instrumental in furthering his career. The success of Kiefer Sutherland as an actor in his turn brought the name into use.

Kieran

This is a form of the Irish name **Ciaran**, meaning "dark-haired." It was the name of 26 Irish saints and in the last two or three decades it has become increasingly popular. It is sometimes spelled **Cieran, Keiran**, or **Kieron**.

Kim

Probably from Old English *cynebeald*, meaning "royally bold," developing through the surname Kimball. Rudyard Kipling's hero in the novel *Kim* (1901) used a shortened form of his true name,

Kimball O'Hara, showing the use of the surname as a first name.

Kiran
An Indian name deriving from the Sanskrit for "ray of light, sunbeam."

Kirk
A Scandinavian name for "church," brought to prominence as a first name by the actor Kirk Douglas. It would originally have been the surname of someone who was connected with the church or lived near one.

Krishna
The name of a popular Hindu god, a partial incarnation of Vishnu, and deriving from a Sanskrit word for "black." In northern India it occurs as **Kishen**; other regional forms include **Kishan, Krishan**, and **Kistna**.

Kumar
The boys' name derives from the Sanskrit for "boy," but it is usually taken to mean "prince."

Kurt *see* **Conrad**

Kushal
An Indian name meaning "clever."

Kyle
This is a Scottish place and surname meaning "a strip of land."

L

Lachlan
From Gaelic **Lachlann** or **Lochlann**. Primarily a Highland name, it was introduced as a term for Viking settlers there, but was taken by Scottish emigrants to Australia and Canada where it flourished. Short forms are **Lachie** and **Lochie**.

Lal
An Indian name and endearment. As a Hindi term of address, Lal means "darling boy," though it derives from a Sanskrit word meaning "caress." The name has been in use since the Middle Ages.

Lancelot
A name of disputed meaning,

possibly from the Old French for "servant." It can also be spelled **Launcelot** and was used in Britain from the 13th century due to the popularity of Sir Lancelot, the knight without equal, in stories of King Arthur. The short form **Lance** is more common today.

Landon
Old English meaning "long hill," Landon has quickly become a popular first name in the United States.

Laurence, Lawrence
From the Latin, meaning "of Laurentium," a town that took its name from the laurel plant, symbol of victory. It became common in the 12th century. St. Laurence, the 3rd-century Archdeacon of Rome, was a favourite medieval saint. The name was popular in Ireland because of St. Laurence O'Toole, a 12th-century Archbishop of Dublin, whose real name was **Lorcan** (Irish for "fierce"). **Larrie** or **Larry** is the usual abbreviation in England, while **Laurie** or **Lawrie** is used in Scotland. **Loren** is a form of

the name used for both boys and girls.

Lee

From the various forms of the surname meaning "meadow." It may have spread from the southern U.S. and probably owes its popularity there to the Confederate general Robert E. Lee (1807–70).

Leo

From the Latin for "lion." Six emperors of Constantinople and thirteen popes were named Leo. **Leon** is the French form.

Leon *see* **Leo, Lionel**

Leonard

From the Old German, meaning "brave as a lion." The 6th-century St. Leonhard was a Frankish nobleman who was converted to Christianity. He became a hermit and devoted his life to helping prisoners, of whom he is the patron saint. His popularity made the name common in medieval England and France and it was revived in the 19th century. The usual shortened forms are **Len(nie)**

and **Lenny**. It is sometimes spelled **Lennard**.

Leopold

From the Old German words meaning "people" and "bold." This name came to Britain through Queen Victoria's uncle, King Leopold of Belgium, after whom she named her fourth son. It has not been used much in the 20th century.

Leroy

A surname from the Old French meaning "the king," which was probably given to royal servants.

Levi, Levon

This is a Hebrew name, meaning "associated." It is occasionally given to girls and has been elaborated into Levon.

Lewis, Louis

From the Old German, Chlodowig, meaning "famous warrior," was latinized into Ludovicus (source of **Ludovic**). This became **Clovis** in Old French, which was the name of the founder of the French monarchy. His name later became Louis, the name of

18 other French kings. The Normans brought the name to England, where it became Lewis. Use of the French form, Louis, is comparatively recent. Other forms include **Ludwig, Luigi,** and **Luis**. Short forms are **Lou(ie)** and **Lew(ie)**.

Lex *see* **Alexander**

Liam

A variant of **William**, Liam is a Top 10 boys' name in Canada and is 5 times more popular in Canada than the United States.

Lindsey

From the Scottish surname meaning "pool island." Together with its other forms, **Lindsay, Linsey,** and **Linsay**, this name is used for both boys and girls. The form Lindsay tends to be the more usual one for boys. At the moment all forms of the name are used much more frequently for girls than for boys.

Lionel

This name means "young lion." A French diminutive of **Leon**, it thus derives from the same root as **Leo**. It was the name of one of King Arthur's knights and was given by Edward III of England to his third son, later Duke of Clarence. The name was very popular in the Middle Ages and survived into more recent times, particularly in the north of England, where it has come back into general, though infrequent, use.

Lloyd

A Welsh name meaning "grey." **Floyd** is a variant form that has arisen due to the difficulty of pronouncing the Welsh "ll," and that appears to come from the United States.

Logan

This Scottish place name, meaning "little hollow," became a surname, which led in turn to its use in Scotland as a first name. Since 1990 the name has become one of the Top 50 names for boys in the United States and is becoming more popular in Canada too.

Lorne

The masculine form of **Lorna**, a name created by R. D. Blackmore for the heroine of his novel *Lorna Doone*, published in 1869. In the book she was the lost daughter of the Marquis of Lorne, an ancient Scottish first name sometimes used for boys.

Lucas

A variant of **Luke**, Greek name, latinized as Lucas, meaning "a man of Lucania" in southern Italy. St. Luke the Evangelist is the patron saint of doctors and also of painters, and the name was often given by a craftsman to his son. The name appeared in the 12th century as Lucas, but a century later it was well established in the English form, Luke.

Lucius

From the Latin word *lux*, meaning "light." The masculine form Lucius and its variants **Lucien** and **Lucian** are much less common than the feminine forms.

Luther

From the Old German, meaning "people's warrior." The modern use of Luther as a first name is entirely due to Martin Luther, the German leader of the Reformation, and to the American civil rights campaigner Dr. Martin Luther King, Jr., named after him.

M

Madoc, Madog

A Welsh name meaning "fortunate." It is rarely used outside Wales (see also **Marmaduke**).

Magnus

This is a Latin adjective meaning "great." The spread of this name was due to the Emperor Charlemagne, Carolus Magnus in Latin. Some of his admirers took Magnus for a personal name, and among those who christened their sons after him was St. Olaf of Norway. The name spread from Scandinavia to Shetland and Ireland. From Shetland the name became well established in Scotland. In Ireland it became **Manus**, hence the common Irish surname McManus.

Mahomed, Mahommed *see* **Mohammed**

Malcolm
From the Gaelic *mael Colum*, "follower of St. Columba." This was a very popular Scottish name, borne by four kings of Scotland. It was used very occasionally in medieval England, but only became common in the 20th century. Short forms are **Mal** and **Col(u)m** (see **Callum**).

Malik
From the Arabic for "king." The black activist and leader of the Nation of Islam, otherwise known as Malcolm X, took the name El-Hajj Malik El-Shabazz, which has led to the use of this name in the United States.

Marius
From a Roman family name that was adopted as a first name during the Renaissance. It has never been common in the U.K., although the Spanish and Italian form **Mario** is much used throughout Europe and in the United States. The name is probably derived from Mars, the Roman god of war, and so related to **Mark**.

Mark, Markus
These names are probably derived from Mars, the Roman god of war, and were used as Roman family and personal names. Although it occurs from the Middle Ages in Britain, Mark, the modern form of the name, has only become common since the 1950s. The French forms are **Marc** and **Marcel**, the latter derived from the Latin, diminutive of the name, **Marcellus**.

Marlon
A name of unknown origin, brought into use through the fame of the actor Marlon Brando (b. 1924). **Marlin** and **Marlo** have also been used for both sexes in the United States.

Marmaduke
From the Irish *mael Maedoc*, meaning "servant of Madoc." The name is mainly confined to Yorkshire, where Celtic civilization lingered after the Norse invasions of northern England. **Duke** is sometimes used as an abbreviation, but in America its use usually derives from the title.

Martin
From the Latin *Martinus*, a diminutive of Martius, meaning "of Mars," the Roman god of war. According to popular legend, St. Martin was a 4th-century soldier who cut his cloak in half to share it with a beggar one winter's night; he later became Bishop of Tours in France. Martin has been used since the 12th century. **Martyn** is the Welsh spelling, and **Marty** a short form.

Marvin *see* **Mervyn**

Mason
The surname, which comes from the occupation, used as a first name.

Mathis
The German counterpart of the name **Matthias**. From the Hebrew, meaning "gift of God."

Matthew
From the Hebrew, meaning "gift of God," and the name of one of the Evangelists. The name was particularly popular from the 12th to the 14th centuries. After the Reformation the Greek form, **Matthias**, was adopted.

In the Bible it is used for the name of the apostle chosen to succeed Judas Iscariot. The usual short form is **Matt**.

Maurice, Morris

From the Latin *Mauritius*, meaning "a Moor." The spread of the name was due to St. Maurice, a third-century martyr in Switzerland, after whom the town of St. Moritz was named. The Normans brought the name to England as **Meurisse**, which was soon anglicized to Morris. The more modern French form, Maurice, has now to a large extent replaced the English form. There is a Welsh equivalent, **Meurig**, which occurs from the fifth century. Short forms are **Morrie** and **Maurie**.

Maximilian

Maximus in Latin means "greatest." Two third-century saints bore its derivative, Maximilian, yet it is popularly thought to have been invented by German Emperor Frederick III, combining the last names of Quintus Fabius Maximus and Scipio Aemilianus, two Roman generals. His son, later Emperor Maximilian I, was a huntsman and fighter, and the name became very popular in German-speaking countries. It has recently become more popular in Britain and North America, particularly in its short form, **Max**. **Macsen** is the Welsh form of **Maximus**. **Maxime** is used in France for both sexes, but in Britain this, or **Maxine**, tends to be used for girls, keeping **Maxim**, also a Russian form of the name, for boys. Max can also be a short form of **Maxwell**, from a Scottish surname and place name meaning "Mac's well."

Melvin, Melvyn

Various theories have been put forward as the source of this name. It seems likely that it comes from a surname, which can come from a variety of sources, several of them Scottish. **Mel** is the short form.

Meredith

From the surname from the ancient Welsh **Maredudd** or **Meredydd**, "great chief." It can be spelled **Meridith** and has **Merry** as a short form. Use of the name for girls was a 20th-century innovation.

Merle

This is the French for "blackbird" originally derived from Latin. It was adopted as a first name in the 19th century. It became well known as the name of the film actress Merle Oberon (1911–79). As a boys' name it is less common.

Mervyn

From the Welsh name **Myrddin** ("sea fort"), which is the true form of **Merlin**, the name of King Arthur's legendary magician. It is also spelled **Mervin**. Merlin has recently come to be used for girls. **Marvin**, also a common surname, is probably a form of Mervyn, although some would dispute this.

Micah

A variant form of **Michael**. Micah, the name of a minor prophet in the Old Testament, was used in the 17th century among Puritans and can now be found used for both sexes, sometimes as **Mica** or **Myka**.

Michael

From the Hebrew, meaning "who is like the Lord?" In the Bible Michael was one of the seven archangels and their leader in battle, and he therefore became the patron saint of soldiers. Michael has short forms **Mike** or **Mick(y)**. The surname **Mitchell**, derived from Michael, is also used as a boy's name, with the short form **Mitch**. **Mis(c)ha** is in Russia a short form of Michael, but because of the "a" ending is sometimes thought of as a girls' name. The Spanish form is **Miguel**. Mike is the most common name for NHL players.

Milan

In Europe this name usually derives from the Czech for "grace." As an Indian name the derivation is from a word meaning "union."

Miles

An old name of unknown meaning. The Normans brought to Britain the forms Miles and **Milo**. It has also been used to transliterate the Irish **Maol Mhuire** ("devotee of Mary") and its Gaelic form **Mael Moire**. A variant spelling is **Myles**.

Milton

From the Old English surname derived from a place name meaning "mill-enclosure." Initial use as a first name may have been due to the poet John Milton (1608–74). It has been particularly popular in the U.S.

Mohammed

The name of the Prophet of Islam, which comes from the word "praise." It is probably the most popular Islamic name and is spelled in various ways, **Muham(m)ad, Mahom(m)ed,** and **Moham(m)ad** being the common variants.

Mohan

In early times a name of **Krishna**'s; from the Sanskrit for "attractive, bewitching."

Montagu(e), Montgomery

The founder of the ancient noble family of Montague was Drogo de Montacute, William the Conqueror's companion who received estates in Somerset. He took his name from Mont Aigu, a "pointed hill" in Normandy. Montagu(e)'s first-name use dates from the 19th century, when many aristocratic surnames, e.g., **Cecil, Howard, Dudley, Mortimer, Percy,** were adopted by the public. It shares **Monty** as a short form with Montgomery, from the Old French meaning "mountain of the powerful one."

Morgan

In its earliest form, **Morcant**, this name meant "sea-bright," but it later absorbed another name, **Morien**, meaning "sea-born." Its earliest celebrated male bearer was the first recorded British heretic, who was known as Pelagius, a Greek translation of the name. It was almost always a male name until the 20th century but now is more common for girls.

Mortimer

An aristocratic surname adopted as a first name in the 19th century. The surname was derived from a French place name meaning "dead sea." The Mortimer family connect it with the Dead Sea in Palestine, where their ancestors fought in crusading times. The short form **Morty** was also used independently in Ireland as a form of the Irish name **Murtaugh** or **Murty** ("skilled sailor"). The short form **Mort** is also used.

Moses

The meaning of this name is uncertain and it is possibly Egyptian rather than Hebrew. It became common among Jews after their return from captivity in Babylon. In Britain it first appears in the Domesday Book as **Moyses**, which became **Moyse** or **Moss** in general use. The present form, Moses, which was not used until the Reformation, is the form used in the Authorized Version of the Bible. **Moosa** or **Musa** is the Arabic form of the name.

Muhammad *see* **Mohammed**

Muhsin

A popular name in the Arab world, derived from an Arabic word meaning "charitable" or "benevolent."

Mungo

This name was originally a term of affection given to St. **Kentigern** by his followers, and in Gaelic means "beloved." Kentigern was a 6th-century Bishop of Glasgow and is generally known as St. Mungo. The name is confined to Scotland and the most famous bearer was Mungo Park, the 18th-century explorer of the River Niger.

Munir

From the Arabic for "brilliant" or "illuminating." The name has the alternative form **Muneer**.

Murdo, Murdoch

This Scottish name is derived from the Gaelic meaning "seaman," and is equivalent to the Irish **Murtaugh** (see **Mortimer**).

Murray

From the Gaelic meaning "sea." The Scottish clan of Murray, or Moray, probably took its name from the Moray Firth in the northeast of Scotland. James Stewart, Earl of Moray, was half-brother of Mary, Queen of

Scots, and he acted as Regent when she was imprisoned in Lochleven Castle. His fame gave rise to the use of **Moray** as a first name in Scotland, but today the form Murray is more common, with **Murry** a variant.

Murtaugh, Murty *see* Mortimer

Musa *see* Moses

Mustafa

From the Arabic, meaning "chosen." It is one of the names used to describe the Prophet Muhammad.

Myca *see* Micah

Myron

The Greek word for "fragrant." It was the name of a famous sculptor in the fifth-century B.C.

N

Nadim

This Arabic name refers to a "drinking companion" or "friend." It is also spelled **Nadeem**.

Naim

From the Arabic, word meaning "comfortable," "contented," or "tranquil." Some families prefer to spell the name **Naeem**.

Nathan, Nathaniel

Nathan comes from the Hebrew, meaning "gift." It was the name of the prophet in the Old Testament who condemned King David for killing Uriah by putting him in the front line of battle, so that David could marry his widow, **Bathsheba**. The name shares the short form **Nat** with Nathaniel, meaning "gift of God." It was the name of the apostle who was better known by his second name, **Bartholomew**. Both names are increasingly popular.

Nayan

An Indian name derived from the Sanskrit for "eye."

Neal, Neil *see* **Nigel**

Neville

From the French surname Neuville, meaning "new town." It was introduced into England at the time of the Norman Conquest, when the Neville family, which came over with William the Conqueror, was very powerful. Their influence continued, but the name was not adopted as a first name until the 17th century. **Nevil** is a variant spelling.

Niall *see* **Nigel**

Nicholas

From the Greek, meaning "victory of the people." The name was common in the Middle Ages as a result of the popularity of St. Nicholas, the patron saint of children and sailors. The usual form then was **Nicol**. In Latin the name is *Nicholaus* and the use of **Claus** in "Santa Claus" is taken from **Klaus**, the modern German development of the Latin. **Nick(o)** and **Nicky** are the short forms.

Nigel, Niall, Neal, Neil

The origin of these names goes back to an Irish name, the meaning of which could be "champion," "cloud," or "passionate." Niall is the Irish spelling of the name, but it early on developed different spellings. When medieval scribes wanted to write the name in Latin documents, they gave it the form *Nigellus*, as if it were a name that came from the Latin, *niger* meaning "black"; and when interest was strong in all things medieval in the 19th century, this Latin form was adopted as Nigel.

Nelson

Nelson is an old surname meaning "Neal's son."

Nikhil

An Indian name derived from the Sanskrit for "entire," "complete."

Nikita

Nikita was originally a Russian, masculine name, from the Greek meaning "unconquered" and adopted by Russians in honour of a second-century pope. However, in many languages it looks like a feminine name, and after its use for a woman in the successful 1990 French film *La Femme Nikita* and the subsequent American television series based on it, it has come to be used as a girls' name. Nikita or **Nikhita** is also an Indian name used for both sexes, from the Sanskrit for "the earth."

Ninian
The name of a fifth-century saint who converted the Picts in the south of Scotland to Christianity. It is mainly found in Scotland.

Noah
A Hebrew name meaning "rest" has been rare in the past, but its use is now increasing in Canada and the United States.

Nolan
Best known from the former major league baseball pitcher, Nolan Ryan. A common surname, it derives from the Gaelic word meaning "champion" or "famous."

Norman
From the Old English for "Northman," used first of all for the Vikings, and then for the descendants of the Viking settlers in France who were known as "Normans." It was

popular in Scotland, and for a while was considered a purely Scottish name, being used as a substitute for the Gaelic **Tormod** ("protected by Thor"), itself originally a Viking name. **Norm** and **Norrie** are short forms.

O

Oberon *see* **Aubrey**

Octavius
A Roman family name derived from the Latin, meaning "eighth." It was also used as a given name for an eighth child in the 19th century, but now that such large families are rare it is used without regard to its original sense. **Octavian** is an alternative form. The short forms **Tavia(n)** and **Tavius** are sometimes used independently.

Odysseus *see* **Ulysses**

Oengus *see* **Angus**

Oisin *see* **Ossian**

Olaf *see* **Oliver**

Oliver
In Old French legend Oliver was one of Charlemagne's greatest knights. Since these knights were of Frankish origin—that is to say of Germanic ancestry—their names are likely to be from Old German. Thus it is thought that this name goes back to the same source as the Scandinavian **Olaf** ("heir of his ancestors"). However, users probably associate it with the more obvious source of the olive tree, symbol of peace. Variants include **Ol(lie)** and **Olivier**.

Omar
A popular name from the Arabic for "flourishing, long life." It was the name of the Prophet Muhammad's lifetime companion and supporter. Another form of the name is **Umar**. **Omari** is the Kiswahili form.

Orlando
This is the Italian form of **Roland**. Italian names were

fashionable in the 16th century and Shakespeare used this one in his play *As You Like It* (1600).

Orville
A name invented by the 18th-century novelist Fanny Burney for the hero of her novel *Evelina*. It is fairly rare in Britain. A famous American example was Orville Wright, aviation pioneer and brother of **Wilbur**.

Osbert
From the Old English, meaning "bright god." It shares **Oz** and **Ozzy** as short forms with **Oswald**.

Oscar
In the 1760s James Macpherson gave this name to **Ossian**'s warrior son in his poems on the legendary past of Scotland, and Napoleon's enthusiasm for the Ossianic legend caused him to give the name Oscar to his godson, later King of Sweden. The Scandinavian spelling is **Oskar**. It probably means "deer-lover."

Ossian
In legend Ossian ("little deer")

is the son of **Finn** and father of **Oscar**. It is spelled **Oisin** in Irish, while **Osheen** reflects the Irish pronunciation, although it is usually pronounced as it is spelled in England.

Oswald
From the Old English, meaning "god power." Oswald, King of Northumbria in the 7th century, was killed fighting the Welsh at Oswestry. He was later canonized, and the place is said to take its name from him. A second St. Oswald helped St. Dunstan with his church reforms in the 10th century. Because of these two saints, the name was popular in the Middle Ages and has never entirely died out. **Oz(zie)** and **Ozzy** are short forms shared with **Osbert**.

Owen, Owain
This is one of the most popular of all Welsh names, but its origin is uncertain. It may well have come from the Greek name **Eugene** meaning "well-born," or from Welsh *oen*, meaning "lamb." There are many bearers of the name in Welsh history and

legend, but the best known is Owen Glendower, who fought for Welsh independence in the 15th century.

Oz, Ozzie, Ozzy *see* **Osbert, Oswald**

P

Paddy, Padraig *see* **Patrick**

Padma
This Indian name, usually identified with the goddess Sri or Lakshmi, derives from a Sanskrit word meaning "lotus." In some parts of India Padma and **Padman** are used as boys' names.

Pascal
A French name meaning "Easter," which has come into general use since the 1960s.

Patrick
From the Latin *patricius*, meaning "nobleman." St. Patrick adopted this name at his ordination. He was born in Britain in the late fourth century,

captured by pirates when still a boy and sold as a slave in Ireland. Although he escaped, he wished to convert the Irish to Christianity, so after training as a missionary in France, he returned to devote his life to this cause. **Pat** and **Paddy** are short forms, and **Padraig** the Irish form. Other forms include **Patrice, Patrizio, Patricio,** and **Patryk**.

Paul

From the Latin *paulus*, meaning "small." The New Testament tells how **Saul** of Tarsus adopted this name after his conversion to Christianity. The name was not common until the 17th century. It was often coupled with the name **Peter**, as the saints Peter and Paul share the same feast day.

Payton *see* **Peyton**

Percy, Percival

Percy is an English aristocratic family name, ultimately from a village in Normandy. It became popular in the 19th century, partly due to the fame of the Romantic poet Percy Bysshe Shelley (1792–1822). It is also a short form of Percival (**Perceval**), the name, in the medieval story, of one of King Arthur's knights, although as a surname it also comes from a village in Normandy. Both names can be shortened to **Perce**; and Percival can become **Val** as well.

Peregrine

From the Latin *peregrinus*, meaning "stranger" or "traveller" and hence "pilgrim." There was a seventh-century saint of this name who was a hermit near Modena in Italy. **Perry** is used as a short form.

Perry

This name sometimes occurs as an abbreviation of **Peregrine**, but it is also a surname used as a first name. It was the surname of two 19th-century American admirals, one of whom inflicted a defeat on the British while the other led the expedition that opened up Japan to the West. The singer Perry Como, who helped spread the popularity of the name, was born **Pierino**, a short form of **Peter**.

Peter

From the Greek *petras*, meaning "rock." Cephas is the Aramaic equivalent that Jesus gave as a nickname to Simon bar Jonah, to symbolize steadfastness in faith. Peter was chief of the Apostles and became the first Bishop of Rome. He was a favourite saint of the medieval church and his name was very popular throughout Christendom. In England the name is first recorded in the Domesday Book in the Latin form, Petrus. The Normans brought over the French form, **Piers** (or **Pierce**), which was usual until the 14th century, when Peter became predominant, although Piers is now quite fashionable once again. The name was unpopular after the Reformation because of its association with the papacy and did not return to fashion until 1904, when James Barrie's *Peter Pan* was published. A short form is **Pete**. Other forms include **Pierre, Pietr(o)**, and **Pedro**.

Peyton

An Old English place name meaning "a warrior's home." Also spelled **Payton**.

Philip
From the Greek, meaning "lover of horses." It was common in the Middle Ages on account of Philip the Apostle. However, in Elizabeth I's reign Philip of Spain was the arch enemy of England, and the name suffered accordingly. It was revived in the 19th century. **Phil** is now the most usual short form, although **Pip** and **Flip** are sometimes used. **Phillip** is a variant spelling reflecting the form usually found in surnames.

Poojan
This Hindi name, which can also be spelled **Pujan**, means "worship." **Poojit** is also found as **Pujit**, meaning "worshipped."

Pratik
A Hindi name that means "a symbol."

Priya
An Indian name from the Sanskrit for "beloved."

Punit
A Hindi name that means "pure."

Q

Qasim
The name of a son of the Prophet Muhammad, this comes From the Arabic, and refers to a "distributor," one who distributes food and money among the people.

Quentin, Quintin
From the Latin for "fifth," originally a name for a fifth son. Quentin was the French form that the Normans introduced to England. It became obsolete after the Middle Ages except in Scotland, although it revived in the 19th century, possibly due to Walter Scott's historical romance *Quentin Durward* (1823). **Quinton** and **Quinten** are other forms of the name.

Quincy
A surname taken from a French place name. Its use in the United States may have been due to the prominent New England family of that name in colonial times. John Quincy Adams (1767–1848), the sixth president, may have received his middle name in honour of this family, or it may have been taken from Quincy, Massachusetts, where he was born. It can also be found as **Quincey**.

Quinn
Quinn is an old Irish family name, literally meaning "descendant of Conn" (see **Conor**), but used to indicate "chief, leader." It has recently come into use for both sexes.

R

Radhakrishna
The masculine form of **Radha**, the name of the cowherd loved by Krishna. It derives from the Sanskrit for "success." Radhakrishna is a blend of this and **Krishna**, and is meant to symbolize the male and female nature of the supreme god. In southern India it appears as **Radhakrishnan**.

Rafe *see* **Ralph**

Rahim
From the Arabic, meaning

"merciful" and "compassionate." The fuller form of the male name is AbdurRahim "servant of the Merciful," a reference to one of the attributes of Allah. The spelling **Raheem** is also found.

Raja

An Arabic name that means "hope."

Rajan

An Indian name derived from the Sanskrit word for "king." Similar names include **Rajesh** and **Rajendra**.

Rajnish

This Indian name derives from the Sanskrit words meaning "ruler of the night," the reference being to the moon. **Rajneesh** is a variant spelling of the name.

Ralph

From the Old Norse words meaning "counsel" and "wolf." In its earlier form, **Radulf**, this name was fairly common in England before the Norman Conquest, and it was reinforced by French use. The medieval spellings were **Ralf** and **Rauf**, which were pronounced with the same vowel sound as the word "ray." **Rafe** was the common form in the 17th century and Ralph appears in the 18th century. The current usual pronunciation with a short "a" and pronouncing the "l" is 20th-century practice. **Raoul** is the French form of the name, and **Raul** the Spanish.

Rama

From the Sanskrit for "pleasing." As the seventh incarnation of Vishnu, Rama is widely worshipped in India. Rama's full name is **Ramachandra**, or **Ramachander** in southern India.

Ranald *see* Ronald

Randolph

From the Old English Randwulf, meaning "shield wolf," which in the Middle Ages became **Ranulf** and **Randal(l)**. The short form, **Randy (Randi)**, has been used as a name in its own right.

Raphael

This is the name of an archangel, meaning "God heals" in Hebrew. It is often found in the Spanish spelling **Rafael** in the United States. Use is currently increasing.

Raqib

A Muslim name from an Arabic word meaning "guardian" or "supervisor," especially in religious matters.

Rashad

This Arabic name means "integrity" or "maturity."

Rauf, Raul, Raoul *see* Ralph

Ravi

The Indian name of the sun god, from the Sanskrit for "sun." **Ravindra** is another name based on the same word.

Raymond

From the Old German, meaning "counsel protection." The Normans brought the name to Britain and it was particularly popular in crusading times. Two 13th-century saints bore the name. One of them spent much of his life rescuing Spaniards captured by the Moors. **Redmond** or **Redmund** is a form of the name that developed in Ireland. The short form, **Ray**, is sometimes given independently.

Reginald
From the Old English Regenweald, meaning "power force." It was not a common Anglo-Saxon name but was reinforced at the time of the Norman Conquest by the French equivalent **Reinald** or **Reynaud**, and developed into **Reynold** or **Reynard**. It can be abbreviated to **Reg(gie)** or **Rex** (see also **Ronald**).

Reilley *see* **Riley**

René
The French name derived from the Latin *renatus*, meaning "reborn." The Latin form was sometimes used by Puritans in the 17th century, and the French form has been used in Britain in the 20th century.

Reuben
From the Hebrew, meaning "behold a son," it appears in the Bible as the name of a son of Jacob, the founder of one of the tribes of Israel. The form **Ruben** is also found.

Rex
This is the Latin for "king," which has been used as a first name only in recent times. It is also found as an abbreviation of **Reginald**.

Reynard, Renaud, Reynold, *see* **Reginald**

Richard
This name first appears in Anglo-Saxon as Ricehard meaning "strong ruler," which was later developed into Ricard. It was the Normans who spread the present form of the name, the softer, French Richard. The short form **Dick** appears as early as the 13th century, and this is still very common, though **Rich(ie), Dickie, Rick(ie), Ricky**, and **Dickon** have been used at various times.

Rick, Rickie, Ricky *see* **Derek, Eric, Richard**

Ridley
An Old English place name meaning "red meadow."

Riley
From the Gaelic meaning "courageous," it is also found as **Rylee, Ryleigh**, and **Ryley**.

Rio
From the Spanish word for "river," and is also the short form of the glamorous Brazilian city of Rio de Janeiro. In the United States **River**, as in the late River Phoenix (1970–93), is more usual.

Rishi
An Indian name that means "sage" or "wise man."

Robert
This name is derived from the Old German meaning "famous and bright." Although there was an equivalent Anglo-Saxon name, it was the French form that took hold in Britain after the Norman Conquest. King Robert the Bruce popularized the name in Scotland where it has the local short forms **Rab** and **Rabbie. Rob(bie), Bob(bie)**, or **Bobby** and **Bert** are used in England. **Robin** or **Robyn**, a French short form of Robert, is now popular in its own right (see also **Rupert**).

Robin *see* **Robert**

Rocco

This is a name that has become fashionable since it was chosen by the singer Madonna for her son. It is the Italian form of the name of the 14th-century saint, patron of the sick from his work with plague victims, called St. **Roch**. It has also been anglicized to **Rock**, a source of the name **Rocky**. It means "rest."

Roderick

From the Old German, meaning "famous rule." The Goths took the name to Spain where it became Rodrigo, and it was established there at least as early as the eighth century. In Britain the name is most common in Scotland where it was first used to transliterate the Gaelic name **Ruairi**. In Wales it is used as an English form of **Rhodri**, meaning "crowned ruler" or **Rhydderch** ("reddish-brown"). Short forms are **Rod, Roddy**, and **Rory**.

Rodney

This means "reed island" and was originally a surname. It was not used as a first name until Admiral George Rodney gave it heroic associations in the 18th century. Short forms are **Rod** and **Roddy**.

Roger

Hrothgar, meaning "famous spear," was an Anglo-Saxon form of this name. It became famous as the name of a legendary king, but it was the Normans who gave us the present form, which was derived from Old German. Roger was a favourite name in the Middle Ages, but from the 16th to the 19th centuries it was thought of as a peasant name and consequently fell from esteem. The ancient short form **Hodge**, once a name for a farm labourer, has been replaced by **Ro(d)ge**.

Rohan

This name comes from a Sanskrit word that can mean either "ascending" or "medicine," although some like to interpret the meaning as "sandalwood." In Sri Lanka it is the name of a sacred mountain, also known as Adam's Peak, which has on its summit a mark like a footprint which features, with different interpretations, in the legends of all three of the island's great religions—Muslim, Hindu, and Buddhist.

Roland

From the Old German *Hrodland*, meaning "famous land." Roland was the most famous of Charlemagne's warriors, and the Normans brought the name to England. **Rowland** is both the medieval spelling and the form of the surname that comes from this name. They are shortened to **Roly** or **Rowley**. **Orlando** is the Italian version of the name.

Rolf

From the Old German, meaning "famous wolf." **Rollo** is a Latin form and Rollo the Ganger ("Walker") was a 9th-century Norwegian exile who, with his followers, founded the Norman race. Rolf developed in Normandy and came to Britain at the time of the Norman Conquest. It was soon absorbed into **Ralph** but revived in the late 19th century.

Romeo
From a name meaning "pilgrim to Rome," it is most widely recognized as the hero of Shakespeare's *Romeo and Juliet*. This name was recently brought to public attention when the Beckhams chose it for their second son.

Ronak
This Indian name is from a Sanskrit word meaning "radiance, embellishment."

Ronald
Ronald and **Ranald** are Scottish equivalents of **Reynald** and **Reginald**, but they are from the Norse (Viking) not the Old English forms. Ranald is still almost exclusively Scottish, but Ronald is now widespread. A short form commonly used is **Ron(nie)**.

Ronan
An Irish and Scottish name meaning "little seal," borne by a number of early saints.

Rory, Rorie
From the Irish and Gaelic

Ruairi, meaning "red-haired." The name became popular in Ireland due to the fame of the 12th-century King Rory O'Connor. It is also widely used in the Scottish Highlands and is sometimes found in England as an abbreviation of **Roderick**. It can also be spelled **Ruari** and **Ruaridh**.

Roshan
A name from the Persian for "shining" or "famous," used by many in India.

Ross
From the Gaelic for "of the peninsula," and the name of a Scottish clan. Its use as a first name has spread throughout the English-speaking world.

Rowan
From the Irish **Ruadhan**, meaning "little red-(haired) one." It was the name of an Irish saint. Once used exclusively for boys, it is now also found as a girls' name.

Roy
From the Gaelic *ruadh*, meaning

"red." The famous Highlander Robert Macgregor, who was involved in the Jacobite Rising of 1715, was commonly known as Rob Roy because of his red hair. Walter Scott's novel about him may have contributed to the name's popularity.

Ruadhan *see* **Rowan**

Ruairi, Ruari, Ruaridh *see* **Roderick, Rory**

Ruben *see* **Reuben**

Rudolph
From the Old German Hrodulf, meaning "famous wolf," the same name that gives us **Rolf**. **Rudolf** is the Modern German form of the name. The spread of this name was undoubtedly helped by the widespread adoration of Rudolf Valentino (1895–1926), the American film star. Another American, the singer **Rudy** Vallee (1901–86), made the short form, found in Germany as **Rudi**, well known.

Rufus
This is a Latin word meaning

"red-haired." William Rufus was the second son of William the Conqueror, and became King William II of England. It gained popularity as a given name during the 19th century.

Rupak
An Indian name from a Sanskrit word meaning "beautiful." Other names based on the same word are **Rupesh**, **Rupchand** ("as beautiful as the moon"), and **Rupinder** ("of the greatest beauty").

Rupert
This name has the same origin as **Robert** and means "bright fame." In Germany it became **Rupprecht**, and Rupert is an English form of this. Prince Rupert of the Rhine was the nephew of Charles I and a brilliant general. He came to England to support the Royalist cause during the Civil War, and was much admired for his dashing bravery. It was because of him that the English form of the name was coined and became popular.

Rupesh, Rupinder see **Rupak**

Russell
This is primarily a surname and is derived from the Old French *rousel*, which means "little red-(haired) one." It was a surname which came into use as a first name along with other family names in the 19th century. **Rus(s)** and **Rusty** are short forms.

Ryan
A common Irish surname perhaps meaning "little king," now used as a first name. Its spread was greatly helped by the success of the film star Ryan O'Neal (b. 1941). It is also found as **Rian**. It is now beginning to be used for girls.

Ryder
Old English for "horseman."

Rylan
Old English for "land where rye is grown," Rylan and its variants **Ryland, Rylin**, and **Rylun** are increasing in popularity in Canada.

Rylee, Ryleigh, Ryley see **Riley**

S

Sacha
A Russian short form of **Alexander**. Although originally a man's name, the "a" ending has led to its use for girls. **Sasha** is an alternative form.

Sa'eed
Sa'eed or **Sa'id** is an Arabic name meaning "happy, lucky."

Sagar
An Indian name from the Sanskrit meaning "ocean." The spelling **Saagar** is also used.

Sage
This is one of the most recent plant names to come into fashion as a first name, its use boosted by several American entertainers choosing it for their children. The aromatic plant sage gets its name from the ancient belief tea made from its leaves boosted memory and wisdom. The

spelling **Saige** is occasionally used for both boys and girls.

Sahil
An Indian name from the Sanskrit for "guide."

Sajan
This Indian name comes from the Sanskrit for "beloved."

Sajjad
This Muslim name refers to one who "prostrates" himself, or worships God. The name is sometimes spelled **Sajad** or **Sajid**.

Salah
A popular name from the Arabic for "goodness, righteousness." The name is sometimes spelled **Saleh**.

Salima, Salman
An Arabic name that means "safe" or "unharmed."

Samir
An Arabic name that means "one whose conversation in the evening or at night is lively," thus an entertaining companion. The spelling **Sameer** is also used.

Samuel
From the Hebrew, meaning "heard by God." In the Old Testament the prophet Samuel was the leader of the Israelites who chose Saul and later David as their kings. In Scotland and Ireland it was used to transliterate the Gaelic **Somhairle**, a name anglicized as **Sorley**; this derives from the Old Norse term meaning "summer wanderer," that is, "Viking." Currently a popular choice, a short form is **Sam(my)**.

Sanjay
From a Sanskrit word that means "triumphant," but referring specifically to the charioteer of King Dhritarashtra in classic Hindu epics. The name was made familiar by Sanjay Ghandi, son of the former Indian prime minister, and, more recently, through a character in the TV series *EastEnders*.

Saul
From the Hebrew, meaning "asked for (child)." The name occurs in the Old Testament as that of the first King of Israel,

and in the New Testament as St. **Paul**'s name before his conversion to Christianity. It was initially used as a first name in Britain in the 17th century.

Scott
This is a surname, meaning "a Scot," used as a first name.

Seamas
This is an Irish form of **James**. It is also spelled **Seamus**, and the Gaelic form is **Seumas** or **Seumus**. **Shamus** is a modern phonetic version of the name (see also **Hamish**).

Sean
The Irish form of **John**, developed from the French **Jean**. It is also spelled as it is pronounced, **Shaun** or **Shawn**. **Shane** is a variant form.

Sebastian
From the Latin *Sebastianus*, meaning "man of Sebasta." The name of this town in Asia Minor was derived from the Greek meaning "majestic" or "venerable." St. Sebastian was executed by being shot with arrows, and his martyrdom was

a particularly popular subject for paintings. The name took hold in Spain and in France, where it was shortened to **Bastien**, and taken by fishermen across the Channel from Brittany to the West Country, where the form **Bastian** took root. The name did not spread to the rest of Britain until modern times, but Sebastian is now reasonably common, having the short form **Seb(bie)**.

Seth
This is a biblical name meaning "appointed," which was given to the third son of Adam and Eve.

Seumas, Seumus, Shamus *see* **Seamas**

Shahid
An Arabic name that means "witness" or "martyr."

Shahin
An Arabic name that means "falcon." **Shaheen** is a variant spelling.

Shakil
An Arabic name meaning "beautiful, handsome." It can also

be spelled **Shakeel**, and among English speakers take a form such as **Shaquil(le)**.

Shakir
An Arabic name meaning "grateful."

Sham *see* **Shyam**

Shannon
This is the Irish river and place name, meaning "the old one." It is less common for boys.

Shaquil(le) *see* **Shakil**

Sharad
From an Indian word for "autumn." **Sharadchandra** means "autumn moon." **Sharadindu** has a similar meaning.

Sharif
This Arabic name means "eminent" or "honourable." It is also used as a title for descendants of the Prophet Muhammad.

Shea
An Irish surname meaning "descendant of the fortunate one"

now used as a first name. **Shay** is also used.

Shiva
The name of the Hindu god, from the Sanskrit meaning "benign." Similar names are **Shivaji, Shivesh, Shivlal, Shivraj**, and **Shivshankar**, which mean "Lord Shiva."

Shyam
From the Sanskrit for "dark," but identified with **Krishna**. In some parts of India it takes the form **Sham**.

Sidney, Sydney
This is a surname used as a first name from at least the beginning of the 18th century. The spelling Sydney did not appear until the 19th century, and the city in Australia was named after Viscount Sydney, who was then Secretary of State. The short form is **Sid**. Sydney is more common as a female name.

Silvester, Sylvester
The Latin for "wood-dweller." There have been three popes of this name, which was quite common in both forms in

the Middle Ages. The New Testament name **Silas** is probably a form of Silvester.

Simon

This is the better-known English form of the New Testament **Simeon**, the name of the man who blessed the baby Jesus in the Temple. The popularity of Simon in the Middle Ages was due to Simon **Peter**, the Apostle, whose popularity was great at that period. The short form is **Sim**.

Sion *see* **John**

Skye, Skyler

Skye is the name of the Scottish island used as a fashionable name, comparable to the older use of **Iona**. The name's associations with the word "sky" may have helped its rise, and it is sometimes found as **Sky**. The same sound may have helped make the Dutch surname Skyler, "scholar," a popular first name in the United States, for it is often shortened to Sky. This, in the original Dutch form **Schuyler**, has been in use since at least the late 19th century. It is the

surname of a family prominent in New York since the mid-17th century, and was originally used in honour of Philip Schuyler (1733–1804), congressman, senator, and hero of the American Revolution.

Snehin

From a Sanskrit word meaning "friend."

Somhairle *see* **Samuel**

Spencer

This name, originally a surname given to the steward of a great household, but later an aristocratic surname, was made famous by the actor Spencer Tracy.

Srikant

From the Sanskrit words meaning "beautiful throat," a name applied to the god Shiva. **Shrikant** is an alternative spelling.

Stacey, Stacy

A short form that has become popular as an independent name. For men it was a short form of **Eustace**. Currently, it is mostly given to girls.

Stanley

This was originally a surname derived from an old Anglo-Saxon place name meaning "stony field." It was used as a first name from the mid-19th century partly because of its association with Sir Henry Morton Stanley, the famous explorer. It has the short form **Stan**.

Stefan, Steffan *see* **Stephen**

Stephen, Steven

From the Greek *stephanos*, meaning "crown" or "wreath." The laurel wreath was the highest honour a man could attain in the classical world. Stephen was a common personal name in Ancient Greece and was borne by the very first Christian martyr. Steven is the alternative spelling. **Steve** and **Stevie** are the modern short forms. There is a Welsh form, **Steffan**, and also a German form, **Stefan**.

Stuart

From the Old English *sti weard*, an official who looked after animals kept for food. Though it has changed its meaning somewhat, it survives as "steward" today. The co-founder of the Scottish royal house of Stewart or Stuart in the 14th century was William the Steward, who married the king's daughter and whose son later became king. **Stewart** is a common alternative and **Stuert** is also used.

Suhayl

An Arabic name that refers to a bright star, Canopus, in the southern constellation Carina. **Suhail** is a variant.

Sujan

A Hindi name that means "honest."

Sunil

This is a puzzling name, as it comes from an obscure, ancient Sanskrit word meaning "very dark blue." Its use as a first name is modern. It has become a popular choice for parents in India and is sometimes interpreted as "sapphire."

Suraj

This Hindi name means "the sun."

Surinder

This is a development of the name **Indra** and can be interpreted as meaning "mightiest of the gods." It is also found in the form **Surendra**. It is less often used for girls than for boys, and as a boys' name can be shortened to **Sunni**.

Syed

This is a common way of spelling the Arabic name **Sayyid**, meaning "noble" or "master."

Syril *see* **Cyril**

T

Tahir

An Arabic name that means "pure" and "virtuous."

Tanner

A surname, from the job, used as a first name.

Tara

Tara is the name of the hill where the ancient High Kings of Ireland held court and which plays an important part in Irish legend. It has been used as a first name only since the end of the 19th century. It is occasionally used for boys. As an Indian name it means "star."

Tarun

This is part of a group of names with varied origins. Tarun is an Indian boys' name, from the Sanskrit for "young, tender." In addition, the American author Lloyd Alexander coined the name **Taran** (probably based on **Tara**) for the hero of his Celtic fantasy novels *The Chronicle of Prydain*. Many other variants of these names have appeared in recent years.

Tashan

While Tashan is a common Turkish surname, as a first name it appears to be a new creation, in use since about the 1970s.

Taylor

This English surname, indicating an ancestor who was a tailor, has been made familiar as a first name for both boys and girls.

Teagan

A variant of *tadhg*, Gaelic for "poet." Other variants of Teagan include **Tadhgh, Taig, Teige, Teague**, and **Thady**.

Ted, Teddy *see* **Edmund, Edward, Theodore**

Terence

This is from the Latin Terentius, the name of a famous Roman comic playwright. Short forms are **Terry** and **Tel**. It is now also found in the forms **Ter(r)ance, Terrence**, and **Terrell** (although this could also be from the name of an American city). Terrell is a comparatively modern name, having come from Ireland, where it was used to transliterate the native **Turlough** ("tar-loch," pronounced as if Scottish), meaning "instigator" (see also **Theodoric**). Terry as an independent name can also come from Theodoric (see **Derek**).

Tevin

This recent name is probably a development of **Kevin**, although some would link it to a French surname, **Thevin**, which comes from an old form of **Stephen**.

Theodore

From the Greek, meaning "gift of God." There are 28 saints called Theodore in the Church Calendar. In England the name did not become general until the 19th century, but in Wales it has long been used as a form of **Tudur** or **Tudor**, which in fact probably comes from a Celtic name. The usual abbreviation in North America is **Ted(dy)**, as in the case of President Theodore Roosevelt who gave his name to the teddy bear. **Theo** (sometimes used as an independent name) is a more common abbreviation.

Theodoric *see* **Derek, Terence**

Thomas

From the Aramaic nickname meaning "twin." It was first given by Jesus to an Apostle named Judas to distinguish him from Judas Iscariot. The abbreviation **Tom** appears in the Middle Ages. **Tam** and **Tammy** are the Scottish short forms. The use of **Tommy** as a nickname for a British private soldier goes back to the 19th century, when the enlistment form had on it the specimen signature "Thomas Atkins."

Tilak

An Indian name that refers to the *tika* or *tilak*, the red mark worn as a caste-mark or decoration by Hindus. It is also placed as a blessing on the forehead of an honoured guest.

Timothy

Timotheos is an old Greek name meaning "honouring God." Its use as a first name is due to Timothy, the companion of St. **Paul**. It was not used widely until the 16th century when many classical and biblical names were introduced. **Tim** and **Timmy** are the abbreviations. In Ireland Timothy has long been used as an equivalent for the native **Tadhg** ("tieg") which means "poet."

Titus

This is a Latin name of unknown meaning. Two well-known

holders of the name were a follower of St. Paul and, in contrast, the infamous Titus Oates, an English conspirator and perjurer in the 17th century.

Toby

Toby is the English form of the Greek **Tobias**, itself derived From the Hebrew, name that means "the Lord is good." The story of "Tobias and the Angel," which is told in the Apocrypha, was a favourite one in the Middle Ages. Punch's dog Toby is named after the dog that accompanied Tobias on his travels.

Tod, Todd

Originally a surname meaning "fox," now used as a first name.

Tom, Tommy *see* **Thomas**

Toni, Tonio, Tony *see* **Anthony**

Tormod *see* **Norman**

Torquil

This is the English rendering of the Norse name Thorketill ("Thor's cauldron"). The first element is the name of the Norse thunder god, **Thor**. The original became **Torcall** in Gaelic, which was anglicized into Torquil. It is used in Scotland, especially in the Outer Hebrides and among the Macleod family, and it has occasionally been given in England.

Travis

A surname, notably that of William B. Travis (1809–36) U.S. commander at the Battle of the Alamo, used as a first name. It comes from the French word *traverser*, meaning "to cross" and would have been given originally to a toll-collector.

Trevor

From the Welsh **Trefor**, meaning "great homestead." Trevor is the English spelling. **Trev** is the short form.

Trey

Trey is an old word for "three" in card games, and has been used, particularly in the United States, as a pet name for the third bearer of the same name to distinguish him from his grandfather and father (often called "Junior"). More recently it has been used as a given name, when it can also appear as **Tre** and (sometimes for girls) **Trea**.

Tristan, Tristram

This is a name of obscure origin, possibly Pictish. It appears as the name of the noble hero of the medieval love stories of Tristram and **Isolda**. When Tristram is escorting Isolda to be married to his uncle, they unknowingly drink a magic love-potion intended for the newlyweds and are doomed to adulterous love until their tragic deaths. **Tristran** is also found. Variants include **Tristen, Tristi(a)n, Triston**, and **Trystan**.

Troy

Troy was the ancient city in Asia Minor besieged by the Greeks for 10 years. Its use as a first name was boosted in the 1960s by the actor Troy Donahue (1936–2001, given name **Merle** Johnson). It has been popular in Australia and is much used in the United States.

Tudor, Tudur *see* **Theodore**

Tulsi
This Indian name is from the Sanskrit word meaning "sacred basil," a plant which symbolizes Vishnu.

Turlough *see* **Terence**

Tyler
A surname, from the job, used as a first name. It has been popular for some years and can be shortened to **Ty**.

Tyrone
The name of the Irish county, which means "Eoghan's land," used as a first name. It was used in the past by the actor Tyrone Power (1913–58) in the United States and by the British theatre director Sir Tyrone Guthrie (1900–71). **Ty** is the short form, although Guthrie was known to his friends as **Tony**. **Tyree**, another Celtic district name, is also used.

Tyson
The name Tyson, which is a favourite in Western Canada, may be popular because of cowboy folk singer Ian Tyson. In the United States, it has declined in popularity, possibly because of its association with disgraced boxer Mike Tyson.

U

Ulick *see* **Ulysses, William**

Ulysses
This is the Latin name for the Greek hero **Odysseus**, whose tale is told in Homer's *Odyssey*. Though little used in England, Scotland, or Wales, it has been used in Ireland as an equivalent for **Ulick**, an Irish form of **William**. James Joyce's most famous novel bears this name. In the United States, where it also appears as **Ulises**, use of the name probably comes from the fame of General Ulysses S. Grant (1822–85), hero of Appomattox and the 18th American president.

Uthman
A name from an Arabic word meaning "baby bustard." Uthman was the son-in-law of the Prophet Muhammad. The Turkish form of the name, **Usman**, is also much used, though often westernized as **Osman**. The name of the Ottoman Empire derived from this name's Latin and Italian plural form.

V

Valentine
From the Latin *valens*, meaning "strong" or "healthy." St. Valentine was a third-century Roman priest martyred on February 14, the eve of the celebrations of the pagan goddess Juno, when lots were drawn to choose lovers. The feast was absorbed into the Christian calendar. **Valentin** is an alternate spelling. **Val** is a common diminutive.

Vaughn, Vaughan
From the Welsh *fychan*, meaning "small one."

Vernon
Richard de Vernon was a companion of William the Conqueror. The surname comes from a French place name that means "alder grove." It was not

used as a first name until the 19th century, when many such aristocratic names were taken into general use.

Victor

This is the Latin for "conqueror." Although it occurs in medieval England, it was not common until the 19th century when it was used as a boy's form of **Victoria**. The most common short form is **Vic**.

Vijay

This Indian name is from a Sanskrit word meaning "victory."

Vikesh

A Hindi name that means "the moon."

Vinay

An Indian name that means "educating to act in a proper way." For Buddhists it suggests the modest behaviour appropriate to a monk.

Vincent

This name comes from the Latin word for "conquering." There was a third-century Spanish martyr of this name, and it occurs in English records from the 13th century. But the 17th-century St. Vincent de Paul popularized the name when he founded the Vincentian Order of the Sisters of Charity. Vincent became quite common in the 19th century. Its usual short form is **Vince**. Variants **Vincente** and **Vincenzo** are also frequently found.

Viral

This Indian name comes from the Sanskrit for "priceless, rare."

Virgil

The name of the great Roman poet. The original spelling of his name was **Vergil**.

Vishal

An Indian name that means "immense, spacious."

Vitus *see* **Guy**

Vivian, Vivien

From the Latin *vivianus*, which means "lively." Vivian is now used for both sexes but was originally the masculine form, with Vivien mostly used for girls.

W

Wallace

From the surname of Sir William Wallace, the great Scottish patriot of the 13th century. The use of his surname as a first name started about a hundred years ago. The surname comes from the same root that gives us the word "Welsh," but which was once used of the British in the north as well. Another spelling of the name is **Wallis**, found in North America where it is used for both sexes. The short form, **Wal(ly)**, is shared with **Walter**.

Walter

From the Old German Waldhar, meaning "army ruler." The name was very popular among the Normans and quickly became established in England. Sir Walter Raleigh is a very well-known later example and he used the short form **Wat** for his son. **Wal(t)** and **Wally** are more popular short forms in use today, and Walt is used as an independent name.

Waqar
This Arabic name means "dignity" or "soberness."

Warren
From the surname, which can either be from an old German tribe name, Varin, or from a Norman place name meaning "a game-reserve." The Normans introduced the forms Warin and Guarin to England and these led to the surnames Warren, Waring, and Garnet.

Warwick
The name of the English town, which means "houses by the weir," used as a surname and then as a first name. **Warrie** is a short form.

Wasim
An Arabic name that means "handsome" or "graceful."

Wayne
This is a surname meaning "cart" or "cart-maker."

Wesley
John and Charles Wesley were the founders of Methodism,

and the name came to be used as a first name in their honour. As a surname it means "west meadow." **Wes** is a short form.

Whitney
Originally a surname meaning "(living) at the white island." Its use as a first name in the United States may be due to its being the surname of both a wealthy family prominent in national politics and arts, and of Josiah Dwight Whitney (1819–96), geologist and surveyor, after whom the United States's highest mountain outside Alaska, Mount Whitney in south California, is named.

Wilbur
From the Old German, the meaning is unknown. The most famous example was Wilbur Wright, who, with his brother **Orville**, made the first successful powered flight in 1903.

Wilfred, Wilfrid
From the Old English Wilfrith, meaning "desiring peace." St. Wilfrid was an important figure

in the 7th century, and his name was particularly popular in Yorkshire, where he preached and founded the bishoprics of Ripon and Hexham. The name did not survive the Norman Conquest but was revived by high-church Anglicans in the 19th century. It has the short form **Wilf**.

William
From the Old German, meaning "desiring protection." William was always a popular name with the Normans, who brought it to England, and, until the 13th century when it was ousted by **John**, it was the most common of all names in England. **Will(ie)** is the old short form but **Bill(ie)** is more usual today. **Gwilym**, shortened to **Gwill**, is the Welsh form of the name, and **Liam** a short form which has spread from Ireland; **Ulick** (see **Ulysses**) is another Irish form.

Winston
This is the name of a small village in Gloucestershire, which became a surname. The name

has been used in the Churchill family since 1620, when Sir Winston Churchill, father of the first Duke of Marlborough, was born. His mother was Sarah Winston. It has come into use in honour of Sir Winston Churchill (1874–1965) to mark his contribution to world affairs.

Wyatt
The use of this surname, from medieval short forms of both **Guy** and **William**, as a first name is mainly restricted to the United States, where it is well known from Wyatt Earp (1848–1929), famous from the gunfight at the OK Corral.

Wyn, Wynfor, Wynne *see* **Gwyn**

X

Xavier
The surname of St. Francis Xavier (1506–52) used as a first name. It is also occasionally spelled **Javier, Zavia**, or **Zavier**.

Y

Yasin
A name formed by the names of Arabic letters from an important passage in the Koran. Yasin features in a well-known Egyptian tale fighting social injustice.

Yehudi *see* **Jude**

Yusuf
Yusuf or **Yusif** is a popular boy's name, the Arabic equivalent of **Joseph**.

Yves *see* **Ivo, Ivor**

Z

Zachary
The English form of **Zacharias**, the Greek for the Hebrew **Zachariah** or **Zechariah**, meaning "the Lord has remembered." Zachary was used occasionally in the Middle Ages, but did not become at all common until the Puritans

adopted it in the 17th century. It has variant forms **Zachery** and **Zackery** and the short form **Za(c)k**. **Zacchaeus** and **Zakki** are other forms of the name.

Zahid
An Arabic name that means "abstinent."

Zake
An Arabic name meaning "pure, chaste."

Zander *see* **Alexander**

Zane
The American author Zane Grey (1872–1939, given name Pearl Grey) took his pen name from his home town of Zanesville, Ohio. The town was named after its founder Ebenezer Zane; the meaning of his surname is not known.

Zavia, Zavier *see* **Xavier**

Zeb
This can be a short form of such Hebrew names as **Zebulun** ("exaltation") or **Zebedee** ("my

gift"), or it can simply be an attempt by parents to find an unusual name. Similarly **Zed** can be seen as a short form of **Zedekiah** ("justice of the Lord").

Zechariah *see* **Zachary**

Zed, Zedekiah *see* **Zeb**

Zeke *see* **Ezekiel**

Acknowledgements

We are extremely grateful to those who shared stories about choosing names. As well, we dealt with many people from government departments who were helpful, patient, and even cheerful in dealing with our never-ending requests. We would especially like to thank Frances Beer (Manitoba); Gary Brown (Yukon); Robert Breau (New Brunswick); Pat Cambridge (Saskatchewan); Dianne Campbell (Ontario); Ted Hickey (Nunavut); Eoin Kenny (Alberta); Terry McMahon (British Columbia); Margaret Nokkitok (Nunavut); Lindsay Scott (Saskatchewan); Sharon White (Prince Edward Island); the Vital Statistics Council of Canada. Special thanks also to Anna Olejarczyk, Wenda Crawford, and Nancy Perrin. Thanks to Dan Liebman, Amy McKenzie, and Duncan McKenzie for developing the Canadian content.

Notes